DECIPHERING SUN TZU

DEREK M. C. YUEN

Deciphering Sun Tzu

How to Read 'The Art of War'

OXFORD
UNIVERSITY PRESS

OXFORD

UNIVERSITY PRESS

Oxford University Press, Inc., publishes works that further
Oxford University's objective of excellence
in research, scholarship, and education.

Oxford New York

Auckland   Cape Town   Dar es Salaam   Hong Kong   Karachi
Kuala Lumpur   Madrid   Melbourne   Mexico City   Nairobi
New Delhi   Shanghai   Taipei   Toronto

With offices in

Argentina   Austria   Brazil   Chile   Czech Republic   France   Greece
Guatemala   Hungary   Italy   Japan   Poland   Portugal   Singapore
South Korea   Switzerland   Thailand   Turkey   Ukraine   Vietnam

Oxford is a registered trade mark of Oxford University Press in the UK
and certain other countries.

Published by Oxford University Press, Inc
198 Madison Avenue, New York, New York 10016

Published in the United Kingdom in 2014 by C. Hurst & Co. (Publishers) Ltd.

www.oup.com

Oxford is a registered trademark of Oxford University Press

Library of Congress Cataloging-in-Publication Data is available for this title
Derek M C Yuen
Deciphering Sun Tzu
How to Read 'The Art of War'
ISBN 978-0-19-937-351-2 (hardback)

Printed in the USA

Dedicated to my late grandparents,
Robert and Nancy Yuen

CONTENTS

ACKNOWLEDGEMENTS

This is the first book I have written, and it owes its existence to Michael Dwyer, my publisher, who has devoted so much time and effort in helping to bring this project to fruition. I would also like to thank Oxford University Press for agreeing to co-publish my book in North America, and Jon de Peyer, Daisy Leitch, and Kathleen May at Hurst for guiding and supporting this layman through the publishing process.

Deciphering Sun Tzu is the product of over a decade of research and writing. Its origins can be traced back to when I studied for my Masters at the London School of Economics and later PhD research at the University of Reading. I owe a special debt to my intellectual mentor, Professor Christopher Coker, who has given me invaluable advice and support since my first days at LSE. This book as well as my academic career would not have been possible without the guidance of Professor Colin S. Gray. As my PhD supervisor and an acknowledged master of war and strategy, Professor Gray laid the foundation for my strategic education; his supervision and consultation served as a veritable dialogue between Western and Chinese strategic thought to me. I am also grateful to Dr David Lonsdale, Dr C. Dale Walton, and to my fellow PhD mates at Reading University, who played an important role in making my years there the most cheerful and fruitful of times.

Though the errors in this book are mine alone, its publication would never have occurred without the support, advice, and helpful critiques of many colleagues. I am indebted to my teachers at the University of Hong Kong, particularly Professor James T. H. Tang, to Professor Richard W.

ACKNOWLEDGEMENTS

X. Hu, and to Professor Joseph C. W. Chan, for nurturing me and setting me on the academic path. I would also like to thank Professor Roger T. Ames for his helpful advice and encouragement.

My deepest thanks go to my parents Elmer and Tania, and my family for their unconditional understanding and support. Without them, I could not have survived the hard times. I owe special thanks to Raymond Yuen, who played an indispensable role in shaping my personality and reading habits. Above all, this book is dedicated to my late grandparents Robert and Nancy.

Hong Kong   *July 2014*

CHRONOLOGY

c. 1600–c. 1046 BC	Shang Dynasty
c. 1046–771 BC	Western Zhou (Chou) Dynasty
c. 1046 BC	Tai Gong (Jiang Ziya) founded the state of Qi (齊)
770–256 BC	Eastern Zhou (Chou) Dynasty
770–403 BC	Spring and Autumn Period
685–643 BC	Reign of Duke Huan of Qi (Qi Huan Gong 齊桓公)
685 BC	Guan Zhong appointed Prime Minister of Qi
684 BC	Battle of Zhang Shao (長勺之戰)—between Lu and Qi
651 BC	The height of Qi's hegemony
638 BC	Battle of Hong Shui (泓水之戰)—between Chu and Song (Sung)
512 BC	Sun Tzu met the King of Wu and presented to him *The Art of War*
506 BC	Battle of Bo Ju (柏舉之戰)—between Wu (Sun Tzu led an army) and Chu
403–221 BC	Warring States Period
221–206 BC	Qin (Ch'in) Dynasty
206 BC–9 AD	Western (Former) Han Dynasty
9–25 AD	Xin Dynasty
25–220 AD	Eastern (Later) Han Dynasty
220–265 AD	Three Kingdoms Period
265–316 AD	Western Jin (Chin) Dynasty
317–420 AD	Eastern Jin (Chin) Dynasty

CHRONOLOGY

420–589 AD	Southern and Northern Dynasties
581–618 AD	Sui Dynasty
618–907 AD	Tang Dynasty
907–960 AD	Five Dynasties and Ten Kingdoms
960–1127 AD	Northern Song (Sung) Dynasty
1127–1276 AD	Southern Song (Sung) Dynasty
1271–1368 AD	Yuan Dynasty (Mongols)
1368–1644 AD	Ming Dynasty
1644–1911 AD	Qing (Ch'ing) Dynasty (Manchu)

INTRODUCTION

SUN TZU IN THE WEST

Sun Tzu: The Art of War (*Sun Zi Bing Fa* 孫子兵法) is an ancient Chinese military treatise that was written 2,500 years ago (*c*.512 BC). It did not reach the West until 1772, when the text was translated into French and published in Paris by Father Jean Joseph Marie Amiot, a French Jesuit who had spent many years in Beijing.[1] The fact that the French discovered *The Art of War* shortly before the French Revolution has often led the Chinese to claim that Napoleon had applied Sun Tzu's teachings in his military campaigns. But there is no evidence that Napoleon ever read the work. And as thoughts and things Chinese were no longer as popular in nineteenth-century France as they had been in the eighteenth century, no post-Revolution reference to Sun Tzu can be found until 1900.[2]

The first English translation of *The Art of War* came at a much later date. In 1905, Captain E. F. Calthrop, RFA, then a British army language student in Japan, translated the text into English. It was first published in Tokyo under the title *Sonshi*.[3] Yet *The Art of War* still remained largely unknown in the English-speaking world until Lionel Giles's much-renowned translation in 1910. The English-speaking world has since used *The Art of War* as a primary source to understand and interpret Chinese strategic thought, as well as China's mindset and international behavior.

There has long been a tendency in the West to rely on *The Art of War* when accounting for China's strategic decisions and international behavior, something that is not entirely unjustified in light of the paramount role Sun Tzu has played in Chinese strategic thought. Thus Mao Yuan Yi

1

(茅元儀 1594–1640), the editor of the most comprehensive military manual and encyclopedia in Chinese history,[4] asserts that *The Art of War* contains everything written before it—works after *The Art of War* never surpass it, while other works are nothing more than mere commentaries on it. Sun Tzu's work has been at the center of the Chinese strategic worldview ever since its first appearance; even *Tao Te Ching*, the Taoist canon that contains considerable strategic wisdom, has been unable to sway its dominant status.

New translations of *The Art of War*, as well as archeological discoveries, are often the primary means through which Western Sinologists and scholars seek to evaluate the current state of research on Sun Tzu. However, while developments such as these have made valuable contributions to the existing scholarship, new translations and archeological evidence are unable to serve the needs of those Western readers and strategists who aim for a more complete understanding of Sun Tzu's ideas—when attempting to decipher Sun Tzu this is not where the real breakthroughs have taken place.

For those wishing to understand Sun Tzu's work, the most significant developments have instead resulted from the integration of aspects of Chinese strategic thought into Western strategic thinking, with the work of Basil H. Liddell Hart and John Boyd being particularly important in this regard. Liddell Hart and Boyd, two of the most influential strategic thinkers of the twentieth century, redefined and re-theorized Western strategic thought in a way that made it more attuned to Sun Tzu's ideas. In so doing, they in turn made Sun Tzu's work more comprehensible to the Western world.

Liddell Hart was not only among the first in the West to rediscover Sun Tzu—he also made a remarkable contribution to our understanding of Sun Tzu by employing one of Sun Tzu's dual-concepts, namely that of *ch'i* (unorthodox 奇) and *cheng* (orthodox 正). This dual-concept played a vital role in informing Liddell Hart's so-called "indirect approach," which he used to reinterpret Western military history from ancient Greece to the Second World War. Although Liddell Hart's adoption of Sun Tzu's ideas was selective and partial, his work clearly demonstrated the validity of Chinese strategic thought and its broader applicability to modern

Western settings. John Boyd, who was heavily influenced by Liddell Hart and saw the enormous potential of Chinese strategic thought, aimed for a more extensive adoption of Sun Tzu's thesis into the Western strategic framework. But he took a different approach. He recognized that simply borrowing Sun Tzu's principles, as his predecessors had, was ineffective and insufficient: any adoption of Chinese strategic thought would be unsuccessful without first grasping the Chinese way of thinking, world-view, and logical and dialectic system. Boyd's insistence on the need to capture the basis of Chinese strategic thought eventually bore fruit, leading to substantial progress in Western understandings of Sun Tzu, as well as in bridging the gap between Chinese and Western strategic thought. This book seeks to augment Boyd's unfinished endeavor.

What Translations of The Art of War *Can't Do*

Unlike many great classics that are more frequently heard about than read or understood, *Sun Tzu: The Art of War* is often heard of and read but seldom understood in the West; despite its popularity in the Western world, *The Art of War* has rarely been understood correctly with due understanding of its Chinese context and Taoist roots. One of the main reasons for this is the fact that research on *The Art of War* has thus far remained in the translation phase. While Sun Tzu started to gain currency among Western, particularly American, scholars, business people, and military officers from the 1980s onwards, book-length works on Sun Tzu have been limited to translations and general introductions describing the period in which he lived and the most important concepts used in the translations themselves. Those in the West who aspire to a deeper understanding of Sun Tzu's ideas are consequently faced with an intellectual lacuna. There is almost nothing in the current market that involves direct research on Sun Tzu and Chinese strategic thought aimed at a Western audience. As this has seriously affected the Western understanding of Chinese strategic thought and strategic culture, as well as China's strategic worldview and international behavior, it is far from a trivial matter.

The second obstacle to a better understanding of Sun Tzu stems from the translations themselves. Not only is there a great deal of variation in the quality of the translations and the emphases of different translators, but there is also a mismatch between the translations and the expectations and knowledge of their intended audience. Ralph D. Sawyer's translation of *The Art of War*, for example, is by far the most widely accepted edition in the English-speaking world.[5] Yet its popularity does not reside in its sophistication, but in the fact that the translation is easy to comprehend. The translations of Thomas Cleary and Roger T. Ames, in contrast, are far more accurate, but are much less approachable than Sawyer's given the emphasis they place on the philosophical aspects of Sun Tzu and Chinese strategic thinking.[6] Cleary and Ames are well aware that these aspects are vital for advancing the Western understanding of Sun Tzu, yet they cannot avoid the fact that most Western readers encounter problems when trying to understand them. In the absence of any prior knowledge of Taoism and other Chinese elements, readers will inevitably find the text both impractical and incomprehensible. Moreover, as the existing research on Sun Tzu tends to consist of mere translations with brief introductions, they are unable to illustrate the system of Sun Tzu's thought as a whole by analyzing the text on a chapter-by-chapter basis. Above all, the existing translations fail to examine Sun Tzu's treatise from its original strategic perspective, and consequently fail to reveal its military and strategic significance. Yet demonstrating the significance of *The Art of War* is supposedly what the translations are intended for in the first place.

Given the sorry state of Western research on Sun Tzu and Chinese strategic thought, it is hardly surprising that the West's understanding of Sun Tzu, despite the passage of thousands of years, has never moved beyond facile references to short one- to two-sentence axioms, aphorisms, and phrases from *The Art of War*. Worse still, this tendency to treat Sun Tzu's thought as nothing more than maxims in a decontextualized manner without considering the history, philosophy, and overall design of Sun Tzu's thesis has become a common practice. All of this has led the study of Sun Tzu astray, and it may take a long time to reverse this trend.

In view of the current impasse in the study of Sun Tzu and Chinese strategic thought, there needs to be a revolution in the way that Sun Tzu is studied in the West. The starting point for any such approach requires analysis of the subject matter itself, rather than translations and introductions alone, based on extensive research that fully examines Sun Tzu, his ideas, and the period in which he lived. An analysis of this kind also needs to meet a number of requirements, the first of which is to view *The Art of War* from a strategic perspective that accurately reflects the system and purpose of Sun Tzu's thought. Second, such an approach must provide a detailed historical analysis that helps trace the origins of Sun Tzu's thought and that presents this history in relation to the concepts and philosophy of Sun Tzu. Third, the Taoist foundation and associations of *The Art of War* need to be identified, with philosophical and cultural commentaries to help uncover aspects of Chinese philosophy, culture, and language that are essential for a better understanding of Sun Tzu. Lastly, and perhaps most importantly of all, the new approach needs to make these Chinese concepts readily communicable in Western terms, with Western equivalents being provided whenever possible.

This book seeks to fulfill these requirements and aims to spark a renaissance in the Western study of Sun Tzu. It aspires to be used as a practical, companion volume to the translations of *The Art of War* that many Western readers will already possess in their libraries.

Aim and Scope

This book begins where existing translations of *The Art of War* leave off. The book's examination of Sun Tzu from historical, philosophical, strategic, and cross-cultural perspectives was only made possible due to the author's knowledge of Chinese language, history, culture, and philosophy, as well as Chinese and Western strategic thought. Even so, the readers can be free of these burdens, for this new synthesizing approach offers a more promising way to understand the essence of Sun Tzu and Chinese strategic thought by pinpointing and elucidating the elements that are most essential to the comprehension of the subject, which is less dependent on the prior understanding of the historical and philosophical aspects regarding Chinese strategy. The book does not aim to provide an exhaustive literature review on the subject but instead seeks to offer a useful synthesis of what Western readers need to know about Sun Tzu from various fields. The fact that a much-needed reconciliation between the needs of readers and the existing literature is long overdue means that practicality should come first in the discussion of strategic thought, particularly as pragmatism has always been the guiding principle and underlying nature of Chinese thought and philosophy.

The book seeks to advance the study of Sun Tzu and Chinese strategic thought in four ways. The first of these is in providing an overall theoretical framework for understanding Chinese strategic thought. This will help Western readers understand the different components as well as the horizontal and vertical dimensions of Chinese strategic thought—in other words, the system of Chinese strategic thought as a whole. Second, the book aims to provide a more detailed historical analysis of the factors and developments responsible for the making of *The Art of War*. The book explores the military, strategic, diplomatic, and cultural origins of *The Art of War* and Sun Tzu's zeitgeist, thereby providing an analysis that transcends the old and ineffective method of studying Sun Tzu's maxims in a decontextualized and almost purely theoretical manner.

The third major contribution this book makes is in highlighting the recently discovered relationship between Sun Tzu, Lao Tzu, and the works named after them: *The Art of War* (*Sun Tzu*) and *Tao Te Ching* (*Lao Tzu*). It has long been believed that *The Art of War* and Taoism are interlinked. Yet recent findings suggest that the relationship between the two may well have worked both ways: whereas Lao Tzu (the person) appears to have had an impact on Sun Tzu's thought, it also appears that *Tao Te Ching* (i.e. Lao Tzu the book) may have borrowed extensively from *The Art of War*, as the latter precedes *Tao Te Ching* chronologically. This new development not only enhances our understanding of the philosophical basis of *The Art of War*, but also the subsequent development of Sun Tzu's thought and the final "completion" of what we today understand as Chinese strategic thought by *Tao Te Ching*. It also helps rectify the current overreliance on *The Art of War* for understanding Chinese strategy.

Fourth, *The Art of War* is a military and strategic treatise and should ultimately be examined through a strategic lens. Nothing can be more beneficial to Western readers in this regard than a close examination of the links between the thought of Sun Tzu and the ideas of Western strategic thinkers, and the continuing synthesis of Chinese and Western strategic thought. The book tries to recapture the original meanings of the most important concepts in *The Art of War* by elucidating them with the aid of Western strategic works, including those of Carl von Clausewitz, Basil H. Liddell-Hart, J.C. Wylie, and John Boyd, and by cross-referencing them to other classical Chinese strategic works. The book also identifies a number of "successors" to Sun Tzu in the West who reproduce many of his key ideas in order to illustrate how they have infused Chinese strategic thought into the Western strategic framework.

The focus of this book is not solely limited to an examination of Sun Tzu; it also makes use of existing analyses and findings on Sun Tzu to open new avenues for further research that can play an essential role in enhancing the Western understanding of Chinese strategy, including:

- the foundations of Chinese strategic thought and strategic culture;
- the introduction of *Tao Te Ching* as a strategic text and the inquiry of Lao Tzu's place in Chinese strategic thought;
- Chinese military dialectics;
- the epistemology of Chinese strategy;
- the "Easternization" of Western strategic thought;
- the future direction of the study of Chinese strategic thought and culture; and
- the establishment of a general theory of strategy transcending the East and West.

Organization of the Book

The book consists of six chapters: Chapters 1–3 explore the life and ideas of Sun Tzu with the aim of recapturing the Chinese and Taoist contexts that are absent in the Western study of Sun Tzu. Chapters 4 and 5 approach Sun Tzu from a Western perspective in order to show that *The Art of War* and Clausewitz's *On War* are not distinctively different, as had originally been thought. Moreover, some Western strategic thinkers, whether knowingly or otherwise, have reproduced Sun Tzu's most important ideas, thereby embedding them in Western strategic thought. Chapter 6 specifically examines China's current strategic culture paradigm and the important role this plays in shaping the Western understanding of Chinese strategic thought.

Chapter 1 provides the philosophical background for the analysis of later chapters by outlining the system of Chinese strategic thought and the way in which this differs from its Western counterpart in almost every sense. It argues that Chinese strategic thought runs contrary to the military and strategic "common sense" of the West and many major tenets of Western strategic thought. What makes Chinese strategic thought even more difficult to decipher is the fact that the Chinese employ logical principles that differ markedly from the formal logic of the West. This is something which can be found in the frequent use of paradox or contradiction in Chinese military and strategic treatises. The chapter introduces the system of Chinese strategic thought by outlining the two grand schemes that systematize Chinese strategic thought in horizontal and vertical dimensions, namely the Four Schools and the Three Levels of Chinese Strategic Thought. These two underlying schemes demonstrate how the Chinese strategic framework is heavily influenced by Sun Tzu and Taoism. The chapter also discusses the potential significance of these schemes for establishing a general theory of strategy and for exploring the epistemology of strategy, two currently underdeveloped areas of Western strategic thought.

Chapter 2 investigates the military, strategic, diplomatic, and cultural origins of The Art of War as well as Sun Tzu's zeitgeist. It looks at the history and culture of the state of Qi (齊, present-day Shandong Province), the home country of Sun Tzu, and explores their role in the formation of Sun Tzu's thought. The chapter also examines the major developments in the period of tremendous upheaval in which Sun Tzu lived, and the way in which these informed the ideas that Sun Tzu sets out in The Art of War.

Chapter 3 puts forward a new argument with regard to the development of Chinese strategic thought. While Sun Tzu can be seen as the founder of Chinese strategic thought, the chapter argues that the tradition of Chinese strategic thought cannot be considered "complete" without the transformation of Sun Tzu's ideas in Tao Te Ching. The chapter introduces Tao Te Ching as a strategic text and explores its development of Sun Tzu's thought. The chapter identifies Chinese military dialectics, the condition–consequence approach, and the Taoist methodology and worldview that form the cornerstone of Chinese strategic thought. Although these are all inherent in Chinese strategic thought and philosophy, they have rarely been understood correctly in the West.

Chapter 4 aims to recover the hidden premises of *The Art of War* that have been lost in translation. In order to achieve this goal, the chapter examines some of the most important aspects of Sun Tzu's thought from a Western strategic perspective. It explores a number of Sun Tzu's most important ideas and systematizes them in a way that can be better understood in the West. By pinpointing some Western equivalents of Sun Tzu's ideas, the chapter advances the claim that the basic logic of strategy is universal and that a single general theory of strategy is attainable.

Chapter 5 seeks to demonstrate the potential role that a synthesis of Chinese and Western strategies can play in informing the creation of a general theory of strategy. It argues that there are a number of "successors" to Sun Tzu in the West who have reproduced many of his main ideas, the most distinguished of whom are Liddell Hart and John Boyd. Liddell Hart's rediscovery of Sun Tzu not only resulted in the aforementioned "indirect approach," but also the recognition of the Chinese condition–consequence approach as well as the establishment of the concept and schemes of grand strategy in Western strategic thought. Boyd, on the other hand, aimed to integrate Sun Tzu's thought into the Western strategic framework. Unlike other Western "successors" to Sun Tzu, Boyd insists on the need to capture the cognitive and philosophical bases of Chinese strategic thought, because he realizes that it is impossible to get to the heart of Chinese strategy without doing so. In order to achieve this, Boyd repackages, rationalizes, and modernizes Eastern thought, using a range of Western scientific theories.

Chapter 6 focuses on Chinese strategic culture. It critiques Western scholarship on Chinese strategic culture, particularly Alastair Iain Johnston's Cultural Realism and Andrew Scobell's "Chinese Cult of Defense." The chapter examines the Confucian-Mencian and realpolitik/parabellum strategic cultures framework, which is currently the most common paradigm for explaining Chinese strategic culture, and explores how it has shaped the Western understanding of Chinese strategic culture and thought. The chapter argues that this paradigm—and indeed the strategic culture approach as a whole—is sorely deficient for understanding the essence of Chinese strategic thought, which is predominantly historical and philosophical in nature. The chapter consequently advocates returning to a close textual reading of Chinese history and philosophical thought in order to comprehend Chinese strategic traditions.

As this book covers a wide range of topics, readers may choose to read each of the chapters selectively, depending on their interests and level of knowledge. Chapter 1 should be read by all readers as it introduces the most important assumptions in Chinese philosophy and strategic thought. It also plays a vital role in the book as it introduces the overall theoretical framework of Chinese strategy as well as the way in which the subject should be studied. For those readers with a limited knowledge of Sun Tzu and Chinese strategic thought, Chapter 4 could be read first in order to gain some familiarity with some of the Sun Tzu's key schemes, which the chapter interprets and discusses in a manner that will be more readily approachable for a Western audience. Readers who are more interested in this historical analysis of *The Art of War* could begin with Chapter 2 before returning to Chapter 1 at a later stage. Yet Chapter 3, on Sun Tzu and Lao Tzu (Taoism), should only be read after Chapters 1 and 2, as they contain philosophical and epistemological discussions that are essential for a better understanding of Chapter 3, while Chapter 2 covers the relationship between Sun Tzu and Lao Tzu. Similarly, readers should have covered Chapters 1 to 3 before reading Chapter 5, for the part on Boyd in Chapter 5 requires prior knowledge of the foundations of Chinese strategic thought to follow Boyd's endeavor in reproducing Chinese strategic thought in the Western strategic framework.

A Note on the Translation, Pronunciation, and Definition

This book uses existing English translations whenever possible. The book uses three major translations of *The Art of War* by Ralph D. Sawyer, Thomas Cleary, and Roger Ames. As Sawyer's translation is the most widely accepted in the Western world, it is used as the primary source of English translation in this book. Conversely, as Cleary's and Ames's translations place more emphasis on the philosophical aspects of Sun

Tzu's thought, they are used whenever Sawyer's translation is unable to bring out the true meaning behind Sun Tzu's text.

Given that there are two major Romanization systems for the Chinese language—Wade-Giles and Pinyin—and as most previous translations employ the older Wade-Giles system, the latter is used for important terms that are already familiar to Western readers, such as Sun Tzu and Lao Tzu (vis-à-vis Sunzi and Laozi), ch'i (unorthodox 奇 vis-à-vis ji) and cheng (orthodox 正 vis-à-vis zheng), and Tao (Dao). The remaining Chinese terms are all in Pinyin. This should help Western readers become accustomed to the Pinyin system, which is currently more widely used. Readers can refer to the glossary of Chinese terms and expressions for further information.

For easier identification, "The Art of War" in this book automatically refers to Sun Tzu: The Art of War and "The Art of Warfare" to Sun Bin: The Art of Warfare. However, as Lao Tzu the person and Lao Tzu the book (i.e. Tao Te Ching) receive different treatment in this book, Lao Tzu and Tao Te Ching are not to be used interchangeably.

When using the division between "the East" and "the West" in this book, "the East" solely refers to China and Japan, whereas China or "the Chinese" is used in discussions that refer to China specifically. "The West," on the other hand, generally refers to the part of the Western world that shares a more or less common tradition of strategic thought and practices, comprising Europe (including Russia), North America, and Oceania.

Readers will notice that the book provides rather limited definitions for Chinese strategic and philosophical concepts. The primary reasons for this are that the Chinese language is highly contextual and most of these Chinese concepts are purposefully abstract and ambiguous in nature—on most occasions they have multiple meanings. Hence knowing their definitions does not imply one has understood them; indeed, they seldom have precise definitions, as the Chinese are not fond of providing definitions or even of the idea of definition itself. Thus, knowing that Tao is the ultimate order of the universe, for example, would not make much difference unless one comes across it in practice. The book consequently aims to guide readers through these concepts in each of its chapters so that they will understand them both rationally and intuitively when they come across them.

1

THE SYSTEM OF CHINESE STRATEGIC THOUGHT[1]

The dominant Western understanding of Chinese strategic thought is based on translated sayings and principles. But such limited material cannot encapsulate Chinese strategic thought in its entirety. To arrive at a truly comprehensive understanding, China's language, culture, history, and philosophy must also be understood, to say nothing of the Chinese logical system, which is fundamentally different from the West's. This chapter aims to overcome some of these difficulties by providing a systematic overview of Chinese strategic thought, and the theoretical assumptions underlying the tradition of Chinese strategic thinking. In so doing, the chapter offers a means to grasp the essence of Chinese strategic thought in a way that goes beyond the simplistic and selective repetition of well-known maxims and aphorisms.

The tradition of Chinese strategic thought differs substantively from its Western counterpart. Indeed, in many ways, Chinese strategic thought runs contrary to Western military and strategic "common sense." As a result, even those in the West who are well versed in the principles of Western strategic thought are likely to find the Chinese strategic tradition utterly baffling.

Chinese Strategic Thought: Assumptions

In the West, definitions of strategy tend to focus on the use of force and concepts such as the rational model of behavior with its emphasis on ways, means, and ends. Yet Chinese strategic thought places no particular emphasis on these conceptual traditions and can remain operational without them. With respect to the major tenets of Western strategic thought, Chinese strategic thought is not necessarily about the use of military force: it does not rely on and in fact renounces the means–ends rational model. Nor does it need to work as a bridge linking the political and the military spheres. Given these differences from Western norms, it is no wonder that many in the West choose to emphasize only those parts of Sun Tzu's thought that they are able to comprehend, with the result that Chinese strategic thought first took root in the West in the form of axioms from *The Art of War*. However, while Western readers may well find these axioms fascinating and easy to understand, on most occasions this selective reading has only led to further confusion.

This narrow reading of *The Art of War*, and the fact that Sun Tzu was himself a general, led many in the West to conclude that the real object of Chinese strategy is warfare. However, Chinese strategic thought is not military-centered, or at least it is far less military-centered than its Western counterpart; its real object is war rather than warfare alone.

Chinese strategic thought is grand-strategic and systemic in nature. It is grand-strategic because it views war from a holistic perspective and employs all possible powers and means rather than military ones alone. It is systemic because it deals with nothing in isolation, but as an organic whole, with a full appreciation of relationships and contexts. Even though *The Art of War* is primarily about warfare, for example, it not only integrates matters concerning organization and supplies into strategic thinking, but also the economic cost of war and the moral and practical state of the country involved in it.[2] This represents a more holistic approach to war, and it is only through this approach that Sun Tzu's famous maxim "subjugating the enemy's army without fighting" can be considered an achievable goal.

Thus, whereas Western strategic thinkers tend to equate "strategy" with military strategy (the word does of course have a more general meaning and is now also used in numerous other fields), the Chinese, even those with little military or strategic knowledge, are likely to form a more grand-strategic (i.e. holistic) picture. The same applies to the word "war"—while the West uses "war" and "warfare" almost interchangeably, the Chinese have adopted a much wider meaning that could refer to struggles of all kinds, and not just those pertaining to warfare.

Alongside these cultural and psychological factors in the more holistic Asian worldview,[3] a further explanation for the fundamental difference between the Western and Chinese views of war and strategy is the fact that the Chinese tend to equate strategy (i.e. a plan designed to achieve a predefined aim) with stratagem (i.e. a plan intended to outwit an opponent). This gives Chinese strategic thought an orientation that places a much higher premium on brain power than on sheer force and technology, and in turn makes grand-strategic struggle rather than warfare a more "legitimate" form of conflict. Hence the West has mistakenly interpreted the Chinese way of war as "unrestricted warfare," yet a more precise understanding would be "unrestricted war."[4] This emphasis on stratagem has enabled Chinese strategic thought to reach outside the military realm, leaving its mark on other sectors of human activity, such as diplomacy and politics.

The Chinese Use of Paradox/Contradiction

Any student of Chinese strategic thought will quickly recognize the distinct and frequent use of paradox or contradiction in Chinese military and strategic treatises. Paradoxes and contradictions are often expressed in the form of pairs of opposites, or polarity; yin-yang, strong-weak, offense–defense, unorthodox–orthodox, vacuity–substance, and so on and so forth. In terms of strategic thought, the use of paradox and contradiction thus denotes the use of a different logical system in the Chinese strategic tradition. As a result, Chinese strategic thought is able to provide an entirely different way of interpreting and formulating strategy.

As Chinese logic is dialectical in nature, it may seem familiar to many in the West because there has been a dialectical tradition in Western thought since the time of Kant, Fichte, and Hegel.[5] However, the Chinese dialectical system is not identical to the Hegelian dialectical system, in which thesis is followed by antithesis, which is resolved by synthesis, and which is "aggressive" in the sense that the ultimate goal of reasoning is to resolve contradiction. Chinese dialectics is based on the principle of yin and yang and uses contradictions to understand relations between objects or events, to transcend or integrate apparent oppositions, or even to embrace clashing but instructive viewpoints.[6] Not only is the Chinese dialectical system far less prone to the cognitive deadlock that results from paradox, but it also provides a powerful tool to arrive at a better understanding of certain situations.[7]

The secret to the Chinese dialectical system lies in the yin-yang principle. As yin and yang are at once interconnected, interpenetrating, and interdependent in an uninterrupted manner, the polarity of the situation essentially rests in them (or the yin-yang continuum). In the same way, in warfare, the polarity of the situation stems from the antagonism between the forces involved. This illuminates why Chinese thought, which conceived of reality in terms of polarity, was predisposed to strategy.[8]

It is impossible to understand how the Chinese dialectical system works without first recognizing that there is not necessarily any incompatibility in the Chinese intellectual tradition between the belief that A is the case and the belief that not-A is the case. On the contrary, in the spirit of the Tao or yin-yang principle, A can actually imply that not-A is also the case, or at any rate that it will soon be the case.[9] In other words, the law of identity, which holds that a thing is itself and not some other thing, and the law of non-contradiction, which holds that a proposition cannot be both true and false, do not always apply in Chinese thought. Far from being two irreducible or even mutually exclusive states, yin and yang (or A and not-A) are two consecutive stages that are produced by the deployment of reality.[10] This idea is represented in one of Lao Tzu's sayings: "do nothing and let nothing be undone" (無為而無不為, Chapter 48). The "and" that is used to link the two propositions together might appear contradictory—at once contrary and consecutive. The saying could also be read as "do nothing *but* let nothing be left undone" or "do nothing *so that* nothing is left undone." The "empty word" in Chinese (*er* 而) that links the two parts of the sentence serves to express both the non-exclusion of contraries and the connection between them.[11] The same logical principle applies to Sun Tzu's maxim of "subjugating the enemy's army without fighting" (Chapter 3) as well as Lao Tzu's "Nothing in the world is more flexible and yielding than water. Yet when it attacks the firm and the strong, none can withstand it, because they have no way to change it" (Chapter 78). After all, the Chinese dialectics not only gives guidance to action and plays an active role in problem-solving, but actually helps eliminate the problem of "externality" in strategy altogether. The enemy and even the situation are part of the overall "system" and have been taken into consideration in the first place (since whatever is the opposite is always complementary, as implied in the logic of interaction).[12]

This chapter also aims to explore the underlying basis of Chinese strategic thought in two dimensions: horizontal and vertical. The horizontal dimension investigates the scope and components of the schools of Chinese strategic thought. The purpose of this discussion is not only to help readers understand Chinese strategic thought; it will also argue that Chinese strategic thought can play a fundamental role in establishing a general theory of strategy, something which has long been incomplete, if not entirely absent, in the Western strategic framework. The vertical dimension refers to the way Chinese strategic thought evolves and progresses from the most basic level to the highest level; this discussion presents the ideal of Chinese strategic thought and how to attain it. It touches upon the most important elements of Chinese strategic thought, such as yin–yang and Tao, which bring into being the Chinese epistemology of strategy and give Chinese strategy a dimension that its Western counterpart lacks.

It is important to note that the strategic thought examined here refers largely to ancient or classical Chinese strategic thought. However, this does not affect the broader applicability of this chapter or the value of Chinese strategic thought, as ancient Chinese strategic thought is still widely applied in modern Chinese strategy, as well as worldwide in numerous non-military fields.

The Horizontal Dimension of Chinese Strategic Thought

No scheme of Chinese strategy portrays the horizontal dimension better than the so-called "Four Schools of Chinese Strategic Thought." The Four Schools were defined by Jen Hung (Ren Hong 任宏) in the "Record of Literary Works" (*Yi Wen Chih* 藝文志), a section of the *History of the Han Dynasty* (*Han Shu* 漢書, Former Han: 206 BC–AD 8). The most accessible source of the Four Schools for Western students is the *Questions and Replies between T'ang T'ai-tsung and Li Wei-kung*, which is one of the books in *The Seven Military Classics of Ancient China*. In Sawyer's translation, the book contains the following exchange:

The Tai-tsung said: "What is meant by the Four Types [Schools]?"

Li Ching said: "These are what Jen Hung discussed during the Han. As for the classes of military strategists, 'balance of power and plans' comprises one type, 'disposition and strategic power' is one type, and 'yin and yang' and 'technique and crafts' are two types. These are the Four Types [Schools]."[13]

There are two reasons why the West seldom takes notice of the Four Schools. First, the Four Schools are only mentioned in the last book of *The Seven Military Classics of Ancient China*, a work far less known than *Sun Tzu: The Art of War*. The second reason is that Ralph Sawyer's translation of the pertinent section is not sufficiently accurate to show the significance of the passage. Sawyer also fails to offer any explanation of the Four Schools and their role in the Chinese strategic tradition.

Sawyer's translation of the passage is a literal one. The "balance of power and plans" is completely mistranslated, while "yin and yang" is meaningless without further clarification because it does not refer to yin and yang as these terms are now commonly understood in the West. Only "disposition and strategic power" and "technique and crafts" remain clear and close to their original meanings. Thus further elucidation of the Four Schools is clearly needed before we can continue our discussion.

1. The School of Strategy (quan mou 權謀)

Jen Hung provides a formal definition of the Four Schools in the "Record of Literary Works." His definition of the first school (*quan mou*; Sawyer's "balance of power and plans") is as follows:

The school of quan mou refers to governing the state by being straightforward [*cheng*/orthodox/the ordinary form 正] and waging war by being crafty [*ch'i*/unorthodox/the special form 奇]; assessing and laying plans before waging

18

wars/battles. It has incorporated the schools of "xing shi" [hsing and shih 形勢] [i.e. the second school; Sawyer's "disposition and strategic power"], "yin and yang" [the third school], and "technique and crafts" [the fourth school].

Literally, quan mou denotes the processes of weighing a situation and planning or strategizing about it. It essentially covers what is today referred to as strategy and grand strategy. It is therefore more appropriate to call quan mou the School of Strategy rather than, as Sawyer has trans-lated it, "balance of power and plans." This is true even though it is widely recognized that "strategy" in Chinese is usually interchangeable with "stratagem." In addition, Jen Hung includes a saying of Lao Tzu, "governing the state by being straightforward and waging war by being crafty," thereby highlighting the inherent political dimension in the School of Strategy, a dimension not present in the other three schools.

After defining quan mou, Jen Hung lists all the books he knows on the subject. As the School of Strategy essentially incorporates the other three schools, most of the important works of Chinese strategy, such as those of Sun Tzu, Sun Bin, and Wu Tzu, belong to this school.

2. The School of Operations and Tactics (hsing and shih 形勢)

Jen Hung describes the School of Operations and Tactics (Sawyer's "dis-position and strategic power") as follows:

The school of hsing and shih stresses moving like the wind and thunder, setting out after your enemies but arriving before them, understanding the art of divid-ing and combining as well as the way of fighting in friendly and enemy territo-ries, changing and transforming with no constant form, and subduing the enemies with speed and mobility.

Clearly, the strategic dimension found in the School of Strategy is absent from the School of Operations and Tactics. This school is strictly operational and tactical in nature as hsing and shih are the central themes in the operational and tactical concepts used in the Chinese tradition. Translating it as the School of Operations and Tactics should give Western readers a better sense of the school. However, a fuller under-standing of hsing and shih is still essential in order to comprehend its true meaning and significance.

Most of the works Jen Hung lists under the School of Operations and Tactics have been lost. The sole extant work is commonly known as *Wei Liao Tzu*, which is one of the seven texts in *The Seven Military Classics of Ancient China*. There is disagreement, however, as to whether the *Wei Liao Tzu* listed in the "Record of Literary Works" is the same as the one in *The Seven Military Classics*, as the *Wei Liao Tzu* in *The Seven Military Classics* is quite strategic and grand-strategic in its content and does not match Jen Hung's description of the School of Operations and Tactics.

3. The School of Yin and Yang (陰陽)

Jen Hung describes the School of Yin and Yang as follows:

The school of yin and yang emphasizes waging war by following the seasons and days, the employment of punishments and virtues, observing the stars, utilizing the "Five Elements," and borrowing the awesomeness and spirituality from the spirits to one's advantage.

It is noticeable that the yin and yang in this description differs somewhat from the concept of yin and yang described earlier. Jen Hung's yin and yang involve seasons, climates, the Five Elements (*Wu Xing* 五行), and even spirits. To clarify these seemingly mystical and superstitious practices, Sawyer notes that the practices or techniques of yin and yang encompassed classifying natural phenomena, including astronomical events and stellar objects, within a matrix of auspicious and inauspicious indications.[14] However extraordinary the practices may sound to modern students, T'ai-tsung and Li Ching assert that they are essential:

The T'ai-tsung said: "Can the [divinatory] practices of yin and yang be abandoned?"

Li Ching said: "They cannot. The military is the Tao of deceit, so if we [apparently] put faith in yin and yang divinatory practices, we can manipulate the greedy and stupid. They cannot be abandoned."[15]

From this passage it is evident that such practices were still widespread in the Sui (AD 589–618) and Tang (AD 618–907) periods. They conform to Sun Tzu's teaching that it is essential for generals to be "able to stupefy the eyes and ears of the officers and troops, keeping them ignorant."[16]

Despite the obsolescence of divinatory practices in modern warfare, the School of Yin and Yang formed the foundation of ancient Chinese military meteorology and geography,[17] and it also has contemporary significance.

4. The School of Technology (技巧)

Jen Hung's definition of the fourth school is as follows:

The school of technique and crafts gives emphasis to martial arts, mastery of weapons and equipments, and the use of military techniques and crafts that help to bring victories in offense and defense.

The School of Technique and Crafts consequently teaches the practical arts of combat and siege. As is true of the School of Yin and Yang, all of the works listed as belonging to the School of Technique and Crafts have been lost. Nevertheless, Mozi (Mo Tzu 墨子), one of the most famous philosophers in ancient China, is undoubtedly the leading figure of this school, given his thoughts on siege and defense as well as other examples of his military expertise. However, it is important to note that his work is not included under the School of Technique and Crafts, for Mozi was better known as a philosopher than as a military technician. The case of Mozi's work is similar to *The Method of the Ssu-ma*, one of the most renowned military classics of ancient China, which is categorized under ritual rather than military works. In modern terms, the School of Technique and Crafts can be better understood as the "School of Technology."

Sun Tzu and the Four Schools

There is a clear relationship between the structure of Sun Tzu's *The Art of War* and the Four Schools. The first three chapters of *The Art of War*—"Initial Estimations," "Waging War," and "Planning Offensives"—examine issues on strategy and grand strategy or *quan mou* (i.e. the School of Strategy). The next three chapters—"Military Disposition" (*hsing*), "Strategic Power" (*shih*), and "Vacuity (Emptiness) and Substance"—deal with topics that belong to the School of Operations and Tactics (the second school). Notions from the School of Yin and Yang are scattered throughout Chapters 7 to 12—"Military Combat," "Nine Changes," "Maneuvering the Army," "Configurations of Terrain," "Nine Terrains," and "Incendiary Attacks." Sun Tzu's final chapter—Chapter 13, "Employing Spies"—deals exclusively with spies and does not correspond to any of the schools.[18] It is noteworthy that the issues addressed by the School of Technique and Crafts do not appear in any of the thirteen chapters. However, a lost text from The Art of War that was recently recovered from an ancient tomb contains thinking from all four schools, including the School of Technique and Crafts.[19]

There is consequently a clear correlation between Sun Tzu's ideas and the Four Schools of Chinese strategy as defined by Jen Hung in the "Record of Literary Works." Yet it is hard to identify whether the two were influenced by each other, and, if they were, in which way the influences occurred. Chronologically, The Art of War (c.512 BC) appeared at a much earlier date than the "Record of Literary Works" (c.AD 100). However, the "Record of Literary Works" indicates that The Art of War has eighty-two chapters and nine scrolls of diagrams, not the thirteen chapters of the existing edition. This raises the question as to whether the Four Schools may have had an influence on the subsequent editing of The Art of War.[20]

There are three possible scenarios: (1) Sun Tzu influenced the formation of the Four Schools; (2) the Four Schools influenced the existing edition of Sun Tzu; or (3) the first and original edition of Sun Tzu influenced the formation of the Four Schools, but the Four Schools shaped later editions of Sun Tzu. There is of course one last possibility: namely that neither influenced the other. But this is highly unlikely given the clear congruity between Sun Tzu and the Four Schools.

On balance it is likely that the first edition of The Art of War influenced the Four Schools. While there is no clear evidence that Cao Cao (曹操 AD 155-220)—the first commentator on The Art of War and a renowned strategist—reedited The Art of War on the basis of the Four Schools, it also seems likely that the Four Schools will have exerted at least some influence over the subsequent editing of The Art of War into its current edition.

THE SYSTEM OF CHINESE STRATEGIC THOUGHT

Although the parallels between the order and content of the Four Schools and the structure of Sun Tzu are clear enough to show a link between the two, a factor that better explains the formation of the Four Schools has long been overlooked. That factor is found in *Sun Bin: The Art of Warfare*. Sun Bin was a descendant of Sun Tzu, whose work incorporated many of the latter's ideas. According to Sun Bin:

In general there are four factors in the way (*dao* 道) of warfare: military formation and display (*zhen/chen* 陣/陳), strategic advantage (*shi* 勢), adaptability (*bian* 變), and weighing with the lever scales (*quan* 權). A thorough understanding of these four factors is the way to crush a strong enemy and to capture its fierce commander.

... He who has a grasp of these four factors is on a safe heading, but he who loses them is on a death course.[21]

Sun Bin's reference to the "four factors" appears to have been based on myths dating back to the era of the legendary Yellow Emperor. The four factors or notions were modeled on the sword (*zhen/chen*), the bow and crossbow (*shi*), the boat and chariot (*bian*), and the long-handled weapon (*quan*). The Yellow Emperor says further that the four factors are "all uses of weapons."[22] The four factors resemble the Four Schools. Weighing with the lever scale (*quan*) is comparable to the First School (*quan mou*). Strategic advantage (*shi*) is equivalent to the Second School (*hsing* and *shih/shi*). Adaptability (*bian*) appears to correspond to the Third School (*yin* and *yang*), although the analogy between adaptability (*bian*) and *yin* and *yang* is not as straightforward as the other pairs. It involves a transformation in the notion of *yin* and *yang* from Sun Tzu's time to Sun Bin's period, an issue which will be discussed further below. Lastly, military formation and display (*zhen/chen*) resembles the Fourth School (technique and crafts), as it encompasses the fundamentals of military technique.

As this account demonstrates, the Four Schools of Chinese Strategic Thought are modeled on the four factors of Sun Bin, who was in turn influenced by Sun Tzu. Nevertheless, if the four factors are "all uses of weapons," the factors are originally operational and tactical concepts. Hence what Jen Hung has actually done is to confer strategic implications upon the four factors so that they become a systematic scheme (i.e. the Four Schools) that can effectively incorporate all Chinese strategic thought. What is more remarkable is that while Sun Bin gives all four factors equal weight, Jen Hung ranks them: he picks out the School of Strategy as the leading school and effectively incorporates the other three into it. The reason behind this transformation is not hard to explain. Toward the end of the Warring States Period (403–221 BC) it was widely recognized that Sun Tzu and Wu Tzu were the best works on war and strategy (they were commonly known as "Sun and Wu"), but Sun Tzu gained an even greater reputation thereafter. As was discussed earlier, what distinguishes Sun Tzu and Wu Tzu from other strategic and military works is their inherent political dimension. There is no doubt that Jen Hung took this characteristic and emphasis into consideration and that it played an important role in the formation of the Four Schools. It is also evident that the ranking of the Four Schools largely imitates the structure of *The Art of War*.

The formation of the Four Schools, as well as its inclination toward political and grand-strategic dimensions, had significant implications for the subsequent development of Chinese strategic thought. With respect to Sun Tzu, it is known that *The Art of War* had been expanded in Jen Hung's time to eighty-two chapters (although not under the direction of Sun Tzu) from its original thirteen chapters, and that the added material belongs mostly to the School of Yin and Yang and the School of Technique and Crafts. Due to the shallowness of the discussion in these additional chapters, however, as well as their divergence from Sun Tzu's original meanings, Cao Cao decided to restore the original face of *The Art of War* by taking out all sixty-nine additional chapters. This was undoubtedly an important event for *The Art of War*, since it largely determined how the text would appear for every generation thereafter.

With regard to the overall development of Chinese strategic thought, the Four Schools' emphasis on political and strategic dimensions, rather than on military and operational ones, together with the growing popularity of Sun Tzu, molded Chinese strategic thought so that it became increasingly political, grand-strategic, and oriented toward theory. It focused far less on operational and tactical matters or on technical and technological aspects. It would not be an exaggeration to say that the Four Schools of Chinese Strategic Thought and their collective orientation had a significant effect on the subsequent development of China's history and its foreign relations. This may also explain why *Sun Bin: The Art of Warfare*, a work of great significance to Chinese strategic thought, was lost for over 1,000 years. Its last official mention appears in the "Record of Literary Works," and it did not reappear until the excavations at Yin-ch'ueh-shan (Silver Sparrow Mountain 銀雀山) in 1972. Even though Sun Bin belongs to the School of Strategy (the first and most dominant school), the loss of the work suggests that it perhaps lacked the political and strategic dimensions of Sun Tzu and that such works quickly lost their appeal after the Han Dynasty.

The Four Schools and Modern Strategy

Although the Four Schools are over 1,900 years old, they may still have considerable significance because they can help solve one of the gravest problems of modern strategy: the absence of a general theory of strategy. The works of Sun Tzu and Clausewitz are often regarded as first-class general theories of strategy. However, *The Art of War*, and indeed Chinese strategic thought as a whole, is actually grand-strategic and theoretically oriented. Although Clausewitz's *On War* touches upon strategy, it is essentially a general theory of war, or at least most readers choose to read it in that way. In fact, Clausewitz and Sun Tzu are in many ways best read together as complementary texts, and combining the two into an informal general theory may be sufficient on some occasions. But such an approach lacks an overall scheme that can correctly identify the scope and key components of a general theory. In this respect, the Four Schools offer a much better conceptual framework; they are better balanced than Sun Tzu and have a more strategic orientation than Clausewitz. Since the original purpose in setting up the Four Schools was to categorize all existing military and strategic works in the Han period, this necessarily included several less useful, even outdated works, such as those from the School of Yin and Yang regarding spirits and divinatory practices. Therefore, before we can use the Four Schools as a common theoretical framework for Chinese and Western strategy, we need to make a few revisions.

The Four Schools all have modern equivalents. The School of Quan Mou covers what is today referred to as strategy and grand strategy. The School of Hsing and Shih essentially concerns operations and tactics. The School of Technique and Crafts clearly points toward technology. The School of Yin and Yang appears to be the only exception. The school established the foundation of ancient Chinese military meteorology and geography, yet its divinatory practices are completely out of date and unscientific.

Nevertheless, the phrase "yin and yang" in this military context means something slightly different from what it has come to mean today. The use of the phrase "yin and yang" in meteorological and geographical terms, like the way it was used when describing the School of Yin and Yang, was only the practice in Sun Tzu's time and before. As Sun Tzu states: "Heaven encompasses yin and yang, cold and heat, and the constraints of the seasons."[23] In the period that followed, the concept underwent a number of changes, which led it to assume the philosophical and metaphysical connotations that are now associated with yin and yang. It is understood as opposing yet interdependent forces or entities that gave rise to each other in turn. In the 150 years from the time of Sun Tzu to that of Sun Bin, yin and yang had become one of the most important concepts in Chinese culture and philosophy. As Sun Bin says, "The correlations between yin and yang should be used to assemble the troops and engage the enemy in battle."[24] Already in this passage, yin and yang has become a collective phrase that generally represents *ch'i* and *cheng* (unorthodox and orthodox) as well as vacuity and substance.

The transformation of the concept of yin and yang is of great significance. Once the concept and the yin–yang continuum are established, we can then "translate the situation into the *yin–yang* vocabulary of complementary opposites: strong–weak, fast–slow, many–few, and so on."[25] This is a necessary step, for we must make distinctions in order to evaluate circumstances and manipulate them in advance.[26] While yin and yang helps us look at things from the opposite viewpoint and hence, get a more complete picture of a situation, we should not forget the *dynamic* nature of yin and yang—they are at once interconnected, interpenetrating, and interdependent. Also, as we can see in the Tai Chi diagram (*T'ai Chi*

T'u or *Taijitu* 太極圖), all correlative pairs, not just offense and defense, are in a constant process of shifting from one end to the other. Such an organic paradigm is essential for acquiring fundamental insights and enhancing our adaptability. Since the yin and yang concept was originally derived from observations of nature (yin and yang originally represented the shady and sunny sides of a mountain), it offers a universal way of describing the interactions and interrelations of natural physical forces. And because of its emphasis on wholeness and its dynamic nature, the yin and yang concept is also able to deal with social and human systems, and, in the case at hand, with war as a system.

Such an all-embracing paradigm should form the very core of a general theory of strategy. As well as offering the theory a dynamic and naturalistic worldview, yin and yang is based on an entirely different logical system to that of Western strategic thought, and is thus able to offer new insights with regard to strategy. As Thomas Cleary contends, understanding this practical aspect of Taoist philosophical teachings helps to cut through the sense of paradox that may be caused by seemingly contradictory attitudes, and it can even resolve contradiction and paradox.[27] It is the use of yin and yang which ultimately explains why the strategic thought of Sun Tzu and Mao looks so fundamentally different from that of their Western counterparts.

If we reexamine the definition of the first and leading school of Chinese strategic thought (i.e. the School of Strategy), we notice how the logic of yin and yang is there from the start and plays a dominant role in shaping Chinese strategic thought as a whole.

The School of Strategy is the only school with an inherent political dimension. Jen Hung defines the school using Lao Tzu's saying, "governing the state by being straightforward (*cheng*) and waging war by being crafty (*ch'i*)." In other words, politics is *cheng* (orthodox) and war is *ch'i* (unorthodox), or, in the simplest sense, politics is yang and war is yin. Yang generally represents the active, dominating side. From this perspective Jen Hung's definition, which is based on Lao Tzu's saying, can be read as "war is the continuation of politics by other means," just as Clausewitz said. This commonality is often seen as evidence that Clausewitz had a greater influence on Mao Zedong and his strategic thought than Sun Tzu did. This, however, is a complete misunderstanding. In Mao's essay, "On Protracted War," he states, "'War is the continuation of politics.' In this sense war is politics and war itself is a political action; since ancient times there has never been a war that did not have a political character."[28] Mao says "war is the continuation of politics," but what he truly means is "war is politics." He takes a stance in which war and politics are welded together, without interruption or suspension; there is no such thing as "pure war" that can be separated from politics:

In a word, war cannot for a single moment be separated from politics. Any tendency ... to belittle politics by isolating war from it and advocating the idea of war as an absolute is wrong and should be corrected.[29]

Nevertheless, Mao recognizes that there is still a need to distinguish between politics and war even if they are two sides of the same coin:

But war has its own particular characteristics and in this sense it cannot be equated with politics in general. "War is the continuation of politics by other means." When politics develops to a certain stage beyond which it cannot proceed by the usual means, war breaks out to sweep the obstacles from the way.[30]

Mao's interpretation corresponds exactly to Jen Hung's definition (and Lao Tzu's saying), "governing the state by being straightforward (cheng) and waging war by being crafty (ch'i)." Politics employs "the usual means" and is the orthodox form, whereas war, as an unorthodox form, takes over when things can no longer proceed by "the usual means." Put even more plainly, Mao maintains that "politics is war without bloodshed while war is politics with bloodshed."[31] He uses "bloodshed" as a boundary to distinguish between cheng (orthodox/yang) and ch'i (unorthodox/yin). Thus Mao's perspective on the relationship between politics and war can only be fully understood by viewing it through the lens of yin and yang, a practice passed on all the way from Sun Tzu to Mao.

The concept of yin and yang has not only played a crucial role in shaping Chinese strategic thought—it can also be employed as the universal logic of war and strategy that has been missing so far, and is fundamental to the formation of a general theory of strategy. Some may claim that such logic of strategy has already been identified by thinkers, such as

Edward Luttwak, in the form of paradoxical logic: a different logic that pervades the entire realm of strategy that routinely violates ordinary linear logic. When the paradoxical logic of strategy assumes a dynamic form, it becomes the coming together, even the reversal, of opposites.[32] The paradoxical logic of strategy resembles yin and yang in many ways, but it is far less useful: while paradoxical logic is often seen as contradictory, and thus of a problematic and inexplicable nature, the logic of yin and yang essentially embraces and makes use of contradiction and paradox; paradox is often thought of as a standard device of Taoist psychology, used to cross imperceptible barriers of awareness.[33] Its application is further explained by François Jullien:

Instead of excluding each other, contraries mutually condition each other, and this constitutes the logic from which a sage [i.e. a strategist] derives his strategy. For, instead of seeing no farther than the opposed aspects of things, as common sense pictures them, and keeping them isolated, the sage is able to discern their interdependence and to profit from it. This is what he exploits instead of wearing himself out in efforts of his own.[34]

Furthermore, in the Chinese view, it can be a mistake to reject conclusions because they seem formally contradictory; such conclusions are merely reflections of things, and it can sometimes be more sensible to admit that an apparent contradiction exists than to insist that either one state of affairs or its opposite is the true one.[35] As a result of this framework, which is capable of bringing much added interpretative power and flexibility, Chinese strategic thought, using yin and yang as its logical and dialectic engine, has a proven record that dates back to the time of Sun Tzu and reaches forward into the present and Mao's wars against both his Eastern and Western opponents. In short, yin and yang appears to offer an indispensable logic for a general theory of strategy because it is a real guide to action that allows us to better understand the world and to improve our ability to adapt to unfolding circumstances.

The Four Schools and a General Theory of Strategy

After reinstating the School of Yin and Yang in a more constructive role, it is now time to illustrate how the Four Schools can be used as a common theoretical framework for both Chinese and Western strategy. Renamed in modern terms, they become the schools of Strategy, Operations and Tactics, Yin and Yang, and Technology. These should be the four key components in a general theory. Clearly, the School of Strategy and that of Operations and Tactics comprehend the study of grand strategy and strategy, and of operations and tactics, which together constitute the levels of war. The School of Yin and Yang serves as the branch for the study of the logic of war. The main concern of the School of Technology should be technology, as well as its applications in and impacts on the practices of war on different levels. These areas and aspects are essential to a meaningful general theory.

Although the Four Schools is a Chinese system, its use as a scheme for a general theory of strategy takes into consideration the strengths and weaknesses of both Chinese and Western strategic thought. The concerns addressed by the School of Strategy and the School of Yin and Yang are clearly the strengths of Chinese strategic thought—Sun Tzu has gained recognition in the West primarily because of his grand-strategic orientation, while the logic of yin and yang is a Chinese specialty. Conversely, in the area of operations and tactics, as well as in technology and its applications, the West clearly has an edge over the Chinese. Overall, Chinese strategic thought tends to be more theoretical, while its Western counterpart is more practical in nature. Even though the Four Schools were originally proposed by the Chinese, it is clear that a well-balanced, comprehensive system can be fully realized only with inputs from both Chinese and Western strategic thought.

It is beyond the scope of this book to propose a general theory of strategy that follows the system of the Four Schools. A few remarks should, however, be made regarding the School of Yin and Yang and the School of Technology.

The importance of yin and yang lies in the concept's capacity to transform our way of understanding the important concepts on all levels of war. Almost all important concepts of Chinese strategic thought are expressed in the form of correlating pairs on the basis of yin and yang. We have already seen through the example of Mao how the relationship between politics and war can be transformed from "war is the continuation of politics by other means" to "war is politics." The two interpretations do not contradict each other and there is no necessary incompatibility in terms of a yin–yang relationship. We also know that Chinese operational concepts such as *ch'i* and *cheng*, as well as vacuity and substance, are established on the basis of yin and yang. The logic of yin and yang shapes and transforms both the notions of strategy and of operations and tactics. Hence the School of Yin and Yang does not work independently—it constantly interacts with and transforms concepts on all levels of war, both within the School of Strategy and within the School of Operations and Tactics. It unites correlating pairs and turns them into an organic, dynamic whole, in addition to helping envision future developments by creating a systemic view.

The need for a School of Technology does not imply advocacy of technology-driven wars. Nevertheless, strategy has always required that we study how new technologies apply to the practice of war, for technology is one of the most changeable factors in war, and it is of great importance to identify technological developments and trends that signal revolutions or transformations in the conduct of war. Needless to say, the study of this school is inescapably scientific, technological, and technical in nature. Yet what is more essential to strategy as a whole is the identification of the political and socioeconomic implications behind technological changes so that these changes can be correctly evaluated in the strategic context. In this respect, we should emphasize studies and analyses such as the generations-of-war model and how the rise of a scientific paradigm or regime can change our way of war.[36] As is true of the School of Yin and Yang, the key aspect of the School of Technology is not technology itself, but how it interacts with all levels of war.

The Vertical Dimension of Chinese Strategic Thought

An understanding of Chinese strategic thought is not complete without mastering its vertical dimension. The vertical dimension refers to the avenue along which Chinese strategic thought evolves and progresses from the most basic level to the highest level; it is about the ideal of Chinese strategic thought and how to attain it. In essence, it represents the epistemology of Chinese strategy.

Again, the excerpt that best illustrates the vertical dimension of Chinese strategic thought comes from the *Questions and Replies between T'ang T'ai-tsung and Li Wei-kung*. This is not a coincidence. The early Tang period marked the height of Chinese power and influence as well as the pinnacle of classical Chinese strategic thought, and the dialogue between T'ai-tsung and Li Ching contains a great deal of sophisticated discussion that reflects the latest developments of the ideas of Sun Tzu and Chinese strategic thought as a whole:

The T'ai-tsung said: "What is of [the highest level of difficulty] in military strategy?"

Li Ching said: "I once divided it into *three levels* to allow students to gradually advance into it. The first is termed *Tao*, the second *Heaven and Earth*, and third *Methods of Generalship*. As for the Tao, it is the most essential and subtle, what the *I Ching* refers to as 'all-perceiving and all-knowing, [allowing one to be] spiritual and martial without slaying.' Now what is discussed under Heaven is yin and yang; what is discussed under Earth is the narrow and easy. One who excels at employing the army is able to use yin to snatch the yang, the narrow to attack the easy. It is what Mencius referred to as the 'seasons of Heaven and advantages of Earth.' The Method of Generalship discusses employing men and making the weapons advantageous—what the *Three Strategies* means by saying that one who gains the right officers will prosper, and the *Kuan-tzu* by saying that the weapons must be solid and sharp."

The T'ai-tsung said: "Yes, I have said that an army which can cause men to submit without fighting is the best; one that wins a hundred victories in a hundred battles is mediocre; and the one that uses deep moats and high fortifications for its own defense is the lowest. If we use this as a standard for comparison, all three are fully present in Sun-tzu's writings."[37]

The three levels of strategy (Tao, Heaven and Earth, and Methods of Generalship) are clearly derived from the five factors listed in Chapter 1 of *Sun Tzu: The Art of War*:

Warfare is the greatest affair of state ... Therefore, structure it according to [the following] five factors ... The first is termed the Tao, the second Heaven, the third Earth, the fourth generals, and the fifth the laws [for military organization and discipline].[38]

Just as Jen Hung did with the Four Schools, Li Ching has ranked the five factors proposed by Sun Tzu, which originally were more or less on the same level, into three levels, with the Tao being the most advanced. This change was made possible only because of certain intellectual developments that took place after Sun Tzu's time. In the period in which Sun Tzu lived, the Tao was considered more or less equivalent to politics. However, during the Warring States Period, the Tao, as with yin and yang, was given philosophical and metaphysical meanings and became the Tao to which we commonly refer today. With the rise of the concept of yin and yang during the Warring States Period, it became possible to discuss Heaven and Earth in a combined metaphysical manner where Heaven and Earth could be understood in terms of a yin–yang relationship and could thus form an independent level on their own.

T'ai-tsung's and Li Ching's discussion of the three levels relates noticeably to the epistemology of Chinese strategy, for Li Ching claims that students should advance gradually into the issue. However, this discussion later merged with that of Sun Tzu's strategic preferences, and the epistemological aspect was largely forgotten. Even so, it goes without saying that it is logical to interpret the three levels of strategy put forward by Li Ching in terms of intellectual paradigms. If the evolution or progression is from the Methods of Generalship to the Tao, from "employing men and making the weapons advantageous" to "all-perceiving and all-knowing, spiritual and martial without slaying," then the subject under discussion has to be the strategic mind and the strategic mind only. Li Ching has made this very clear because the Methods of Generalship are derived from the last two factors of Sun Tzu's five factors, namely generals and the laws/regulations of military organization and discipline. When combined, generals and laws form the Methods of Generalship, and this phrase encompasses methods, principles, and maxims that are necessarily rigid and mechanical in nature. As a form of strategic and military wisdom, the Methods of Generalship are considered unsophisticated and the least effective; they are the basics, of use only to beginners. Unfortunately, it is precisely that level of Chinese strategic thought that the West knows primarily.

DECIPHERING SUN TZU

Heaven and Earth: A Necessary Step toward the Tao

Heaven and Earth represent a more abstract, sophisticated theory and system of logic. Li Ching's explanation may lead us to think that Heaven and Earth denote factors such as weather and terrain, because he says "what is discussed under Heaven is yin and yang" (yin and yang can also stand for shady and sunny) and "what is discussed under Earth is the narrow and easy" (in terms of terrain). He also refers to an expression by Mencius, "seasons of Heaven and advantages of Earth," which further strengthens such an impression.

Nevertheless, we will know the discussion is far more profound when we read, "One who excels at employing the army is able to use yin to snatch the yang, the narrow to attack the easy." While "using the narrow to attack the easy" may still refer to the use of terrain in war, "using yin to snatch the yang" clearly has no climatic implication. "Using yin to snatch the yang" very possibly refers to what Li Ching has discussed in *Questions and Replies*:

According to Fan Li's book: 'If you are last [striking second] then use yin tactics, if you are first [striking first] then use yang tactics. When you have exhausted the enemy's yang measures, then expand your yin to the full and seize them.' This then is the subtle mysteriousness [ingenuity] of yin and yang according to the strategists.[39]

Fan Li was a famous political figure in the Spring and Autumn Period (Sun Tzu's time), but even though the concept was not fully developed until the later phase of the Warring States Period, it is evident that the central ideas of yin and yang had already been formed and become practicable according to *Sun Tzu: The Art of War*:

In warfare the strategic configurations of power (*shih*) do not exceed the unorthodox and orthodox, but the changes of the unorthodox and orthodox can never be completely exhausted. The unorthodox and orthodox mutually produce each other, just like an endless cycle. Who can exhaust them?[40]

The passage clearly illustrates the dominant feature of yin and yang, namely that yin (the unorthodox) and yang (the orthodox) are opposing yet mutually produce each other. What we need to pay special attention to, however, is the mechanism that allows yin and yang to "never be completely exhausted" and how this affects the application of the unorthodox and the orthodox in warfare. Contrary to common belief, the unorthodox and orthodox are of equal importance, and they are not fixed concepts. As Tai-tsung explains:

If we take the unorthodox as the orthodox and the enemy realizes it is the unorthodox, then I will use the orthodox to attack him. If we take the orthodox as the unorthodox and the enemy thinks it is the orthodox, then I will use the unorthodox to attack him. I will cause enemy's strategic power [shih] to constantly be vacuous, and my strategic power to always be substantial.[41]

The essence of the unorthodox and orthodox does not lie in seeking the unorthodox out of the orthodox. Rather, it is in reaching a realm where "there are none that are not orthodox, none that are not unorthodox, so they cause the enemy never to be able to fathom them. Thus with the orthodox they are victorious, with the unorthodox they are also victorious."[42] This is what is meant by "being formless," and such logic can best be demonstrated by yin and yang. Hence the level of Heaven and Earth is about the attainment of formlessness or "oneness" through fully grasping the logic of yin and yang. In T'ai-tsung's words:

[A]ttacking and defending are one! If you understand that they are the one, then in a hundred battles you will be victorious a hundred times.[43]

Echoing T'ai-tsung, Li Ching believes the attainment rises above knowledge and directly involves one's mindset:

If in attack you do not understand defending, and in defending you do not understand attacking, but instead not only make them into two separate affairs, but also assign responsibility for them to separate offices, then *even though the mouth recites the words of Sun-tzu and Wu-tzu, the mind has not thought about the mysterious subtleties of the discussion of the equality of attack and defense. How can the reality then be known?*[44]

The remarks above are congruent with T'ai-tsung's assessment of the level of Heaven and Earth. He states, "One that wins a hundred victories in a hundred battles is mediocre [the second best]." According to the standard of Chinese strategy, attaining oneness and winning 100 victories in 100 battles is not enough—it leads us only to the doorway to the Tao.

The Tao: The Whole System as One

The comments on the *I-ching* (*The Book of Changes*) defines the Tao as "a yin and a yang is the Tao." Yin and yang are without doubt the constituting blocks of the Tao, but the Tao certainly does not end there. Progressing to the level of the Tao from that of Heaven and Earth marks a paradigm shift that is both philosophical/epistemological and strategic. The key of the level of Heaven and Earth is yin and yang, and the purpose of that level is to help us unite the correlating pairs and turns them into an organic, dynamic whole, so that we can progress to the level of the Tao. Speaking philosophically and epistemologically, therefore, the level of Heaven and Earth is about unifying a duality in a way that transforms the dualism (Heaven and Earth) into dialectical monism (the Tao)—"a yin and a yang is what is called the Tao." The Tao, which is the ultimate term in Chinese thought, itself consists simply in the uninterrupted interplay of yin and yang, for the polarity of the situation rests in them.[45] Unifying the duality is therefore the basic requirement before proceeding to the level of the Tao. Once we realize this, we can then use this mental tool to understand the entire system and to know the interactions and interconnections within. As the Tao is derived from Nature, Taoists assume that the way Nature behaves is the most objective and impartial. Hence the ultimate goal of the level of the Tao is to attain absolute objectivity through grasping the origin of the One. According to Wu Tzu:

Now the Way [Tao] is the means by which one turns back to the foundation and returns to the beginning.[46]

As stated in *Huainanzi*, a part of the Taoist canon from the Han Dynasty:

What is meant by the Way [Tao] is to embody the circular and model the square, carry yin on one's back and embrace yang in one's bosom, on the left to be supple and on the right firm, to tread in obscurity and be capped with brightness, changing and transforming without fixity. *To grasp the origin of the One* so as to respond to the limitless [countless situations], this is what is called [spiritual illumination].[47]

Up to this point, we notice that there are two "onenesses." The first is attained through seeing yin and yang (or any correlative pair) as one, and this is also the goal of the level of Heaven and Earth. The second one corresponds to the Tao and appears only in the level of the Tao. In terms of complexity and difficulty, the second "oneness" is a quantum leap from the first one, because this time the goal is to perceive the whole system, the universe, as one. Only this "oneness" should be called "The One" or the Tao. At this level:

the sage/general has made his conscious mind accessible to everything, because he has dissolved all the focal points to which ideal forms and plan inevitably lead, and he has freed it from the particular obsessions that, through a lack of flexibility, it is liable to foster. In this way, he has liberated it from both the partiality and the rigidity in which an individual point of view, once it has become exclusive, becomes trapped. In other words, finally to put the matter plainly, he has allowed his conscious mind to take in the entire globality or processes, and he kept it in a state that is as mobile and fluid—even evolving—as the course of reality itself. The sage/general is thus in a position to identify with the overall coherence of becoming and can confidently anticipate future changes ...[48]

This is why Tai-tsung draws special attention to Sun Tzu after Li Ching has explained the three levels of strategy—such a systemic view is well rooted in Sun Tzu's thought. Tai-tsung considers "subjugating the enemy without fighting is the true pinnacle of excellence" to be the best strategy not only because it saves lives, but primarily because it causes the least disturbance to the system. "Winning a hundred victories in a hundred battles" is no doubt the best outcome in a military sense, but strategy is more than winning battles, or even wars; it is about winning the peace. The ultimate goal of strategy is to restore the system to a relatively stable condition so that the fruits of victory can be enjoyed. On many occasions, focusing too much on winning battles and wars brings unintended and undesirable consequences that are beyond our strategic capacity to repair. This is the principal reason why Sun Tzu always insists on the need to win wars on the moral and mental levels, while attempting to avoid the physical level.

Even though we are already equipped with everything we need to win 100 victories in 100 battles through mastering the level of Heaven and Earth, this is simply not enough in Chinese strategy, or otherwise the

DECIPHERING SUN TZU

level of the Tao would be unnecessary. We have to understand that even if we have every means to attain victory, causing the least disturbance to the system should remain our main concern. From a strategic point of view, the progression from the level of Heaven and Earth to the level of the Tao is an advance from the military level to the political and grand-strategic level or, according to the nature of Tao, to seeing all levels of war as one.

Conclusion

This chapter introduced two ways in which the Western world can better comprehend the system of Chinese strategic thought, namely the Four Schools and the Three Levels. These two grand schemes systematize Chinese strategic thought in horizontal and vertical dimensions, and enable us to better grasp the breadth and depth of Chinese strategy.

The discussion has not confined itself to presenting Western audiences with an overview of the basic system of Chinese strategy. I recognize in addition that the Four Schools offer a conceptual framework that is more balanced than *The Art of War* and has a more strategic orientation than Clausewitz's *On War*. This framework can also strike a balance between Chinese and Western strategic thought, theory and practice, and among various aspects of strategy. It could well be the most suitable framework within which to establish a general theory of strategy. By identifying the modern equivalents of the Four Schools, we become aware that Chinese strategy can be classified into strategy and grand strategy, operations and tactics, and technology. One additional major component of Chinese strategy, however, is missing in Western strategic thought. That is the concept of yin and yang, the logical and dialectic engine of virtually all Chinese thought. It marks the fundamental difference between Chinese and Western strategy and may possibly explain the greater sophistication of Chinese strategic thought.

We should be able to recognize that yin and yang and the Tao lie at the heart of both the Four Schools and Three Levels—yin and yang is the logical engine, while the Tao is the source of a grand-strategic and systemic orientation. They are the essential dimensions of Chinese strategy.

38

Without first understanding these two concepts, there is no way to prog-ress in the realm of Chinese strategy. The importance of yin and yang is even clearer if we put the Four Schools and the Three Levels together. Because yin and yang constitutes one of the Four Schools, it implies that without reaching the level of Heaven and Earth (which has as its objective mastering the yin-yang relationship), we can never truly understand the horizontal dimension of Chinese strategic thought, let alone reach the ultimate level of the Tao. When studying Chinese strategic thought, we have to set off from the level of Methods of Generalship, and proceed through the level of Heaven and Earth in order to gain access to the height of Chinese strategy. To do so we must abandon the way of learning that solely emphasizes fixed principles. This is the fundamental change students in the West must make to truly start to understand Chinese strategic thought.

2

THE GENESIS OF *THE ART OF WAR*

In the West, the most recent development to have occurred in the study of Sun Tzu was the discovery of a new Sun Tzu text in an archaeological find during an excavation at Yin-ch'ueh-shan (Silver Sparrow Mountain 銀雀山) in China's Shandong Province in 1972.[1] The text was unknown to the Western world until the publication of Roger T. Ames's English-language translation in 1993.[2] There are at least two reasons why the so-called "Yin-ch'ueh-shan Texts" are significant for the study of Sun Tzu. First, the rediscovery of *Sun Bin: The Art of Warfare*, a text that had been lost for nearly 2,000 years, validates the traditional view that Sun Tzu and Sun Bin were two different people who wrote separate treatises.[3] Second, the text containing a chapter entitled "The Questions of Wu," which is omitted from the thirteen chapters of *The Art of War*, serves as further evidence regarding the chronology of *The Art of War*. As the chapter refers to the events surrounding the dissolution of the state of Jin (Chin 晉)—a process that climaxed in 403 BC with the onset of the Warring States period (403–221 BC)—*The Art of War* was almost certainly written no later than the late Spring and Autumn period (i.e. before 403 BC).[4]

However important these developments may have been, no significant breakthroughs have since taken place in terms of Western research on Sun Tzu. But this is not the case in China, where new evidence has been uncovered that has the potential to change the paradigm through which Sun Tzu is studied. Contrary to the long-established view that Lao Tzu's

Tao Te Ching (which was probably written by his disciples, rather than Lao Tzu himself) preceded *The Art of War*, this new evidence suggests that the latter not only preceded the former, but that a number of the core ideas contained in *Tao Te Ching* are heavily indebted to the work of Sun Tzu.[5] As a result, there is a clear need to re-examine the influences behind *The Art of War*: while the influence of Lao Tzu (the person) cannot be excluded, it is highly likely that Sun Tzu was also influenced by factors other than Lao Tzu's thought.

The purpose of this chapter is to identify the military, strategic, diplomatic and cultural origins of *The Art of War*, as well as the zeitgeist in which Sun Tzu formed his ideas. It provides a detailed historical analysis that helps trace the roots of Sun Tzu's thought while presenting this history in relation to the concepts of Sun Tzu in a way that a Western audience will be able to understand.

The State of Qi (Ch'i 齊) and Sun Tzu

In various historical records and strategic texts written after *The Art of War*, Sun Tzu is generally identified as Sun Tzu of Wu (吳) (or "Wu Sun Tzu" 吳孫子), in reference to the state which he had served as a general. However, Sun Tzu was actually born in Qi (Ch'i 齊), in what is today known as Shandong province. Hence *both* Sun Tzu (Sun Tzu of *Wu*) and Sun Bin (often called Sun Tzu of *Qi* 齊孫子) were born in Qi, even though they are customarily recognized by the states they had served. The fact that two of China's most influential military and strategic thinkers came from the same state (Sun Bin may even have been a descendant of Sun Tzu) was no coincidence—both were heavily influenced by the culture and national traditions in Qi. As a result, it is impossible to understand the formation of Sun Tzu's ideas without first examining the unique culture and traditions of the state in which he was born and lived.

Tai Gong (T'ai Kung 太公)

Qi (1046–221 BC) was one of the most powerful states in ancient China throughout both the Spring and Autumn period and the Warring States period. The unique military and strategic traditions associated with Qi can largely be attributed to the role of Jiang Ziya (Chiang Tzu-ya 姜子牙, more famously known as Tai Gong, fl. eleventh century BC). Tai Gong was the first ruler of Qi and he also exerted a significant influence over ancient China's military and strategic thought. Indeed, while Tai Gong's treatise on military strategy, *Six Secret Strategic Teachings*, tends to be viewed in the West as only one of the *Seven Military Classics of Ancient China*, and is often overshadowed by *The Art of War*, Tai Gong can be seen as the father of Chinese military and strategic thought.[6] This is confirmed in *The Record of the Grand Historian* (Shi Ji/Shih Chi 史記), which details Tai Gong's role in formulating and implementing political, military, and diplomatic strategy in Zhou (周 1046–256 BC, the state which Tai Gong served). Tai Gong's most spectacular success in this regard came with the conquest of the Shang Dynasty (c.1600–1045 BC), which served as a model that was subsequently emulated by later Chinese strategists. Hence it has been said that Chinese military strategy and stratagem originated from Tai Gong.

Tai Gong's significance in the Chinese strategic tradition is apparent in "The Record of Literary Works" (Yi Wen Zhi 藝文志), a section of the *History of the Han Dynasty* (Han Shu 漢書, Former Han: 206 BC–AD 8), where a series of 237 chapters was named after Tai Gong. Eighty-one of these formed the book of "Stratagems" (mou 謀), seventy-one formed the book of "Sayings" (yin 言), and eighty-five formed the book of "War" (bing 兵). The three books together constituted the "Three Paths/Doors" of Chinese strategy.[7] Tai Gong was also believed to be responsible for devising the military rites, regulations, laws, and institutions of the Zhou Dynasty. These were partly recorded in the treatise, *The Methods of Si-ma* (The Methods of Ssu-ma 司馬法), which was very likely a different and older version of *The Methods of Si-ma* in *The Seven Military Classics of Ancient China*.

Tai Gong's dominating presence in the military and strategic scenes of the Zhou Dynasty had given his own state, Qi, a substantial edge over the other states in terms of military and strategic thought. Ever since the Zhou period, the Qi system of war has formed the core of the Chinese art of war. This in turn provided fertile soil for Sun Tzu's ideas to flourish.

Even Sun Tzu himself came from an established military family—the state which his ancestors served was none other than Tai Gong's Qi. Although the possibility that Sun Tzu gained his military knowledge directly from his family cannot be eliminated, it is almost certainly the case that both he and his family were heavily influenced by Tai Gong's military and strategic thought. In other words, the work of Tai Gong was an important catalyst for *The Art of War*.

The Culture of Qi

In addition to the military traditions that Tai Gong established, Sun Tzu's ideas were also influenced by the culture of Qi. In *The Culture of Qi and Chinese Civilization* (a Chinese work), the author identifies seven distinct national traits that were associated with the people of Qi, six of which correspond to the values underlying *The Art of War*. The six traits are as follows: pragmatism, adaptability, openness, inclusivity, propriety and righteousness, and intelligence.[8]

Tai Gong played a vital role in cultivating these national traits by laying the socioeconomic basis on which the state would subsequently develop and prosper. One of the earliest and most important policies to be implemented in this regard concerned Tai Gong's efforts to create new forms of commerce and industry, as well as to encourage growth in the fishing industry and in the production of salt.[9] These measures were largely adopted due to the problems that Qi faced as a result of its coastal location, with the high salinity of its soil preventing the land from being used for agriculture.

These economic reforms not only played a vital part in Qi's subsequent economic and demographic growth, leading it to become a major power, but also in shaping the culture of Qi, and the distinct national traits associated with its people. During this period most parts of China were dominated by agriculture, and Qi's departure from this norm thus served to create a unique socioeconomic and cultural environment. Given their exposure to a much wider range of commercial activity, and the need to engage with the mercantile culture, the citizens of Qi inevitably became more pragmatic and valued intelligence—they were even said to be deceitful.[10] This unique cultural and economic environment would undoubtedly have provided a favorable milieu for the evolution of many of Sun Tzu's ideas, and not least the cornerstone of *The Art of War*—"War is the Tao of deception." At the same time, the wide-ranging economic activities taking place in Qi were likely to have provided Sun Tzu with a more realistic sense of the material and economic dimensions of war. This is reflected in the fact that *The Art of War* is the first-ever treatise to contain a formal discussion of the relationship between war and the economy, with such economic considerations giving the work an indispensable grand-strategic orientation (see *The Art of War* Chapter 2).[11]

The culture of Qi did not originate from a single source, but emerged through the influence of four separate cultures:

1. The culture of Dong-yi (i.e. Eastern Barbarians 東夷), the original and local culture in the Qi area;
2. The culture of the "Flame Emperor" of Jiang (Jiang-yan 姜炎), originated from the legendary Chinese ruler, the "Flame Emperor." His homeland is near to the Jiang River (identical to Tai Gong's family name) and he is believed to be the ancestor of Tai Gong himself;
3. The culture of the Shang Dynasty, which influenced the area as well as China as a whole before the Shang Dynasty was overthrown by Zhou; and
4. The culture of the Zhou Dynasty, the culture of the sovereign state to which Qi, a vassal state, was subordinated.[12]

As the period in which Sun Tzu lived came 500 years after the formation of Qi, it is not necessary to examine how each of these four cultures influenced *The Art of War*. Instead, it is simply important to note how the multiple origins of Qi's culture gave rise to its inclusive and all-embracing nature as well as openness, which in turn served as a platform for other traits to take root and flourish. Without it, the coming together of all these qualities seems questionable. However, one interesting point that has been overlooked is that Dong-yi was a clan that was well known for archery—this can be shown by the Chinese pictographic character of "*yi*" (夷) from Dong-yi. It portrays a man (人) carrying a bow (弓) on his back. This suggests that Dong-yi people might have invented the bow and arrow, or at least that they were bellicose and good at hunting.[13] This makes a strong case explaining why *shih* (勢—momentum, potential energy, force, the strategic configurations of power, strategic advantage, etc.) is such a salient theme and plays such an important role in Sun Tzu's thesis, and why it had subsequently become the "trademark" of the Qi school of strategic thought. Obviously, Sun Tzu had a better understanding of the principles behind archery than other strategic thinkers— "So it is with expert at battle that his *shih* is channeled and his timing is precise. His *shih* is like a drawn crossbow and his timing is like releasing the trigger" (Chapter 5).[14]

According to *The Record of the Grand Historian*, the people of Qi had open and flexible minds, and were tactful and argumentative.[15] These attributes resulted from the all-embracing nature and openness of the culture in Qi, which was also reflected in the intellectual attitudes held by those in Qi. The citizens of Qi were not only receptive toward foreign ideas and new perspectives, but they were also active in inventing new ideas and incorporating them into their culture.[16] This quality is more than apparent in *The Art of War*, where ideas drawn from Confucianism, Taoism, and even the Legalist (Realist) School are readily identifiable. As has already been discussed, the integration of numerous, disparate ideas is vital for military and strategic treatises that reach the general theory level, and a cultural setting such as this would have undoubtedly played a vital part in the development of Sun Tzu's work and the Qi School of strategic thought in general.

Another interesting aspect of the culture of Qi is that it contained a number of opposing/contradictory traits: it was militaristic on the one hand while it valued intelligence on the other; it shared a strong moral code but never discounted the value of deception; and it stressed the rule of law while also emphasizing adaptability as its core value. Although the openness of Qi's culture certainly played a major role in these traits, what is more noteworthy, is that the capacity to cope with contradictory values is an important sign of a highly developed culture. In contrast to more homogenous societies, heterogeneous cultures, such as that of Qi, which are able to incorporate contradictory values and put them into practice, suggest that their people share a more sophisticated worldview, enabling them to deal with complex phenomena. This kind of quality is a vital one for strategic thinking, particularly as the formal Western logic tends to encounter problems when dealing with the paradoxes and complex situations that are commonplace during times of war.

All of the qualities associated with Qi's culture are manifested in *The Art of War*, a work in which Sun Tzu was able to incorporate the three contradictory attributes described above while forming a coherent theory, without compromising its practicality. One well-known example of this is Sun Tzu's famous saying: "Subjugating the enemy's army without fighting is the true pinnacle of excellence" (Chapter 3). In this saying, Sun Tzu claims that the highest realization of war is to engage in warfare without fighting. Western students of war and strategy often find this idea hard to understand. However, the fact that it serves as a source of confusion for a Western audience, while being generally accepted by the Chinese, suggests that the qualities associated with the people of Qi had a wide-ranging influence over the Chinese as a whole, something which was passed down over successive generations. This example can thus be seen as a milestone in the development of Chinese strategic thought, leading the Chinese to believe in whatever worked, even if it appeared paradoxical—the paradoxical logic of strategy was no longer problematic.

In addition to the seven traits associated with Qi's culture, Sun Tzu's work was also influenced by the fact that society in Qi was open to reform. By the time of Sun Tzu, the state of Qi had already undergone three major reforms. The first, which was of course facilitated by Tai Gong, had led Qi to become a rich country and a major power. The second and third reforms were initiated by Guan Zhong (Kuan Chung 管仲, c.720-645 BC) and Yan Ying (Yen Ying 晏嬰, d.500 BC), respectively, both of whom were later honored as "Tzu" or "Zi" (i.e. master, like that of Sun Tzu) for their achievements as great statesmen and prime ministers of Qi. Among them, the reform implemented by Guan Zhong was believed to be of special significance to Sun Tzu and his art of war.

Guan Zhong and Qi's Rise to Hegemony

Guan Zhong, who was appointed prime minister in 685 BC, was responsible for implementing a large number of reforms during the reign of the

Duke Huan of Qi (齊桓公). The reforms marked the first large-scale reform to have taken place in the Spring and Autumn Period, and built upon the solid economic foundations that Tai Gong had laid as a result of his policies in the state. It was due to these reforms that Qi was subsequently able to gain economic and military dominance over other states, and eventually became the strongest state of the time. Duke Huan was formally recognized as the official hegemon (Ba 霸) by the King of Zhou (the Chinese sovereign), and had been granted royal authority to hold interstate summits and to undertake military ventures. In many ways, Guan Zhong's importance to Qi and China is comparable to that of Bismarck to Germany and Europe—he forever changed Chinese politics and diplomacy and set valuable precedents for their political practitioners thereafter. It was in this period that slogans such as "respecting the king and defending against the barbarian" and schemes like "rich country and strong army" were devised and practiced. Even though other states later emerged and rose in power, Qi's period of hegemony was the first and most remarkable of all. It should come as no surprise that Sun Tzu, as a countryman of Qi, found the measures that Guan Zhong used in securing Qi's hegemony highly inspiring. There are thus a number of signs in *The Art of War* that Sun Tzu drew on the schemes devised by this prominent figure in Chinese history.

Since Sun Tzu had already had Tai Gong as his beacon in military and strategic thought, there was a possibility that Guan Zhong directly inherited Tai Kung's thought. Yet Sun Tzu's ideas on statecraft and diplomacy were more likely to have originated from Guan Zhong, as they were only possible in the more complex international environment that emerged after the time of Tai Gong. Thus as Sun Tzu says, "when the weapons have grown dull and spirits depressed, when our strength has been expended and resources consumed, then the feudal lords will take advantage of our exhaustion to arise. Even though you have wise generals, they will not be able to achieve a good result" (Chapter 2).[17] This passage shows that there were multiple contending feudal lords (i.e. dukes and princes of the vassal states of the Zhou Dynasty) in the international arena, each of whom was strong enough to wage warfare against the others, and were waiting for the best chance to attack. This was not a common scene in time of Tai Gong.

THE GENESIS OF *THE ART OF WAR*

There are also other passages in *The Art of War* that mention the struggle among the feudal lords that were arguably influenced by Guan Zhong and his thought. The first of these reads as follows:

[S]ubjugate the feudal lords with potential harm; labor the feudal lords with numerous affairs; and have the feudal lords race after profits. (Chapter 8)[18]

The broader discussion to which this passage belongs concerns how to manipulate adversaries by employing "the intermixture of gain and loss" (Chapter 8).[19] By first stating how to manipulate the feudal lords using the schemes in the passage above, Sun Tzu possibly received some inspiration from the measures and schemes which Guan Zhong had pioneered. He then put these political and diplomatic schemes into practice in military operations—"Thus the strategy for employing the army: Do not rely on their not coming, but depend on us having the means to await them. Do not rely on their not taking, but depend on us having us unassailable position" (Chapter 8).[20] This excerpt clearly shows the interrelationship between the ideas of Guan Zhong and Sun Tzu. The same also applies, as we will see below, between the ideas of Sun Tzu and Lao Tzu, albeit on a much more extensive scale.

There is also another passage where the ideas of Guan Zhong are evident, although there is a problem in terms of how it has been translated. The first part of the passage, which most translators have accurately translated, reads as follows:

Now when the army of a hegemon or true king attacks a great state, their masses are unable to assemble. When it applies its awesomeness to the enemy, their alliance cannot be sustained. (Chapter 11)[21]

This excerpt elucidates the importance of strategy and diplomacy in war: these tools of statecraft have to be used to their full extent in order to secure victory, regardless of the qualities of the rulers. All translators are in agreement on this. But a problem arises in the following part of the passage. With the exception of Thomas Cleary, all of the existing translations suggest that the hegemon or true king mentioned in the passage has already found a "way," which is never clearly stated, to prevent the enemy's masses from assembling and to make their alliance unsustainable:

For this reason it does not contend with any alliance under Heaven. It does not nurture the authority of others under Heaven. *Have faith in yourself, apply your awesomeness to the enemy.* Then his cities can be taken, his state can be subjugated. (Sawyer's translation)[22]

This immediately raises the question as to why having faith in oneself and applying one's awesomeness to the enemy will lead to the enemy's cities being taken and his states subjugated. There is no evidence of strategy here; nor would it make any strategic sense in the context of Sun Tzu. The reason for the error is that ancient Chinese tends to omit the subject of a sentence, and the translators are consequently at a loss to explain which king/state the sentence is describing. They automatically assume that the subject of the sentence refers to the hegemon or true king that has been mentioned in the previous sentence. But instead, it refers to those who *do not* follow the way practiced by "a hegemon and true king." This mistranslation has led to a complete reversal of the passage's real meaning.

When translated accurately, the passage should be read as a warning that even the true king has to utilize diplomacy, topography, and informants to secure victory; he should never rely solely on force. For those who "do not compete for alliances anywhere, do not foster authority anywhere, but just extend your personal influence, threatening opponents," their cities will be taken and states subjugated.[23] This is the real meaning of the passage, one which is totally consistent with Sun Tzu's famous dictum: "the highest realization of warfare is to attack the enemy's plans; next is to attack their alliances; next to attack their army; and the lowest is to attack their fortified cities" (Chapter 3).[24] Yet most translators simply choose to ignore this fact. This case of mistranslation highlights the problematic nature of existing translations of *The Art of War*.

What is more notable in the excerpt, that would certainly help enhance our understanding of *The Art of War* and its relationship with Guan Zhong, is Sun Tzu's reference to "a hegemon and true king." Most translators and commentators, as soon as they see the term "hegemony" (*ba wang* 霸王) (which usually appears in non-Yin-ch'ueh-shan versions), immediately take it for granted that the whole passage concerns how hegemons attain domination by force. And this in turn leads to the wrong translation, as discussed above. The notion of hegemon or hegemony, which is equivalent to the terms as understood in the West, had yet to be fully developed in the period in which Sun Tzu lived; nor was hegemony the form of power that Sun Tzu advocated. Hence, regardless as to whether the original expression is "*wang ba*" (王霸) or "*ba wang*" (霸王), there could only be one possible explanation that truly reflects the international settings of Sun Tzu's time—chief duke, like the Duke of Huan of Qi, which was above all other dukes and below the king. The term could also be translated as the "lord protector," but never "king" nor "hegemon," as the King of Zhou still retained the king's title (though he was more or less a figurehead) during the period.[25] As a result, "*wang ba*" (王霸) or "*ba wang*" (霸王) should refer to the Five *Ba* (霸 chief dukes) of the Spring and Autumn Period. There are mainly two versions regarding the choice of Dukes. Below is the most common one:

- Duke Huan of Qi (齊桓公)
- Duke Wen of Jin (晉文公)
- King Zhuang of Chu ((楚莊王)
- Duke Mu of Qin (秦穆公)
- Duke Xiang of Song (宋襄公)

Since the Five *Ba* had only appeared since the age of Guan Zhong, there should be no question that Sun Tzu developed these schemes based on Guan Zhong's original thoughts. The historical lessons and examples derived from the Five *Ba* demonstrate a strong emphasis on political and diplomatic warfare and a belief that "the victorious army first realizes the conditions for victory, and then seeks to engage in battle" (Chapter 4).[26] Although it is impossible to say with absolute certainty, for that reason Sun Tzu's famous dictum, "the highest realization of warfare is to attack the enemy's plans; next is to attack their alliances; next to attack their army; and the lowest is to attack their fortified cities," may actually come from Guan Zhong, the chief architect of Qi's "hegemony."

Sun Tzu and his Zeitgeist

The Spring and Autumn Period (770–403 BC) was an unparalleled age of tremendous change and upheaval in Chinese history. Over 400 battles were fought during this period alone, and this almost certainly had an impact on Sun Tzu. The three ancient Chinese thinkers that are most well known in the West—Lao Tzu, Confucius, and Sun Tzu—all emerged in this period; indeed, they were all contemporaries of each other. From the early to late Spring and Autumn periods, there were a number of currents and climates—political, ethical, intellectual, cultural, institutional, technological, and military—that had led to the revolution in strategic thought in China, and the eventual ascendancy of Sun Tzu.

Among the major developments in this extraordinary period of transition, three are most directly related to the birth of *The Art of War*: the rise of deception as the key principle of warfare, the advent of a new form of warfare, and the bifurcation of officials and generals in the state. Alongside the culture of Qi, these developments also served as important influences in the formation of Sun Tzu's ideas.

The Rise of Deception as the Key Principle of Warfare

"War is the Tao of deception" is today viewed as a timeless concept. Yet in Sun Tzu's time it was an entirely novel idea. During the early Spring and Autumn Period, even after the emergence of superb strategists and generals, such as Tai Gong, warfare often continued to be conducted in accordance with a series of military rites. Rather than strategy and stratagem, it was these military rites that were generally regarded as "the art of war."

The form of warfare that preceded Sun Tzu is not completely unknown in the West. In "On Protracted War," Mao Zedong states:

We are not Duke Hsiang [Xiang] of Sung [Song] and have no use for his asinine ethics. In order to achieve victory we must as far as possible make the enemy blind and deaf by sealing his eyes and ears and drive his commanders to distraction by creating confusion in their minds. The above concerns the way in which the initiative or passivity is related to the subjective direction of the war. Such subjective direction is indispensable for defeating Japan.[27]

The Duke Xiang of Song of whom Mao speaks is one of the five *Ba* (chief dukes) of the Spring and Autumn Period, as mentioned above. Mao condemns the duke's ethics as asinine, and the duke himself as a "stupid pig," because the Duke Xiang of Song had committed a serious military blunder. In 638 BC, the state of Song was engaged in battle with the powerful state of Chu (楚). The Sung forces were already deployed in battle positions when the Chu troops began to cross the river. One of the Song officers suggested that, as the Chu troops were numerically stronger, this was an ideal moment for an attack to take place. But the duke said, *"No, a gentleman should never attack one who is unprepared."* When the Chu troops had crossed the river, but had not yet completed their battle alignment, the officer again proposed an immediate attack. Once again the duke said, *"No, a gentleman should never attack an army which has not yet completed its battle alignment."* The duke gave the order for attack only after the Chu troops were fully prepared. As a result, the Song troops were met with a disastrous defeat in which the duke himself was wounded.[28]

Mao's criticism of the Duke Xiang of Song is unfair, however. From today's perspective, Mao's criticism appears justified, based purely on the result of the battle alone. But the duke was not entirely foolish, and his actions and decisions cannot be explained merely on the grounds of his stupidity. What Mao overlooked was the fact that the duke's decisions were not entirely based on his personal judgment. The duke's resolute refusal to follow his officer's advice instead stemmed from the need to pursue actions that he believed to be "right," not in terms of tactical needs, but those that were consonant with the common practices of his day.

Mao failed to take into account the central role that military rites continued to play in the early Spring and Autumn Period, while the case of the Duke Xiang of Song highlights how the norms and practices of war were gradually changing and would soon give way to tactical needs. The duke's logic and actions were informed by the ancient system of military rites that is best represented in *The Methods of Si-ma*, one of the *Seven Military Classics of Ancient China*.

The Methods of Si-ma is a military treatise of ancient China. Its content on military rites (*li* 禮, military rites—*jun li* 軍禮) may well be the oldest among the seven military classics. The system of military rites which *The Methods of Si-ma* upheld was that founded on benevolence and righteousness—"[The rulers of the antiquity] regard the forms of propriety [*li*] as their basic strength and benevolence as [the foundation of] their victory."[29] Even though this may sound impractical by today's standards, the scheme that the work advocates is undoubtedly a noble one, and it constituted a binding code of conduct for those (mainly aristocrats) who were brought up in this system. The excerpt from the text below shows how the duke arrived at the decisions that were to lead to military disaster:

In antiquity they did not pursue a fleeing enemy more than one hundred paces or follow a retreating army more than three days, thereby making clear their observance of the forms of proper conduct [li]. They did not exhaust the incapable and had sympathy for the wounded and sick, thereby making evident their benevolence. *They awaited the completion of the enemy's formation and then drummed the attack, thereby making clear their good faith.* They contended for righteousness, not profit, thereby manifesting their righteousness. Moreover, they were able to pardon those who submitted, thereby making evident their courage. They knew the end, they knew the beginning, thereby making clear their wisdom. These six virtues were taught together at appropriate times, being taken as the Tao of the people's guidelines. This was the rule from antiquity.[30]

Thus it is clearly the case that the duke was simply following what he believed to be the norm in war. Little by way of actual decision-making was involved. While Mao condemns the duke as following the norm blindly without considering the tactical circumstances, the duke's gravest miscalculation was the fact that he failed to take account of the cultural difference between himself and the Chu ruler/generals. As the king of Chu had openly defied the overlordship of Zhou by proclaiming himself a king, it was highly improbable that he and his generals would fight according to the military rites of the Zhou. Yet the duke may even have been aware of this, but chose to fight in the traditional way because he regarded himself as the defender of the Zhou Dynasty. In this regard, the duke was doomed from the start, given that Sung's forces were much weaker than Chu's. Whatever the truth may be, the duke's military defeat represented the twilight of the system of ancient military rites, which would soon yield to the system of deception that Sun Tzu advocated.

This shift in the spirit and values of war from rites to deception is particularly evident when *The Method of Si-ma* is compared with *The Art of War*. As a commentator on Sun Tzu, Zheng You-xian 鄭友賢 of the Southern Song Dynasty (AD 1127–1279) indicates that *The Method of*

Si-ma is founded on benevolence, and *The Art of War* on deception; *The Method of Si-ma* employs righteousness, and *The Art of War* advantage; *The Method of Si-ma* emphasizes war as the last resort of politics, and *The Art of War* concerns dispersion and concentration in military operations to attain change.[31] Direct comparison of these two treatises is especially revealing in the current context as both military works were the product of the Qi system. Indeed, it has even been claimed that Sun Tzu and Tian Rang-yi (田穰苴, the author of *The Method of Si-ma*, also known as Si-ma Rang-yi 司馬穰苴) were in fact from the same family (i.e. the Tian family). Although this is hard to confirm, it is apparent that the state of Qi had undergone a major shift in the conduct of war and battle. Despite the fact that Tian Rang-yi was a famous general, even his great accomplishments were unable to prolong the "shelf-life" of his principles. By Sun Tzu's time, military practice based on military rites had been abandoned and replaced by the school of deception that Sun Tzu had initiated.

Toward a New Form of Warfare

The rise of deception as the key principle of warfare was a process that did not take place in isolation, but was accompanied by the evolution of warfare itself. The period between the early Spring and Autumn Period and the time in which Sun Tzu lived (he began serving the state of Wu in 512 BC) was characterized by significant changes in almost every aspect of war. During the reign of the Duke Huan of Qi, Qi's army, under the reform of Guan Zhong, was believed to number only 30,000 men, while wars were usually decided through a single battle that would last no more than a day. In the Battle of Zhang Shao (長勺之戰, 684 BC), a major battle during the early reign of the Duke Huan of Qi, Qi was defeated as its army was unable to break the opposing army's line after three assaults, paving the way for a counterattack by Qi's opponent that eventually routed Qi's army. The battle was literally decided after three rounds of drumming (a signal for offensive/assault). Notwithstanding that the above example has shown the scale of war in those days, pitched battles, on the whole, were not so common in the early Spring and Autumn Period, for the duke's aim was to become *Ba* (霸, the chief duke) and to seek hegemony, not to destroy the enemy's state. Thus deterrence and diplomacy, rather than warfare, were often the preferred means to fulfill a ruler's goals.[32]

A new form of warfare began to take shape toward the late Spring and Autumn Period, although it is difficult to say whether the expanding scale of war was the cause or effect of this. In any case, as a result of the reforms carried out by the states, it was during this time that conscription armies became the norm. Moreover, the zone where wars took place had expanded to Southern China, where a number of river systems were located. This in turn led to the development of fleets and water transport, with sea/river battles becoming a matter of course. At the same time, the increasing types of terrain that a force had to encounter led infantry to replace chariots as the main arms of the army, even though joint operations involving both infantry and chariots continued. As the intensity of military operations reached a new level, wars became ever more protracted and violent. This new form of warfare also required additional mobility in order to make penetration, continuous operations, outflanking movement, and encirclement more possible than ever.[33]

Almost all of these new elements were present in the Battle of Bo Ju (柏舉之戰, 506 BC), in which Sun Tzu played a major planning and commanding role, eventually winning a stunning victory against the his state's (Wu) arch-enemy, the state of Chu. The battle marked the conclusion of an eighty-year war between Wu and Chu, though the operations phase itself was swift. The battle involved armies and fleets. The campaign comprised a series of mobile and continuous operations in which the Wu army traversed over 2,000 *li* (里, a Chinese unit of length, 1 *li* was equivalent to 415 meters in Zhou's time) and fought five consecutive battles before entering Chu's capital, Ying (郢). Hence Sun Tzu's depiction of "send[ing] forth an army of a hundred thousand on a campaign, marching them out a thousand *li*" (Chapter 13) was far from an exaggeration.[34] The campaign also corresponds exactly to what is written in *The Art of War*: "The prosecution of military affairs lies in according with and [learning] in detail the enemy's intentions. If one then focuses [his strength] toward the enemy, strike a thousand *li* away, and kills their general, it is termed 'being skillful and capable in completing military affairs'" (Chapter 11).[35] The campaign marked the pinnacle of military operations in the Spring and Autumn Period and represents Sun Tzu's greatest military achievement.

As military conflicts intensified and the scale of war expanded, there was an inevitable progression from a rites-based system of war to a deception-based system. Given the size of the armies now involved, it is hardly surprising that it was increasingly difficult to make decisions during pitch battles. Most wars would eventually turn into wars of attrition in which any victory attained was likely to be a pyrrhic one. Furthermore, it is evident from *The Art of War* that wars during the period placed enormous strain on the economies of the states, leading Sun Tzu to argue that it was entirely justified to seize an enemy's provisions, and that rewards should be given to soldiers who captured an enemy's chariots (Chapter 2).[36] It was in the face of such financial and material constraints that Sun Tzu developed two important principles—"conquering the enemy and growing stronger" and "the army values being victorious; it does not value prolonged warfare" (Chapter 2).[37]

In the passage that best encapsulates Sun Tzu's ideas with regard to the new form of warfare, Sun Tzu says: "Thus the army is established by deceit, moves for advantage, and changes through segmenting [dispersion] and reuniting [concentration]" (Chapter 7).[38] A careful reading of this passage reveals three elements that comprise Sun Tzu's strategic thought. The first and second elements, which are primarily about deception and the ways in which advantages can be employed to establish control over an opponent, are adequately covered in *The Art of War*. By recognizing that the psychological and cognitive dimension of war is the place where victory should be decided, Sun Tzu took deception to the realm of "Tao"—"War[fare] is the way (Tao) of deception" (Chapter 1),[39] which suggests that deception should be called a law of war.

Yet few people have noticed the third aspect in Sun Tzu's scheme, which is a great deal more than dispersion and concentration. In fact, Sun Tzu's mention of dispersion and concentration as a basis of change, as well as numerous examples in *The Art of War*, subtly hints at Sun Tzu's method for resolving military problems by imposing measures from the levels of war above the tactical level or the original level. Even though dispersion and concentration were becoming more common as wars grew in scale, it was Sun Tzu who recognized that this was not only a change, but also an opportunity to impose more control over war and to develop a new way of conducting war. In this case, Sun Tzu was trying to create better conditions through the use of dispersion and concentration before engaging in battle; he sought means to resolve a battle by taking it to the operational level. This is why Sun Tzu says, "the victorious army first realizes the conditions for victory, and then seeks to engage in battle. The vanquished army fights first, and then seeks victory" (Chapter 4).[40] This should be seen as a norm rather than a principle under the conditions of Sun Tzu's time. Although Sun Tzu's scheme differs substantively from the Western norm, whereby decisions are attained through a decisive battle, the scheme itself should still be relatively intuitive to a Western audience.

The use of dispersion and concentration is, of course, only one of the many ways proposed by Sun Tzu to resolve military problems through the imposition of measures from the upper levels of war. A modern example of this hidden teaching of Sun Tzu was performed by Mao Zedong and his generals. It is called "besiege the city and strike the relief forces." "Besiege the city and strike the relief forces" is a stratagem that was often practiced by the Communists during the Chinese Civil War, following Japan's defeat in World War II. Despite the fact that the Red Army laid siege to a city, its real intention was not always to capture the city, but to lure out and destroy the enemy's relief forces. In many cases, not only were the enemy's relief forces wiped out, but the city would also fall as the defenders lost heart once the relief had failed.

A careful examination of this stratagem clearly reveals its resemblance to Sun Tzu's maxim: "Thus the highest realization of warfare is to attack the enemy's plans; next is to attack their alliances; next to attack their army; and the lowest is to attack their fortified cities" (Chapter 3).[41] As the least preferred option was to attack the enemy's fortified cities, the Red Army tried to resolve it by settling it in the battlefield, which is a more preferable option to attacking cities. While this modern example serves to demonstrate only one part of Sun Tzu's dictum, it is clear that the essence of Sun Tzu's lesson is that one should never focus on just one spot in the overall strategic picture. If a problem cannot be resolved at one level, there are always other means available at the levels of war above—operational, diplomatic, political, economic, and even psychological (the control of war and the enemy will be further discussed in Chapter 3). This finally leads to Sun Tzu's ultimate teaching of war: "Subjugating the enemy's army without fighting is the true pinnacle of excellence."[42]

Bifurcation of Officials and Generals in the State

Even though war was a frequent occurrence in ancient China, generals who only specialized in military affairs, particularly in commanding an army during wartime, did not emerge until the late Spring and Autumn Period, when war was increasingly intensified. But this does not mean there had been no position for military affairs in general prior to that time. The "Si-ma" (司馬) referred to in the *The Method of Si-ma* was the name used to describe this position. The text's author, Tian Rang-yi, for example, was popularly known as Si-ma Rang-yi. Although commanding an army was one of the responsibilities of a Si-ma, those who held this post were also responsible for military administration and management, as well as other non-military business. It was frequently the case that high-ranking officials in the government would serve concurrently as generals during periods of war. Thus while Guan Zhong was a famous statesman and had been the architect of reform in Qi, he had also led an army himself on numerous occasions. This combined role of official–general was no more than a norm in the early Spring and Autumn Period; there was no definite division between officials and generals. As a result, politics and military affairs were very much intertwined. This may well explain why *The Art of War* was able to retain its grand-strategic design and orientation; even Sun Tzu himself was close to being a "pure" general.

The bifurcation of officials and generals in the state started to take place in the late Spring and Autumn Period, though the process was not completed until the Warring States Period. One major sign of this transition is the fact that leading military officials started to become more commonly known as generals (*jiang-jun*, 將軍) rather than Si-ma. *The Art of War*, which was written during this period, is revealing in this regard.

DECIPHERING SUN TZU

Despite the fact that the work was first presented to the king of Wu, it was evidently written for generals as well. In the text, there are signs that generals had already broken away from government officials, with the post of "general" becoming a purely military position. Sun Tzu even puts generals on the same level with Tao (politics), Heaven (climate, seasons), Earth (geography, terrain), and laws for military organization and discipline as the five key factors that determine the outcome of a war, and which generals have to understand if they are to be victorious (Chapter 1).[43] Sun Tzu consequently places a great deal of emphasis on the qualities of a general: "The general encompasses wisdom, credibility, benevolence, courage, and strictness," qualities that are quite specific to generalship (Chapter 1).[44] It is also evident that generals were able to defy the ruler's order if the situation required them to do so (Chapters 3 and 10).[45] This bifurcation process encapsulates the fact that China was then undergoing a period of tremendous change and that this transition had yet to be completed. It is only through an awareness of this historical background that the multifaceted and versatile nature of *The Art of War* and its grand-strategic orientation can be properly understood. Even Sun Tzu must have considered it necessary for the proper conduct of war. It originated from the pattern of war and customs of early Spring and Autumn Period to a large extent, while some contents that are dominantly military in nature are the result of new developments toward the end of the Spring and Autumn Period. These new developments, including the advent of a new form of warfare, and the bifurcation of officials and generals in the state, foreshadowed the so-called "militarization of strategy" in the subsequent Warring States Period. This explains why the grand-strategic orientation in *The Art of War* was absent in *Sun Bin: The Art of Warfare*, a military treatise written by Sun Tzu's descendant in the Warring States Period. And as in the West, the more "militarized" strategic thought became, the more pressing was the need for a grand-strategic reorientation—this is one important reason why *The Art of War* is so highly valued. The wisdom of Sun Tzu undoubtedly reached the political and grand-strategic level. However, because of the fact that Sun Tzu made a very crucial move to the military sphere (due to the bifurcation process mainly), the usage of his thought became so much more situation-dependent, and has been largely limited to the military field. In other words, Sun Tzu decided that his ideas should be used and further developed "downstream" toward lower levels of war, at the expense of developing his thought further "upstream," where it could be used in the political realm or other non-military areas. It was the inability of *The Art of War* to answer the needs of strategic thought in the latter that ultimately paved the way for the advent of Lao Tzu's *Tao Te Ching* in filling the void left by Sun Tzu.

Lao Tzu

As *The Art of War* precedes *Tao Te Ching*, it might seem somewhat paradoxical to refer to Lao Tzu as one of the influences on Sun Tzu's thought. Yet it is important to note that Lao Tzu *the person* and Lao Tzu *the book* (i.e. *Tao Te Ching*) appeared at different times in history; Lao Tzu was believed to be contemporary with, though older than, Sun Tzu and Confucius (i.e. in the Late Spring and Autumn Period), whereas *Tao Te Ching*, his magnum opus, is believed to have emerged at a later time in the early Warring States Period.[46] Thus, despite new evidence indicating that *The Art of War* chronologically precedes *Tao Te Ching*, this does not mean that Lao Tzu did not influence *The Art of War*: it was only Lao Tzu *the book* (i.e. *Tao Te Ching*), and not the person, that came after *The Art of War*. Numerous sources indicate that Confucius visited Lao Tzu on more than one occasion to seek his opinion on the Rites (*li*) of the Zhou Dynasty. He did so because Lao Tzu was then a widely acclaimed expert in the subject matter—Lao Tzu was known to be the Keeper of the Archives (or Librarian–historian) of the royal court of Zhou. This reportedly gave him broad access to the historical records and other classics of the time, a privilege that was unavailable to Confucius. The fact that Confucius appears to have met Lao Tzu is important because it is indicative of the latter's fame as a sage, and it is thus unlikely that Sun Tzu would have been unfamiliar with Lao Tzu and his ideas. As there are also a number of notable similarities between the concepts used by Sun Tzu and Lao Tzu, it is extremely likely that Lao Tzu had a significant impact on Sun Tzu's work.

The Art of War features at least two elements which suggest that Lao Tzu, or his school of thought, exerted some degree of influence over Sun

Tzu. The first of these is the text's extensive use of dialectical pairs. The use of dialectical and opposing pairs is more noticeable in *The Art of War* (e.g. near–far, vacuity–substance, attack–defense) and *Tao Te Ching* (e.g. yin–yang, weak–strong, rigid–flexible) than in any of the other Chinese classics. The skill of Sun Tzu and Lao Tzu not only resides in their ability to reveal these dialectical pairs and to recognize how they work in their own respective fields, but also in making full use of these so-called contradictions (*mao-dun* 矛盾) and dialectics to fulfill their goals. The second area in which Sun Tzu was arguably influenced by Lao Tzu, and which is closely related to the first, is in their use of seemingly contradictory means to attain desired ends. In Sun Tzu's case, in "subjugating the enemy's army without fighting is the true pinnacle of excellence," subjugating the enemy's army is the end and achieving it without fighting is the means, while Lao Tzu's "The Way is always uncontrived (*wu-wei* 無為, also known as non-action), yet there's nothing it doesn't do" shares exactly the same logic. Even though there is a possibility that Sun Tzu's line preceded Lao Tzu's (since *Tao Te Ching* emerged at a later time), it is probable that the concept of using contradictory means to attain desired ends itself comes from Lao Tzu *the person* or the ancient classics upon which he drew this concept, for Lao Tzu was a famous sage in Sun Tzu's time. It also seems unlikely that Sun Tzu, who came from an established military family in Qi, and whose career had solely been centered on military affairs, would have been able to formulate these philosophical notions entirely by himself without borrowing from other sources. And given the strong resemblance between the underlying conceptions of Sun Tzu and Lao Tzu, it is extremely likely that the source in question was Lao Tzu.

Hence, it is possible to speculate that there is a relationship between Sun Tzu, Lao Tzu *the person*, and Lao Tzu *the book* (i.e. *Tao Te Ching*), where Lao Tzu influenced Sun Tzu and *The Art of War*, and *The Art of War* in turn influenced *Tao Te Ching*. In this chapter we have focused on the first half, in the next we will work on the second half.[47]

Conclusion

The foundation of Chinese strategic thought was primarily laid in the Spring and Autumn Period, when tremendous changes were taking place throughout China. However, as this period of history is not widely understood in the West, the role that these changes and socio-historical developments played in the work of Sun Tzu has served as a barrier to those seeking to understand Chinese strategic thought.

This chapter has discussed the principal factors and developments during this period that exerted an influence on *The Art of War* and Chinese strategic thought as a whole. One of the most important of these influences was the rising power of the state of Qi and the ascendancy of its specific strain of military and strategic thought, which subsequently became the basis for Chinese strategic thought as a whole. Given his origins in Qi, Sun Tzu consequently had an intellectual advantage over his contemporaries when it came to writing a strategic treatise. Yet it is impossible to understand the formation of Sun Tzu's ideas without reference to the broader zeitgeist of the period in which he lived. The fact that Sun Tzu lived in a transitional period allowed him to incorporate elements and ideas from different periods of time, which has in turn enabled *The Art of War* to transcend time itself. However, it was the same factor that ultimately limited the applicability of his theory. As a result, the transformation and final completion of Chinese strategic thought was left to be fulfilled by the Taoists, who further developed Lao Tzu's thought after embracing Sun Tzu's ideas.

3

FROM SUN TZU AND LAO TZU

THE COMPLETION OF CHINESE STRATEGIC THOUGHT

Lao Tzu's *Tao Te Ching* tends to be understood as a philosophical work in the West. In China, however, the text has often been viewed as a work of strategy. Lao Tzu's famous saying, "governing the state by being straight-forward and waging war by being crafty," as we saw in Chapter 1, was used to define the School of Strategy (*quan mou*), the leading school among the Four Schools of Chinese Strategic Thought. As Sun Tzu was said to belong to this school in the "Record of Literary Works" (*Yi-wen chih*), a strong association between *Tao Te Ching* and Chinese strategic thought as a whole had consequently been identified as early as the Han Dynasty (206 BC–AD 220).

'Tao Te Ching' as a Strategic Text

The identification of links between *Tao Te Ching* and Chinese strategic thought continued over the course of subsequent years. During the Tang Dynasty (618–907), for instance, Wang Zhen (Wang Chen 王真) wrote a volume entitled *The Martial Tao Te Ching* (English translation by Ralph D. Sawyer)[1] which claimed that each of the chapters in *Tao Te Ching* was relevant to strategic thought. In the seventeenth century, Wang Fu-zhi (Wang Fu-chih 王夫之), a Chinese philosopher–scholar, even went so far as to claim that Lao Tzu was the forerunner to Chinese strategic thought, and that the ideas contained in *Tao Te Ching* should be studied by everyone who was interested in war and strategy. It has long been rumored that Mao Tse-tung also regarded Lao Tzu's masterpiece as a work of strategy.

This divergence in terms of the prevailing Chinese and Western interpretation of *Tao Te Ching* raises a question that has seldom been addressed in the West: namely, what is a "strategic volume" (*bing shu* 兵書)? Due to its ancient Chinese roots, *bing* (兵) in *bing shu* (兵書) can stand for soldier, the military, or strategy. Yet only the two latter definitions are relevant in the current context. The absence of a clear distinction between the two terms in ancient Chinese is one of the reasons why *Tao Te Ching* has been regarded as a *bing shu*. While the work could be viewed as a military text, it is more likely to be interpreted as a strategic work owing to the strategic theory and concepts (albeit not necessarily in a military–strategic sense) that it contains. In *Questions and Replies between T'ang T'ai-tsung and Li Wei-kung*, one of the *Seven Military Classics of Ancient China*, Li Ching identifies two major streams of Chinese strategic thought. This classification can serve as a more precise line between the strategic and military streams of Chinese strategic thought:

Li Ching said: "What Chang Liang [Zhang Liang 張良] studied was *The Six Secret Teachings* and *The Three Strategies* of the T'ai Kung [Tai Gong]. What Han Hsin [Han Xin 韓信] studied was the *Ssu-ma Jang-chü* [*The Methods of the Ssu-ma*] and the *Sun-tzu* [*The Art of War*]."[2]

Zhang Liang (d.185 BC) and Han Xin (d.196 BC) are highly prominent figures in Chinese military and strategic history. Zhang Liang was a strategic advisor to the first emperor of the Han Dynasty, Liu Bang (劉邦 256–195 BC), while Han Xin was one of the greatest generals in Chinese history. The excerpt above indicates that Zhang Liang studied the works of Tai Gong, which are more comprehensive in nature and have a political and grand-strategic orientation. Han Xin, on the other hand, studied *The Methods of the Ssu-ma* and *The Art of War*, which are of a primarily military character, although both texts also contain discussions of issues pertaining to politics and grand strategy that are directly related to war. Hence there were two different types of strategist in ancient China: the first type was represented by an all-round strategist-advisor (e.g. Zhang Liang) and the second type by a military strategist-general (e.g. Han Xin, Sun Tzu).[3] It is important to note that both types value the use of stratagem.

As mentioned in the previous chapter, Sun Tzu's swing toward the military strategist-general type served to limit the applicability of his theory to areas other than war. However, the all-round strategist-advisor type that originated from Tai Gong was not the answer either. This is because this stream of strategic thought emerged prior to the bifurcation of officials and generals in the state, and hence at a far earlier date than its counterpart. Consequently, while the works that belong to this stream appear to be more comprehensive in nature, they lack the depth and degree of specialization offered by the military stream. More importantly, they remained military-oriented to a certain extent.

The issue faced by Chinese strategic thought after Sun Tzu was that while *The Art of War* marked a real breakthrough in the study of war and strategy, it also implied that strategic thought under this military strategist-general paradigm was close to maturity. Further developments in the same direction would only lead to works that were largely a response to the increasing militarization of war in the Warring State Period—*Sun Bin: The Art of Warfare* being a prime example of this. On the other hand, unlike its Western counterpart, where a general theory of strategy did not appear until Clausewitz, 2,300 years later, the Chinese had already had a general theory (i.e. *The Art of War*) explaining the nature of war and strategy in 512 BC, and hence they started to seek something different.

There was thus a demand for a new paradigm of strategic thought, and such a paradigm would have to respond to two issues: first, it should not be military-centered—though it would not necessarily need to be fully politically oriented, it should at least view human struggle (not confined to war or warfare) from a political perspective. Second, rather than offering a general theory of strategy, the new paradigm would have to provide specific schemes through which victory could be attained that would offer a means for the weak to defeat the strong—explaining the nature of war and strategy alone was no longer sufficient. In fact, such requirements are already addressed in the definition of the School of Strategy (*quan mou*) in the "Record of Literary Works" (*Yi-wen chih*). The choice of

Lao Tzu's "governing the state by being straightforward and waging war by being crafty" as the key sentence in the definition shows that there was a demand for a more universal theory of strategy, while it also hinted that the answer lay in Lao Tzu.

In response to the first issue, Lao Tzu's *Tao Te Ching* positions itself as a book that encompasses numerous topics, including statecraft, strategy, and stratagem. As a result, *Tao Te Ching* acquired an inherent strategic dimension without losing its applicability to areas other than war. In addition, in order to make his thesis more universal and less situation-dependent, Lao Tzu took his work to a new theoretical and philosophical height—this is consistent with the Chinese tendency to build increasingly abstract theories. Lao Tzu's answer to the second issue is designed to avoid the risk of his universal theory becoming so general that it ceased to be useful. Thus whereas *The Art of War* sets out the necessary means and conditions to defeat an adversary, *Tao Te Ching* proposes practical measures that would enable the weak to defeat the strong, thereby providing a guide that could be used in almost any form of struggle. In order to achieve this, the proposed measures needed to be underpinned by stratagem, and a better understanding of the human mindset and behavior was also required. This kind of approach was not entirely unprecedented. The *Thirty-Six Stratagems*, a Chinese strategic text that gained some popularity in the West, for example, also shares this attribute. However, the text focuses solely on the unorthodox and deceptive means in strategy and consequently lacks the theoretical sophistication of *Tao Te Ching*.

From Sun Tzu to Lao Tzu: The Origin

The relationship between *The Art of War* and *Tao Te Ching* underwent a tectonic shift when Ho Ping-ti (何炳棣) presented substantial evidence that *The Art of War* precedes *Tao Te Ching*. Ho Ping-ti even went so far as to assert that *The Art of War* is China's earliest private compilation (i.e. a text that had not been compiled by the royal court) in existence.[4] This claim has been advanced by Li Zehou (李澤厚), who argues that the political and philosophical dialectics put forward in *Tao Te Ching* bear a strong resemblance to the military dialectics used in the work of Sun Tzu. He consequently concludes that the authors of *Tao Te Ching* (Lao Tzu's students, rather than Lao Tzu himself) have augmented Sun Tzu's military dialectics by applying his approach at the political and philosophical levels.[5] This has led to a great deal of progress in understanding the importance of Sun Tzu in the development of Chinese dialectics and the specific line of thought that is derived from it.

The evolution of Chinese dialectical thought—from military to Taoist dialectics—undoubtedly stems from Sun Tzu's identification of the so-called "Tao of deception": "warfare is the Tao of deception."[6] This concept has revolutionized strategy:

Thus although [you are] capable, display incapability to them. When committed to employing your forces, feign inactivity. When [your objective] is nearby, make it appear as if distant; when far away, create the illusion of being nearby. (Chapter 1)[7]

This of course is nothing more than the most basic principle underlying deception and stratagem. However, the importance of this principle in the current context resides in the way that it has been interpreted in Chinese and Western strategic thought. For Sun Tzu, and Chinese strategic thought in general, "warfare is the Tao of deception": in other words, stratagem and deception are at the heart of the Chinese strategic tradition. Clausewitz, in contrast, dismisses the value of deception in warfare and instead emphasizes his thesis of the concentration of superior force at the decisive point:[8]

[P]lans and orders issued for appearances only, fake reports designed to confuse the enemy, etc.—have as a rule so little strategic value that they are used only if a ready-made opportunity presents itself. They should not be considered as a significant independent field of action at the disposal of the commander.[9]

Consequently, while Clausewitz dismisses the value of deception as a tool of warfare, it is precisely this which Sun Tzu and his Taoist successors use to develop their strategic thought and the practical measures through which strategy can be put into practice.

As the genesis of Chinese strategic dialectics, Sun Tzu's "Tao of deception" is an important milestone in that it not only identifies the differences and contradictions between phenomenon and essence, but it also recognizes the importance of understanding the differences between the two in war—as a matter of life and death.[10] Despite the everyday contradictions between phenomenon and essence as a result of the use of stratagem, in Sun Tzu's discussion of the Tao of deception, the ability to grasp the phenomenon can help to infer the essence upon which a strategist or a general can make his judgments and decisions. In other words, contradictions or yin-yang in war are useful as they offer important clues. As contradictions do not necessarily lead to paradoxes, there is no need for them to be eliminated in war. Therefore, Li Zehou, having learnt about the constructive use of contradictions in war, realizes that Chinese dialectics is highly unlikely to be derived from dialogue, as is the case in the Western tradition. Rather, Chinese dialectics is most likely to come into existence from military experiences: hence it remains practical and utilitarian in nature, and has highly significant empirical value. To paraphrase Li, Chinese strategic dialectics and the way of thinking from which it is derived has always been an empirical generalization of everyday struggles, rather than an abstraction of dialogue.[11]

Rather than a method of argument for resolving disagreement, Chinese military/strategic dialectics is a method of thought for grasping reality. As far as decision-making and actions in war are concerned, ancient Chinese strategists deliberately selected certain topics, while omitting others, in order to reveal and grasp the essence of a particular matter in a focused and definite manner.[12] In order to achieve this, Chinese strategists needed to observe complex and multifaceted phenomena on the one hand, while at the same time employing a general dichotomy derived from the method of thinking that involved the active use of contradictions, in order to discriminate against things and grasp the entirety of the situation for decision-making purposes. Such a general dichotomy is vital for grasping the essence, the reality, in a definite, rapid, and straightforward manner, through actively employing contradictions to generalize the traits of matters. That is why Sun Tzu has used so many contradiction pairs in The Art of War, including enemy-friend, peace-war, win-lose, life-death, advance-retreat, strength-weakness, attack-defense, move-stop, vacuity-substance, fatigued-rested, hungry-full, numerous-few, courage-fear, and so on—using these pairs to represent any situation, circumstance, or matter so that generals and strategists can grasp them easily in such a highlighted form of contradiction. And by doing so they are able to form the basis for planning and conducting war or battle. This, in short, provides an intuitive means for grasping the essence/reality that is non-inductive and non-deductive in nature—it is a simplified yet highly effective method of thought.[13]

A further important feature of the Chinese dialectical system is its ability to identify the interactions between objects in war (e.g. terrain) and the subject (i.e. ourselves/our army); rather than being static, the nature of such objects changes depending on how they are perceived.[14] A general will always view terrain in the form of the advantage it offers and this will change depending on the strategic situation and context. As this is the case, a general will attach a large degree of importance to the interdependence and interpenetration between the two sides of a contradiction pair, while attaching even greater importance to their transformations and the ways in which these can be used to advantage:[15]

Chaos is given birth from control; fear is given birth from courage; weakness is given birth from strength. (Chapter 5)[16]

If they are substantial, prepare for them; if they are strong, avoid them.
If they are angry, perturb them; be deferential to foster their arrogance.
If they are rested, force them to exert themselves.
If they are united, cause them to be separated. (Chapter 1)[17]

This helps explain why Sun Tzu says that "courage and fear are a question of the strategic configuration of power (*shih*)" and "strength and weakness are a question of the deployment [of forces] (*hsing*)."[18] *Shih* and *hsing* are two frameworks that were created in order to understand the dynamics and transformations of the contradiction pairs—courage–fear and strength–weakness, respectively. With the presence of these frameworks, the contradiction pairs cease to be paradoxical and instead serve as an important means for attaining victory, as the quotes above suggest.

We have witnessed how the Tao of deception, the genesis of Chinese strategic dialectics, which at first is simply about the contradictions between phenomenon and essence, has sprouted to a method of thinking that utilizes contradictions, and finally, to which a cyclical movement is added, has further developed into *ch'i* (unorthodox) and *cheng* (orthodox), which resembles yin and yang in *Taiji* (*T'ai Chi* 太極):

> In warfare the strategic configurations of power (*shih*) do not exceed the unorthodox and orthodox, but the changes of the unorthodox and orthodox can never be completely exhausted. *The unorthodox and orthodox mutually produce each other, just like an endless cycle. Who can exhaust them?*[19]

There is a clearly a huge leap involved between identifying the contradictions in war to the utilization of these contradictions as a strategic scheme, and such a transformation was expected to be completed by Sun Tzu himself. The system was later fully incorporated into *Tao Te Ching*, which further stresses the natural propensity of things (i.e. the cyclical movement) and how to put it to full advantage.

From the above description of the evolution of Chinese strategic dialectics, it should be apparent that while the dialectics itself can be arrived at intuitively, it can also be understood and explained logically and rationally. Although the practical application of this dialectical system requires generals or strategists to make an intuitive judgment, the system has solid theoretical foundations that allow it to be explained throughout the process. This contrasts greatly with Clausewitz's *coup d'oeil* (or intuition) of the military genius, or his concept of genius as a whole. Clausewitz has turned the *coup d'oeil* of military genius into a "super-concept," and it has largely remained an intellectual black box throughout his work. That Handel himself has to clarify that the *coup d'oeil* of the military genius, is not irrational; it simply reflects a different mode of rationality in which intuitive decisions can be explained rationally *ex post facto*.[20] Its mechanism has never been spelled out so methodically as in *The Art of War*. This is not to suggest that *The Art of War* is in some way better than *On War* with regard to military genius, but rather that Sun Tzu's strategic dialectical system is able to help illuminate the intellectual black box of military genius. This is a promising avenue of enquiry for the strategic community. In addition, while Western strategic thought has never developed an epistemology of strategy, Sun Tzu has laid a solid epistemological basis for strategic thinking of all kinds, as illustrated in his strategic dialectics. A renewed investigation of Chinese strategic thought will help open these new windows of opportunity.

FROM SUN TZU AND LAO TZU

From Sun Tzu to Lao Tzu: The Transformation

In Western strategic thought there has long been a tradition of seeking a panacea in war that would be capable of defeating the enemy in any situation. The Chinese, in contrast, have tended to focus on the discovery, and refinement, of schemes that would enable the weak to defeat the strong, as merely defeating an adversary of equal or lesser strength is considered unremarkable in Chinese strategic thought. Rather than forming a general theory of strategy similar to that contained in *The Art of War*, the authors of *Tao Te Ching* decided to embark on a general theory setting out how the weak can defeat the strong. But this does not mean that these schemes are entirely absent in *The Art of War*. On the contrary, Sun Tzu's treatise contains the basis upon which *Tao Te Ching* is able to develop its thesis explaining how the weak can defeat the strong.

The Tao of deception, which forms the basis for the Chinese strategic dialectical system, is depicted in the first chapter of *The Art of War* as having three sets or variations of "deception" (Chapter 1).

The first set/variation:

> Warfare is the Way (Tao) of deception.
> Thus although [you are] capable, display incapability to them.
> When committed to employing your forces, feign inactivity.
> When [your objective] is nearby, make it appear as if distant;
> When far away, create the illusion of being nearby.

The second set/variation:

> Display profits to entice them.
> Create disorder [in their forces] and take them.
> If they are substantial, prepare for them;
> If they are strong, avoid them.

The third set/variation:

> If they are angry, perturb them;
> be deferential to foster their arrogance. [If they are humble, encourage their arrogance.]
> If they are rested, force them to exert themselves.
> If they are united, cause them to be separated.[21]

These three sets of four measures form the core of the Tao of deception. The first set constitutes the most basic form of deception, which is
mainly about creating false impressions. The second and third sets, however, go beyond the pure form of deception and involve the active
responses and measures that should be implemented in war: the second
set represents rational responses to certain conditions in war, and the last
set comprises the process through which conditions can be created for the
defeat of an opponent, which predominantly draws on human factors or
irrationalities in war. It is noteworthy that the primary concern of the
second and third sets is creating the conditions for victory, rather than
the outright defeat of the enemy—this corresponds with one of Sun Tzu's
maxims: "the victorious army first realizes the conditions for victory, and
then seeks to engage in battle."[22] But it is the third set of measures that is
truly remarkable: it not only brings human factors and irrationalities into
play, but it also draws on a process of discovering a potential/propensity,
encouraging its impetus and pushing it to the extreme, and finally exploiting it when it reaches the tipping point. In most cases the process in
question involves the use of opposite means—means that are often seen
as counterintuitive. In the third set described above, for example, Sun
Tzu recommends perturbing an angry enemy with the aim of making him
even angrier; if the enemy is humble, Sun Tzu recommends encouraging
his arrogance rather than making him more humble. The logic behind
this can be better understood through the words of Tai Gong:

Now in order to attack the strong, you must nurture them to make them even
stronger, and increase them to make them even more extensive. What is too
strong will certainly break; what is too extended must have deficiencies. *Attack
the strong through his strength. Cause the estrangement of his favored officials by using
his favorites, and dispense his people by means of people.*[23]

For Sun Tzu and the Taoists, assisting the natural tendency is always
preferable to opposing it as everything carries within itself its own seeds of
destruction when it overextends, in much the same way as yin-yang works.
This forms the basis for the Chinese philosophy of struggle and, of course,
the practical ways in which the weak can defeat the strong. This issue will
be returned to below in a detailed discussion of Taoist strategy.

The Tao of deception is consequently about much more than "deception." As it progresses from the first to the second and third variations, it turns into a form of strategic manipulation. Even if the first variation is used in isolation, it is apparent that its purpose is not just to deceive or mislead; the Tao of deception instead aims for a higher goal whereby an enemy can be manipulated and controlled. In Chinese, "deception" (*gui* 詭) in the Tao of deception (*gui dao* 詭道) can also stand for "strange," "anomalous," and even "paradoxical." The Tao of deception can thus be interpreted in a much broader sense, as the anomalous and paradoxical form of Tao (way), and this in turn can help provide a better means to understand the concepts used by Sun Tzu.

The Taoist Methodology

As the third set of measures in Sun Tzu's Tao of deception effectively represent yin-yang in action and are the best suited for the aim of enabling the weak to defeat the strong, it is hardly surprising that it is this set of measures with which the Taoists are most concerned. The use of the Tao of deception is clear in the following passage, which captures the essence of Taoist strategy:

Should you want to contain something, you must deliberately let it expand.
Should you want to weaken something, you must deliberately let it grow strong.
Should you want to eliminate something, you must deliberately allow it to flourish.
Should you want to take something away, you must deliberately grant it.
This is called subtle illumination. (*Tao Te Ching*, Chapter 36)[24]

Cleary's translation was used here because it highlights how the scheme can be facilitated by design ("deliberate") and can thus act as the basis for strategy or stratagem. This in turn constitutes the foundations upon which the weak will be able to defeat the strong, given that the line that follows the key passage is: "Flexible and yielding overcome adamant coerciveness."[25] The Taoists justify this logic by referring to nature:

If you peak in strength, you then age;
this, it is said, is unguided [going against the Tao].
The unguided soon come to an end. (Chapter 30)[26]

As François Jullien observes, Chinese thinkers have stressed the legitimacy of inevitable result.[27] Victories are won through propensity rather than force or actions. One of the most important tasks for a strategist is to recognize and assist natural propensity by encouraging its impetus, with the downfall of an adversary likely to follow as an inevitable result.[28]

This scheme of "natural propensity" and "inevitable result" was incorporated into the Taoist framework because it exhibits the idea that the underlying order of nature is perfectly consistent with Tao, the ultimate law/order of everything. The Taoists call this the theory of "returning":

> Greatness [i.e. another name of Tao] means it goes;
> going means reaching afar;
> reaching afar means return. (Chapter 25)[29]

As the theory of "returning" displays how Tao emulates nature, it helps to rationalize the seemingly paradoxical strategic scheme of the Taoists, which is about encouraging the impetus of natural propensity through means that appear to be contrary to the original goal. The internal logic and methodology behind the Taoist strategy are best encapsulated in the following lines:

> Return is the movement of [Tao];
> yielding is the function of [Tao]. (Chapter 40)[30]

"Return" corresponds to the movement of Tao, according to which everything reverses its course as soon as it has reached its extreme, as exhibited in the working of yin–yang. However, even when the internal logic of Tao has been understood, it will not be transformed into effect automatically. It still requires a corresponding scheme to bring about the effect. And that scheme is "yielding" or "being weak." That is why it is called the function of Tao—*Te* (*De* 德, virtue, not in the moral sense but in terms of efficacy, i.e. "to obtain/actualize"—*Tao* and *Te* are the concepts after which *Tao Te Ching* is named). Therefore, just as Tao is the fundamental principle and *Te* its practical application, "return" represents the fundamental principle while "yielding" denotes its practical application that effects the manifestation of "return" and indeed Tao. By grasping the interaction between the theory of return and the scheme of yielding, one should be able to decipher the paradoxical relationship between means and ends that is repeatedly mentioned in Taoist works:

Be tactful and you remain whole;
bend and you remain straight.
The hollow is filled,
the old is renewed.
Economy is gain,
excess is confusion.
Therefore sages embrace unity [The One, i.e. Tao] as a model for the world.
(Chapter 22)[31]

This leads back to Chapter 1's discussion of the Three Levels of Chinese strategic thought (Tao, Heaven and Earth, and Methods of Generalship). Taoist strategy seems paradoxical because one still has not completed the paradigm shift from the level of Heaven and Earth to the level of Tao, because one still sees opposites as opposites, not as an organic, dynamic whole (i.e. "The One"). Hence "The One" or Tao is essential for understanding the Taoist methodology and putting it into practice. By embracing Tao, sages can draw on contrary means to attain their goals, providing them with an advantage and additional methods for dealing with complex situations. After all, what Lao Tzu and the other authors of *Tao Te Ching* say is no more than "people may gain from loss, and may lose from gain" (Chapter 42).[32] But this marks a real breakthrough in the realm of strategy as it denotes a complete break from the means–end rational framework that is at the heart of modern war and strategy.

The Water Metaphors and the Condition–Consequence Approach

In its simplest sense, strategy can be defined as "[t]he direction and use made of means by chosen ways in order to achieve desired ends."[33] This concise definition implies the use of certain means to achieve desired ends—in other words, it implicitly contains the means–end rational framework. This is the Western tradition of strategy. In Philip Windsor's words, Western strategic thought depends "largely on the assumption that strategic considerations are *causal* rather than *consequential* in nature. It is still part of the process of Weber's rationalization."[34] This assumption is rarely acknowledged in the West, mainly because Western strategists believe that strategic thinking is impossible without it.

Chinese strategic thought, however, is the "Black Swan"—an exception. It has its own system, one that is able to supersede the means–end rationality of the West. As discussed above, the key to Chinese strategy is to rely on the inherent potential of the situation (i.e. *shi/shih* 勢) and to be carried along by it as it evolves. This immediately rules out any possibility of predetermining events in accordance with a more or less definitive plan worked out in advance as an ideal to be realized.[35] According to Jullien, there are at least two different modes of "efficacy" that result from these two different logics: (1) the means–end relationship familiar to a Western audience; and (2) a relationship between conditions and consequences, which is favored by the Chinese.[36] These different modes of efficacy can be described as the means–end rational approach and the condition–consequence approach. It goes without saying, however, that this is a generalization as it is unthinkable that the Chinese would ever act without having any goals or plans in mind, or that causal reasoning is absent in Chinese minds.

The condition–consequence approach, according to Jullien, is a Chinese concept of efficacy that teaches one to learn how to allow an effect to come about: not to aim for it directly, but to implicate it as a consequence.[37] The concept is closely related to Sun Tzu's famous "water" metaphors. Sun Tzu tends to employ his water metaphors in one of two ways, both of which have played an important part in the emergence of the condition–consequence approach. The first usage constitutes the metaphorical basis of the concept of *shih* (potential, impetus, strategic configuration of power, strategic advantage, etc.)—"That the velocity of cascading water can send boulders bobbing about is due to its strategic advantage (*shih*)."[38] The passage constitutes an image of potential, and the concept is concerned with the strategic advantage/potential acquired from closely following the flow and acting in accord with the propensity. Sun Tzu uses this metaphor in order to elucidate an even more important lesson: "The expert at battle seeks his victory from strategic advantage (*shih*) and does not demand it from his men."[39] This suggests that the suitable conditions for something to happen must be created (as a consequence) and that nothing should and can be forced. By creating suitable conditions, the strategic advantage/potential (*shih*) that can later be turned into effects will also be created. Sun Tzu calls the latter *hsing* (形 shape or strategic disposition of force)—"The combat of the victorious is like the sudden release of a pent-up torrent down a thousand-fathom gorge. This is the strategic disposition of force (*hsing*)."[40] This is why Chinese strategists tend to combine and use *hsing* and *shih* as one concept (*hsing shih* 形勢 more commonly understood as "situation" or "the trend of event" with which one has to go along)—nothing is essential except the demands of the situation: the situation is the only thing that matters.[41] *Hsing* is the creation of the suitable conditions and *shih* the strategic advantage being created. The dual-concept of *hsing* and *shih* represents the essence of the condition–consequence approach.

Hence the main difference between the means–end approach and the condition–consequence approach is that the latter views the result to be achieved as a second-order, rather than a first-order effect:

For something to be realized in an effective fashion, it must come about as an effect. It is always *through a process* (which transforms the situation), *not through a goal* that leads (directly) to action, that one achieves an effect, a result.[42]

For Western strategists, the most immediate question this raises concerns why a second-order effect would be preferred to a first-order effect. But the issue is not whether it is first- or second-order, but whether the effect can be realized at all. If we go back to Sun Tzu's water metaphor, it is not just the propensity or impetus upon which one can draw that is a matter of concern; what is of greater importance is the inevitable result it can bring—water races downward and "can send boulders bobbing about," given the right amount of time and velocity (conditions). Unlike the means–end approach, which typically involves a predetermined plan that is liable to disintegrate when put into in practice, the condition–consequence approach is designed to leave as little room for chance as possible. Once a situation has begun to develop, it allows no other way out: one "is bound to go along with it"—the outcome is predetermined.[43] To make this possible:

a good general intervenes *upstream* in the process. He has already identified the factors favorable to him "before they have actually developed" and in this way has got the situation to evolve in the direction that suits him. When the accumulated potential reveals itself to be completely in his favor, he engages resolutely in battle, and his success is assured.[44]

In this passage, "upstream" refers to the need to establish conditions in advance (i.e. *hsing*) in order to enable the desired effects to come about in the "downstream" (i.e. *shih*) in the form of consequence, rather than actions being directed toward a predetermined goal (think Sun Tzu's water metaphor). Yet as strategy always involves more than one party, the full potential of the condition–consequence approach can only be appreciated when the adversaries involved are put back into the equation. This leads to Sun Tzu's second water metaphor.

Sun Tzu's second water metaphor emphasizes the property of water: it has no form and constantly adapts. This metaphor is used in order to emphasize the idea that a predetermined plan is the last thing that a general should follow in warfare:

Now the army's disposition of force (*hsing*) is like water. Water's configuration (*hsing*) avoids heights and races downward. The army's disposition of force (*hsing*) avoids the substantial and strikes the vacuous. Water configures (*hsing*) its flow in accord with the terrain; the army control its victory in accord with the enemy. Thus the army does not maintain any constant strategic configuration of power (*shih*), water has no constant shape (*hsing*). One who is able to change and transform in accord with the enemy and wrest victory is termed spiritual [*shen* 神]. (Chapter 6)[45]

This metaphor is remarkable because it contains no trace whatsoever of means and ends—strategy is solely determined in relation to the enemy. It does not project any kind of plan upon the course of events, and as such there is no need to envisage behavior from a means–end perspective.[46] Indeed, the water metaphor and the condition–consequence approach on which it is based shows how "astrategic" the means–end approach actually is. As war is necessarily the dialectics between two opposing sides, both parties will need to engage in a process of constant adaption. But this is rendered almost impossible within the means–end approach as little consideration can be given to an adversary once a fixed plan has been created; when there is a significant divergence between the plan and reality, a new plan has to be established. Sun Tzu himself may well have reflected upon the attributes of the means-end approach when he formulated his theory.

Sun Tzu's water metaphor is probably the most condensed strategic theory of all existing theories. It contains many timeless lessons while it also avoids being overly general. More importantly, the beauty of the water metaphor is that it is a model suitable for applying in all situations—there is no need to use a number of theories to cope with different situations; all that is needed is to think of the image of water. It is this simplicity which explains why the Taoists tend to resort to nature for inspiration and use metaphors that are naturalistic in essence.

The water metaphor is suitable for use in a range of diverse contexts because it is able to produce patterns that are never definite. This has two significant implications for resolving the problems associated with the means-end approach: it can serve to limit the risk of becoming pinned down during the course of action, and it also offers the ability to attain multiple possibilities instead of a single end. One central theme of Sun Tzu's scheme is about revealing the enemy's pattern (*hsing*) and concealing one's own:

Thus critically analyze them to know the estimations for gain and loss. Stimulate them to know the patterns of their movement and stopping. Determine their disposition of force (*hsing*) to know the tenable and fatal terrain. Probe them to know where they have an excess, where an insufficiency.

Thus the pinnacle of military deployment approaches the formless. If it is formless, then even the deepest spy cannot discern it or the wise make plans against it. (Chapter 6)[47]

Again, it is clear that the means-end approach, as well as the predetermined goals and plans upon which it is based, is counterproductive for realizing Sun Tzu's scheme. In reality, efficacy diminishes as the course of things becomes more definite: the more reality is determined in practice, the more difficult it becomes to manage. The more the conflict takes shape and the farther the process advances, the more our behavior is hampered—the more "action" and effort are required.[48] This in turn makes it easier for the enemy to identify an adversary's intention and to counter their actions, making the entire plan more liable to collapse.

A Chinese general, in contrast, does not elaborate a plan that he projects upon the future and which leads to a predetermined goal before defining how to link together the means best suited to realize the plan in question. As unforeseen circumstances may arise it is not always possible to draw up a plan in advance. Rather, plans contain a certain potential from which, if we are agile and adaptable enough, we can profit. This suggests that, for a Chinese general, there is not an "end" set up in the distance as an ideal, but he continues to make the most of the situation as it unfolds.[49] At the same time, by constantly changing the pattern in which troops are disposed, both in attack and defense, it is possible to avoid becoming bogged down in maneuvers, or even allowing the enemy to glimpse the slightest fixity in the disposition of his troops.[50] This can be achieved by emulating the formlessness of water, where nothing tangible is presented for the enemy to oppose—as the enemy is unable to focus on a particular point or goal, it is impossible for resistance to crystallize.[51] That is why Sun Tzu says, "Intermixed and turbulent, the fighting appears chaotic, but they cannot be made disordered. In turmoil and confusion, their deployment is circular, and they cannot be defeated" (Chapter 5).[52]

Furthermore, unlike the means–end approach, which focuses upon bringing about a predetermined goal, Sun Tzu's scheme is capable of arriving at multiple and thus interchangeable outcomes. This is possible because actions and strategy can be decided in full accord with the demands of the situation and in relation to the actions of an enemy. As Sun Tzu puts it, "One who is able to change and transform in accord with the enemy and wrest victory is termed spiritual [shen]." The use of shen (神, spiritual, god) in this context not only suggests that the general or strategist who is able to put this ideal into practice possesses skills that are comparable to god—it also highlights the idea that the god/creator has the ability to create everything and all the ensuing possibilities. This in turn implies that the scheme created on the basis of the water metaphor can also bring about all sorts of possibilities, depending on the general's skill in taking advantage of the unfolding opportunities and preventing himself from following a definite pattern.

Western authors are of course not entirely unaware of the problems associated with the means-end rational approach, and a number of authors have proposed various ways to overcome these. The German infiltration tactics of 1918 and Liddell-Hart's "Expanding Torrent" theory, for example, represent two attempts to overcome these problems, both of which emulate Sun Tzu's water metaphors. Yet in the absence of a compatible system of thought, such as that underlying the condition–consequence approach, these efforts were always likely to end in failure in terms of producing the desired results.

From the Water Metaphor to the Theory of Tao

Tao Te Ching inherited Sun Tzu's water metaphors but elevated them to a new level. In *Tao Te Ching* they serve as a theoretical basis for explaining how the weak can defeat the strong:

> Nothing in the world is more flexible and yielding than water.
> Yet when it attacks the firm and the strong,
> none can withstand it,
> because they have no way to change it.
> So the flexible overcome the adamant,
> the yielding overcome the forceful.
> Everyone knows this,
> but no one can do it. (Chapter 78)[53]

As Sun Tzu's water metaphors were originally created for military purposes, the Taoists ("the Taoists" hereafter refers to the authors of *Tao Te Ching*, and not necessarily Lao Tzu who was a contemporary of Sun Tzu) had to modify them in order to make them suitable for the aim of creating a theory that would enable the weak to defeat the strong, and for spheres beyond the military sphere. Hence the Taoists have different treatments for the two main aspects of Sun Tzu's water metaphors: *shih* (potential, impetus, etc.) and constant adaptation. He puts the two aspects to different uses and makes major variations to them. These developments were important steps in the transformation and eventual completion of Chinese strategic thought, the principal groundwork for which had been laid by Sun Tzu.

As can be seen in the passage from *Tao Te Ching* above, water's accumulation of power by *shih* continues to be valued by Lao Tzu after Sun

Tzu—it is this which enables something as formless and weak as water to overcome hard and strong objects. Yet there is only one direct reference to *shih* in *Tao Te Ching* (Chapter 51). It appears that the concept of *shih* is deliberately deemphasized. But why? The most immediate and obvious explanation is that the authors of *Tao Te Ching* were seeking to hide the fact that they had borrowed extensively from Sun Tzu. Yet while there could be some truth in this, it is far from a complete explanation: in reality, *shih* is simply insufficient for the purpose of the weak defeating the strong. As mentioned earlier, *shih* is a concept that is inseparable from the condition–consequence approach—suitable conditions have to be created to allow things to happen, and *shih* is the strategic advantage that will eventually be transformed into effect. But this raises an important problem: if an actor is weak, they might lack the resources or power to create the suitable conditions, and accumulate enough *shih* for the effect to come about. The authors of *Tao Te Ching* have to overcome this problem before moving on.

Lao Tzu realized that, despite the fact that *shih* is not an advantage that the weak can always draw on, there is another natural propensity that does not need to be created intentionally and which continually evolves through its own actions, in much the same way that water races downward. Furthermore, this natural propensity can be assisted by encouraging its impetus. As Sun Tzu says: "If they are angry, perturb them; if they are humble, encourage their arrogance." Nevertheless, in Sun Tzu's case, as far as military operations are concerned, an army still has to engage in battle after the conditions for victory have been realized. Lao Tzu, however, draws almost completely on the self-defeat of the enemy, following that the natural propensity has reached its extreme and backfires upon himself:

If you peak in strength, you then age;
this, it is said, is unguided [going against the Tao].
The unguided soon come to an end. (Chapter 30)[54]

So when an army is strong,
it does not prevail. [A country that has a strong army will lead to its own demise]
When a tree is strong,
it is cut for use. [When a tree is strong, it is easier to break (for it lacks flexibility)] (Chapter 76)[55]

This passage constitutes Lao Tzu's theory of "Return": "Return is the movement of [Tao]; yielding is the function of [Tao]" (Chapter 40). Yielding is essential because it prevents one from reaching maturity and thus the extreme prematurely, and it also greatly enhances one's chance to "out-flex" his opponent.

All of the above never goes beyond the concept of yin-yang. However, it is highly probable that Lao Tzu's use of yin-yang as a strategic scheme in fact originated from Sun Tzu. In effect, the Taoists borrowed and combined three aspects of Sun Tzu's thought in order to produce their own scheme of yin-yang, namely the concept of *shih* (i.e. natural propensity evolves itself under right conditions), and that natural propensity can be assisted by encouraging its impetus ("If they are angry, perturb them; if they are humble, encourage their arrogance"), and finally, that any contradiction has a tendency to "mutually produce each other, just like an endless cycle" (just like the movement exhibited in yin-yang/T'ai Chi (Taiji)):

In warfare the strategic configurations of power (*shih*) do not exceed the unorthodox and orthodox, but the changes of the unorthodox and orthodox can never be completely exhausted. The unorthodox and orthodox mutually produce each other, *just like an endless cycle.* Who can exhaust them? (Chapter 5)[56]

It is clear that the three aspects are closely related to, or even part of, the concept of *shih*. As the Taoist methodology is likely to be a variant of Sun Tzu's Tao of deception, the claim that *The Art of War* precedes *Tao Te Ching*, and that the Taoists have in fact adopted Sun Tzu's ideas, thus appears to be even more credible. Indeed, it would in no way be an exaggeration to assert that Sun Tzu is the "grandfather" of yin-yang as a strategic scheme. The strategic use of yin-yang as well as its concept and related vocabulary was not yet fully systematized in Sun Tzu's time, or otherwise Sun Tzu could have used concepts such as yin-yang (in its metaphysical and philosophical sense) and Tao. This was only made possible after the authors of *Tao Te Ching* had actively absorbed and reformed Sun Tzu's ideas.

The Taoist Worldview

Whereas the purpose of Lao Tzu's thesis is to enable the weak to defeat the strong, what he has been advocating is indeed: "The soft [flexible] and weak vanquish the hard and strong." (Chapter 36)[57]—being weak is just one of the two requirements to be fulfilled. *Tao Te Ching* asserts that "nothing in the world is more flexible and yielding than water," something which is clearly related to the second aspect of Sun Tzu's water metaphors—constant adaptation. Yet as with the first aspect, this element of Sun Tzu's water metaphor has undergone significant change in *Tao Te Ching*. While the concept of *shih* has evolved into yin–yang as a strategic scheme, which constitutes the Taoist methodology through which the weak are able to defeat the strong, the theme of constant adaptation has been developed into the Taoist worldview, which plays a major role in bringing about the stark contrast between Chinese and Western strategic thought in philosophical terms.

In order to discern the theme of constant adaption, which the *Tao Te Ching* borrows from Sun Tzu's water metaphors, it is necessary to re-examine the relevant passage:

> Nothing in the world is more flexible and yielding than water.
> Yet when it attacks the firm and the strong,
> none can withstand it,
> because they have no way to change it.
> So the flexible overcome the adamant,
> the yielding overcome the forceful.
> *Everyone knows this,*
> *but no one can do it.* (Chapter 78)[58]

Those who are familiar with *The Art of War* will quickly recognize the section of the text that pertains to the lines cited above. According to Sun Tzu, there is only one concept in *The Art of War* that everyone seems to know on the surface while failing to understand its real working. That is the concept of formlessness (i.e. *hsing*-less):

In accord with the enemy's disposition (*hsing*) we impose measures on the masses that produce victory, but the masses are unable to fathom them. Men all know the disposition (*hsing*) by which we attain victory, but no one knows the configuration (*hsing*) through which we control the victory. Thus a victorious battle [strategy] is not repeated, the configuration (*hsing*) of response [to the enemy] are inexhaustible. (Chapter 6)[59]

The concept of formlessness constitutes one of the major tenets of Sun Tzu's water metaphors—as water best illustrates the concept of formlessness, the metaphors were formed primarily with the aim of attaining this end. However, as with Sun Tzu's work as a whole, the concept of formlessness was put forward as a principle to be applied in the military sphere. In order for the concept to be used in a more general sense, a number of modifications have to be made. As a result, the authors of *Tao Te Ching* abandon the image of water altogether in radically reapplying the concept of formlessness to the most important notion of Taoism—Tao.

As Tao has already been depicted as something that "cannot be spoken of" and "cannot be named" in the first chapter of *Tao Te Ching*,[60] the concept of formlessness is re-manifested in different ways in numerous descriptions of Tao in the text: Tao "is empty, yet use will not drain it" (Chapter 4).[61] It cannot be seen, heard, or touched, and hence cannot be fathomed (Chapter 14).[62] "This is called the shape that has no shape, the image that is without substance" (Chapter 14).[63] "Indistinct and shadowy, yet within it is an image; shadowy and indistinct, yet within it is a substance. Dim and dark, yet within it is an essence. This essence is quite genuine and within it is something that can be tested" (Chapter 21).[64] These excerpts clearly show how the concept of formlessness was "transplanted" on to Taoism. In so doing, formlessness moves from a guiding principle for use in the military sphere to a key feature of Tao, the ultimate order of everything, and from a means to defeat enemy forces to a new worldview.

The idea that Tao cannot be understood, while it simultaneously retains its image, substance, and essence, can be explained by the fact that the Taoists hold a dynamic worldview—reality is constantly evolving. This uninterrupted flow of variance, which is vividly illustrated by the course of flowing water, is regarded as the very course of reality.[65] There is no place for fixed rules or blind adherence to any form or specific model. The only thing that can be said with any degree of certainty about Tao is that it is unchanging simply because it is ever-changing. Li Zehou (李澤厚) argues that people often find Tao extremely difficult to understand due to the indeterminability of Tao, which is precisely the result of the multiplicity and adaptability of Tao in practice, the origins of which can be traced to Sun Tzu. Li even claims that this mysterious quality of Tao can be associated with Sun Tzu's Tao of deception.[66] Thus as Jullien puts it, even though the sage/general knows that there are no rules or norms to codify the future, since the flow of reality is constantly innovating, he feels no anxiety (in contrast to the latest Western mode of ideology—which is concerned with "uncertainty," "turbulence," and "chaos"...) as he has already been equipped with the "toolkit" and worldview of the Taoist and Military Schools that enable him to orient himself under such circumstances.[67]

Although the concept of formlessness was originally intended to be applied in the military sphere, it also has an intrinsic mental and cognitive dimension as the formlessness of the army cannot be attained unless the general himself has acquired a mindset that is compatible with it. The authors of *Tao Te Ching* grasped this mental and cognitive dimension and fully developed its potential, turning it into an essential means for understanding Tao and reality. The most important lesson underlying the Taoist worldview regarding the formlessness of Tao and the constant evolution of reality is the idea that reality possesses no form—it is humans who impose various forms upon it, and these forms are merely mental constructs. While these simplified forms and models may be useful when first trying to make sense of the world, they will eventually become major obstacles for understanding reality as a flow of variance and, more importantly, as one without any distortion. As Lao Tzu says:

> Humanity emulates earth,
> earth emulates heaven,
> heaven emulates the Way [Tao],
> the Way [Tao] emulates Nature. (Chapter 25)[68]

In the passage, "earth," "heaven," and "Tao" can be viewed as different levels of simplification. Tao has the least simplification, as it directly emulates nature. On the other hand, as Lao Tzu indicates, humans tend to emulate "earth," the level of maximum simplification, and make use of highly simplified forms and models to represent reality. When seen through these "lenses," the world is seriously distorted, while the dynamism stemming from the flow of variance is completely lost as an inevitable result. But Lao Tzu has already arrived at a solution to this problem:

> For learning you gain daily;
> for the Way [Tao] you lose daily. (Chapter 48)[69]

As far as Lao Tzu is concerned, "learning" is unable to lead an individual closer to Tao because it involves learning and employing simplified forms and models (usually in the form of experience and knowledge) in order to grasp reality, thereby preventing reality from being grasped as it actually is. In order to avoid using these mental constructs, Lao Tzu suggests that individuals should actively try to "lose" them each day, which is the way to pursue Tao vis-à-vis "learning." "Direct observation" (i.e. without the interference of mental constructs/models) can then be used to arrive at the true face of the reality.[70]

The Taoist worldview has important implications for war and strategy because the defining characteristic of warfare is the distance that inevitably separates the reality of war from abstract theoretical models. The essence of warfare is to betray its model.[71] This is one of the main reasons why it is extremely difficult to formulate theories of war and warfare, with almost all existing theories failing to bridge the gap between theory and practice. This shortcoming has been particularly problematic for the West due to the Western tradition of focusing on well-defined and easily discernible forms, a tradition that stretches back to Plato; while the West is unable to conceive of war without a predefined plan, the latter inevitably clashes with variable circumstances.[72] These two issues are exactly what Lao Tzu has identified and tried to resolve by introducing the Taoist worldview—Tao is formless and reality is constantly evolving. As has long been recognized in warfare, nothing is more dangerous than becoming immobilized in one particular case; there can be nothing worse than the creation of rules and imperatives that subsequently make conduct inflexible and prevent an actor from the variation from which all potential stems.[73] By embracing Tao, it is possible to embrace variations in circumstances, which marks an important step toward a system of variation that is capable of replacing all models. This is why Lao Tzu asserts that "keeping flexible is called strength" (Chapter 52).[74] After all, the evolution from the concept of formlessness to the Taoist worldview helps complete Chinese strategic thought by providing it with the worldview and epistemology that are either missing or incompatible with the requirements of war in its Western counterpart. This also explains why Chinese strategic thought can transcend areas beyond the military sphere.

"Striking Second"

The components of Taoist strategic thought described above were mainly formulated with the aim of enabling the weak to defeat the strong. But *Tao Te Ching* also contains another strategic idea, which, when combined with other aspects of Chinese philosophy, can be said to characterize Chinese strategic thought. This is the idea of "striking second." This translation is derived from the Western concept of initiative, whereby it is necessary to "strike first" against an enemy so that the enemy must respond to the attack. As a result, the idea of "striking second" is likely to puzzle a Western audience—there is almost no way in which the concept can be understood in purely Western terms. "Striking second" is a concept of initiative that is distinctively different from that of the West. Its proper translation should be "to gain mastery by striking only after the enemy has struck" (*hou fa zhi ren* 後發制人).

Sun Tzu has no particular preference with regard to striking first or second. However, he briefly states that:

In military combat what is most difficult is turning the circuitous into the straight, turning adversity into advantage.

Thus if you make the enemy's path circuitous and entice them with profit, *although you set out after them you will arrive before them.* This results from knowing the tactics of the circuitous and the direct. (Chapter 7)[75]

Although these remarks have been viewed as Sun Tzu's "endorsement" of "striking second," what Sun Tzu is actually emphasizing is that in warfare, what is circuitous or straight, adverse or advantageous, is not static and unchanging, but is subject to change due to the subjective efforts of both sides. This is why it is possible to pursue certain circumstances while arriving before them—an idea repeatedly emphasized by Sun Tzu following his introduction of the Tao of deception in the first chapter of *The Art of War*. Nevertheless, we should not overlook that the Taoists too have spotted this very aspect of *The Art of War*, which is inherently inclined to favor "striking second," and further refined it alongside the Tao of deception, finally turning it into the Taoist methodology—the basis enabling the weak to defeat the strong. And the weak can usually only strike second. Hence it is only after the Taoist transformation that "striking second" has essentially become the default mode of Chinese strategic thought.

The condition–consequence approach, as well as the insistence of grasping the enemy's form (*hsing*) before engaging in a battle, contributes to this default mode in a different way. Both are the key rationales behind Sun Tzu's principle: "the victorious army first realizes the conditions for victory, and then seeks to engage in battle." And as a matter of course, creating the necessary conditions for victory and seeking out the enemy's form takes time and cannot be forced. Hence Sun Tzu says, "a strategy for conquering the enemy can be known but yet not possible to implement [force upon]."[76] In other words, one has to wait until the enemy exposes its form, and thus weakness, before a strike should take place:

The prosecution of military affairs lies in according with and [learning] in detail the enemy's intentions. If one then focuses [his strength] toward the enemy, strikes a thousand *li* away, and kills their general, it is termed "being skillful and capable in completing military affairs."[77]

For this reason at first be like a virgin; later—when the enemy opens the door—be like a fleeing rabbit. The enemy will be unable to withstand you. (Chapter 11)[78]

These remarks have made "strike second" a preferred option for Chinese generals and strategists. This is because "wait-and-see" constitutes an integral part of the condition–consequence approach—it has an active purpose in Chinese strategic thought, as time is needed to allow a situation to develop and for conditions to ripen, so that the predetermined outcome can come about. It is because its unfolding is regulated that the general can foresee and wait (foresee the time ahead and wait for it to improve).[79] While it may appear that a general "waits-and-sees," he in fact "foresees-and-waits." It should consequently come as no surprise that Mao Zedong was able to formulate his own theory of revolutionary/protracted war with relative ease. For Mao, revolutionary war was not just about wearing down the enemy and buying time (using guerilla warfare), but also about accumulating potential and factors before they were completely in his favor. When this had been achieved, war could progress to the final and decision phase, with the enemy vanquished in battles, according to Mao's three-stage theory of revolutionary war. This theory represents nothing more than a reapplication of Sun Tzu's ideas in a weak-versus-strong setting on a much larger scale. The related theories and principles have long been laid down by Sun Tzu and other Taoist thinkers.

Furthermore, with the aid of the dynamic Taoist worldview that allows the Chinese general/strategist to better grasp the reality by seeing it without simplified forms and models and that the reality is constantly evolving, Chinese strategic thought has a marked advantage over its Western counterpart in making strategic forecasts. This in turn gives the Chinese a powerful force multiplier that makes both striking second and the weak defeating the strong more possible and lethal. Therefore, "the weak defeating the strong" and "striking second" are but two sides of the same coin. They are the products of the organic structure of Chinese strategic thought.

The Taoist Statecraft and Grand Strategy

As discussed above, the idea that Chinese strategic thought was completed by the Taoists (i.e. the authors of *Tao Te Ching*) after Sun Tzu is based on two premises: that Lao Tzu borrowed extensively from *The Art of War* and that the Taoists have taken Chinese strategic thought to a political height from its military origin. The following saying from *Tao Te Ching* clearly supports both of these premises:

> Govern the state by being straightforward [cheng];
> wage war by being crafty [ch'i];
> but win the empire [world] by not being meddlesome. (Chapter 57)[80]

One should be familiar with the saying because it is used to define the School of Strategy (*quan mou*), the leading school among the Four Schools of Chinese Strategic Thought to which Sun Tzu belonged in the "Record of Literary Works" (*Yi-wen chih*). The saying is significant because it demonstrates that Lao Tzu openly adopted Sun Tzu's dual-concept of *ch'i* and *cheng* (unorthodox and orthodox) while reapplying it in a new way. In their original manifestations, the concepts of *ch'i* and *cheng* were specifically designed for military deployment:

What enable the masses of the Three Armies invariably to withstand the enemy without being defeated are the unorthodox (*ch'i*) and orthodox (*cheng*). (Chapter 5)[81]

The Taoists, however, have turned *ch'i* and *cheng* into a measure of where deceptive means should or should not be used. They insist that only righteous and non-deceptive means (i.e. *cheng*) should be used when governing the state; war is the realm of deception (i.e. *ch'i*). This is because "[t]he more skills [craftiness] the people have, the further novelties multiply" (Chapter 57).[82] If the people are constantly exposed to such influence, they may risk: "The straightforward [*cheng*] changes again into the crafty [*ch'i*], and the good changes again into the monstrous" (Chapter 58).[83] This is a clear sign of the Taoists elevating Sun Tzu's military dialectics to the political level. Moreover, it serves to demonstrate the fact that "governing the state by being straightforward and waging war by being crafty" has long been accepted as fundamental to Chinese strategic thought (c.AD 100)—that strategic thought cannot be military-centered alone; it ought to be political and grand-strategic-oriented. And this cannot be achieved without Taoist contributions.

Yet the essence of Taoist statecraft and grand strategy does not lie in "governing the state by being straightforward and waging war by being crafty." It instead resides in the following line: "win the world by not being meddlesome." "Not being meddlesome" refers to *wu shi* (無事) in Chinese. As well as denoting non-interference or non-intervention, the concept has strong links to one of the core concepts of Taoism—non-action or do nothing (*wu wei* 無為):

[W]hen one does nothing at all [*wu wei*] there is nothing that is undone.

It is always through not meddling [*wu shi* 無事] that the empire [world] is won.

Should you meddle, then you are not equal to the task of winning the empire [world]. (Chapter 48)[84]

A more simple translation of the concept of non-action is "do nothing and let nothing be left undone."[85] This is an important Taoist teaching which suggests that refraining from action (knowing not to act) is the best way to achieve a desired end.[86] However, far from advocating disengagement from human affairs and the world, the non-action of *Tao Te Ching* teaches individuals how to behave in this world in order to be successful.[87] Jullien attributes this Chinese skepticism regarding the efficacy of action to the fact that Chinese thought never developed a cult of action:

as actions intervene in the course of things, an action is always external to it and constitutes an initiative that is intrusive—it is a source of embarrassment; it intervenes as a hindrance. Therefore, action is easy to spot and inevitably provokes elements of resistance.[88] As a result, in any long-term endeavor of a massive scale, with countless interactions such as ruling the state and winning the world, a cult of action is bound to fail:

Whoever takes the empire [world] and wishes to do anything to it I see will have no respite.
The empire [world] is a sacred vessel and nothing should be done to it.
Whoever does anything to it will ruin it; whoever lays hold of it will lose it.
(Chapter 29)[89]

In short, both the empire and the world cannot be objects for action.[90] This kind of thinking might be derived from Sun Tzu's principle of attaining "unremarkable victory":

Perceiving a victory that does not surpass what the masses could know is not the pinnacle of excellence. Wrestling victories for which All under Heaven proclaim your excellence is not the pinnacle of excellence ... Those that the ancients referred to as excelling at warfare conquered those who were easy to conquer. Thus the victories of those that excelled in warfare were not marked by fame for wisdom or courageous achievement.[91]

A remarkable victory shares the same shortcomings as those resulting from taking action, as both a remarkable victory and actions are easy to spot and inevitably provoke (new) elements of resistance. Although they may well prove to be of great value in non-successive moves, their shortcomings will eventually outweigh the benefits they can bring in the long run.

The Taoist lessons regarding statecraft and grand strategy also have systemic and strategic implications. As stated repeatedly, Sun Tzu and the Taoists see war and the world as a system, and they understand that unintended consequences can be, and very often are, devastating. So even though the Chinese are experts in dealing with second-order effects, they would rather choose to avoid the potentially harmful unintended consequences. And engaging in more forms of action and effort are sources of unintended consequences. Moreover, it is impossible to engage constantly in actions and effort as this will simply generate "turbulence," which will in turn bring further disorder and chaos to the system:

Hence a gusty wind cannot last all morning, and a sudden downpour cannot last all day. Who is it that produces these? Heaven and earth. If even heaven and earth cannot go on forever, much less can man. That is why one follows the way [Tao]. (Chapter 23)[92]

In much the same way as gusts of wind and sudden downpours, human actions and efforts are anomalies that disrupt the system but cannot last long. In other words, any continued action and effort to improve the situation in a systemic environment will only be short lived and is bound to fail. At the same time, it also disrupts the system and creates unintended and undesired consequences. In the realm of politics and war, one possible unintended consequence is hatred:

When peace is made between great enemies,
Some enmity is bound to remain undispelled.
How can this [reconciliation] be considered perfect? (Chapter 79)[93]

Unforeseen consequences, such as hatred, frequently take a long time to reverse, and they will eventually hamper progress. Hence the repeated use of action and intervention in a long-term endeavor will in turn create more obstacles of this kind, and one of the foremost tasks of a strategist is to limit any action/interference so as to prevent negative unintended consequences from arising and to eliminate any chance that they will lead to a reversal of the tide. The same also applies to governing a state: "Governing a large state is like boiling [cooking] a small fish" (Chapter 60).[94] If the fish is flipped too frequently it will break—a small fish can be spoiled simply by being handled.[95] Excessive measures and actions are counterproductive and will only disrupt the overall harmony of the system. They only hinder the implicit transformation from taking place.

How, then, is it possible to win the world without meddling? Apart from using the condition–consequence approach that allows effects to come about through processes, there is a Taoist scheme derived from the Taoist methodology that is most applicable to the diplomatic and strategic scenes, and it bears some resemblance to game theory:

Know the male
But to keep to the role of the female
And be a ravine [be humble] to the empire [world]. (Chapter 28)[96]

The message in this passage is about far more than being humble. It is not hard to discern that "male" stands for superiority and "female" inferiority. It is a common understanding that people wish to be superior rather than inferior. As people strive to become superior and states struggle to gain hegemony, however, there will be fierce competition, and most contenders will end up in failure. Therefore, the Taoists see it from another, if not reversed, angle: in order to succeed, one has to first understand both sides—"male" and "female." Yet the key is to renounce the claim to superiority and hegemony and to remain inferior (i.e. "keep the role of the female") while fully understanding the "male" side (i.e. "know the male") and the game itself. By remaining inferior and being humble like a ravine, an individual or a state can win the hearts and minds of other people or states more easily and will ultimately stand a better chance of becoming superior or gaining hegemony. Here we can see how "purely" strategic and effect-based Chinese strategic thought is in nature, even to the degree of forsaking the claim to hegemony. Hence the Taoists are capable of developing a new approach to diplomacy that shares the "female" properties:

A large state is the lower reaches of a river—
The place where all the streams of the world unite.
In the union of the world,
The female always gets the better of the male by stillness.
Being still, she takes the lower position.
Hence the large state, by taking the lower position, annexes [rules] the small state;
The small state, by taking the lower position, affiliates itself to the large state. (Chapter 61)[97]

Even though this sounds idealistic, this already marks a big difference from the old norms of power politics and hegemony—at least both big and small states could get what they want.

Today, we can see that the Taoist statecraft and grand strategy are still being widely practiced by the People's Republic of China, from Hu

Jintao's "avoid self-inflicted setbacks/don't stir up turmoil" (*bu zhe teng* 不折騰) in the domestic scene[98]—that carries the meaning of "governing a large state is like cooking a small fish"—to Deng Xiaoping's "hide our capabilities and bide our time" (*tao guang yang hui* 韜光養晦),[99] and Hu's "Peaceful Rise" in foreign policy. Such concepts cannot be fully comprehended without first comprehending the related Taoist ideas.

Conclusion

The Western way of studying Chinese strategic thought has long been overdue. There has been an overreliance on *The Art of War* to interpret Chinese strategy in a purely theoretical manner. The previous chapter tried to correct the problem by providing a historical perspective of the foundation of Chinese strategic thought. This chapter has introduced the Taoist transformation and final completion of Chinese strategic thought—this shows how unrealistically one tries to understand Chinese strategic thought without recognizing *Tao Te Ching* as a strategic text and the extent it has developed Sun Tzu's ideas. Moreover, the Taoist transformation helps Chinese strategy transcend the military scope to potentially any domain that involves human struggle, further strengthening the Chinese view and practice of "unrestricted war." This in turn results in the invention of many novel ways to wage and win wars and has contributed significantly to strategic thinking per se. Therefore, whether the West is ready for it or not, the study of Chinese strategic thought in the West needs to enter a "post-Sun Tzu era." This of course does not mean we have to thrash *The Art of War* altogether, but that Chinese strategic thought should never again be understood by simply quoting Sun Tzu's maxims, without ever considering its historical background and further developments.

However, as the Taoist strategic thought is highly specialized and has crystallized into a number of schemes, this poses another problem for the West: that the components and schemes, such as the Taoist methodology, the condition–consequence approach, and the Taoist worldview, are culturally alien to the West—they are incompatible with the cultural practices, philosophy, and even logic, of the West. Hence, in the following section, we will investigate the linkage between the thought of Sun Tzu and those of various Western strategic thinkers, and the continuing synthesis of Chinese and Western strategic thought. The main aspects of Sun Tzu's thought will be examined through the lens of Western strategic thinking, and a number of "successors" of Sun Tzu in the West who reproduce many of his key ideas will be discussed.

4

DECIPHERING SUN TZU[1]

"Sun Tzu's *The Art of War* may seem easier on first reading, but it is actually more difficult to understand in depth."[2] Sun Tzu's most famous sayings are frequently cited in the West. But Western readers often find Sun Tzu's work extremely difficult to understand. To a certain extent this results from the translations themselves. Yet there is also a broader problem in that many of the Chinese phrases and concepts in *The Art of War* do not have precise English translations. This situation is further compounded by a lack of understanding of Taoism, which serves as the philosophical basis for *The Art of War*. As Jeremy Black notes, Western readers are frequently confused by the use of paradox in Sun Tzu's work, which is often interpreted in incorrect and misleading ways.[3] The discussion in the preceding chapters partly aspired to provide readers with a better understanding of the use of paradox and contradiction in Chinese strategic thought, and, fortunately, most of Sun Tzu's ideas can still be understood and explained without reference to Taoism.

This chapter aims to show how Chinese strategic thought can be understood in a way that is less dependent on prior knowledge of Chinese philosophy, thereby making Sun Tzu's work more accessible to a Western audience and more practical to Western strategists. In order to uncover the original meaning of Sun Tzu's work, the chapter seeks to explain the concepts used in *The Art of War* by referring to the works of Western strategists, including those of Clausewitz, Liddell-Hart, Boyd, and Wylie. These Western texts, and the strategic concepts they contain, are also discussed in the broader context of other Chinese works.

Clausewitz and Sun Tzu: Their Views on the Complexities of War

When compared to Clausewitz's *On War*, Sun Tzu's *The Art of War* is often perceived to be a collection of maxims and sayings that readers can select or discard depending on context and intention, rather than being a coherent strategic manual on a par with the analytical and theoretical sophistication of *On War*. But such a superficial reading of Sun Tzu's text is largely due to a failure to understand the hidden premises that *The Art of War* contains. Sun Tzu's *The Art of War* is undoubtedly different from Antoine-Henri Jomini's more didactic and prescriptive text of the same name, yet reading Sun Tzu through a Jominian lens (i.e. seeking out and drawing up rules and principles of war) is ultimately no different from treating poetry as a science.

However, contrary to the way it tends to be received and understood in the West, *The Art of War* is indeed a manual with important strategic lessons regarding the conditions necessary for victory in warfare, as well as the ways in which the broader complexities of war can be managed effectively. As a general rule, an actor who is able to achieve the latter goal will almost always be victorious. One way to understand Sun Tzu's ideas with regard to these issues is to read *The Art of War* with reference to Clausewitz's "trinity."

Clausewitz developed the so-called "remarkable trinity" in order to explain the complexities of war. The trinity is comprised of the following elements:

primordial violence, hatred, and enmity, which are to be regarded as a blind natural force; of the play of chance and probability within which the creative spirit is free to roam; and of its element of subordination, as an instrument of policy, which makes it subject to reason alone.[4]

The three elements refer to emotion, chance, and reason. Clausewitz then goes on to connect each of these elements to one of three sets of human actors: the people, the army, and the government.[5] In order to enhance the explanatory power of the trinity, Villacres and Bassford generalize the three elements into three categories of forces:

Far from comprising "the people, the army, and the government," Clausewitz's trinity is really made up of three categories of forces: *irrational forces* (violent emotion, i.e., "primordial violence, hatred, and enmity"); *non-rational forces* (i.e., forces not the product of human thought or intent, such as "friction" and "the play of chance and probability"); and *rationality* (war's subordination to reason, "as an instrument of policy").[6]

Although the use of these categories in the place of Clausewitz's original terminology runs the risk of distorting his arguments, the broader theoretical applicability of Villacres' and Bassford's concepts—irrationality, non-rationality, rationality—means that they can be used in the context of many different kinds of conflict. Moreover, and of greater importance for the purposes of this chapter, reinterpreting the elements of Clausewitz's trinity in this way provides a lens through which to understand the nuances of Sun Tzu's thought in a manner that is compatible with the requirements of a general theory of strategy.

Sun Tzu's work contains many concepts which are similar to those used in the Clausewitzian trinity. As both authors were examining the same subject, it is of course hardly surprising that Clausewitz and Sun Tzu should arrive at similar analyses of the complexities involved in war, particularly as both approached the subject from a holistic perspective. Where Clausewitz and Sun Tzu differ in this regard is the use of analytical discourse in *On War*, something which is clearly absent in *The Art of War*—yet a close reading of the latter reveals that Sun Tzu also employs the three elements and arrives at a number of insights in terms of how they operate in war. Consequently, the Clausewitzian trinity can serve an important role as a conceptual framework for understanding the real value and implications of Sun Tzu's ideas.

When read against this framework, Chapters 1-2 of *The Art of War*—"Strategic Assessments" and "Waging War"—can be viewed as those most closely concerned with what the Clausewitzian trinity describes as "reason" (or rationality), as both chapters focus on the political, economic, and logistical aspects of war. The second element in Clausewitz's trinity, "emotion" (or irrationality), most closely corresponds to the principle of "preservation," which is discussed in Chapter 3, "Planning Offensive." The latter chapter explores the impact of "primordial violence, hatred, and enmity ..." all of "which are to be regarded as a blind natural force." It is this chapter which contains some of Sun Tzu's most well-known maxims, including "subjugating the enemy's army without fighting is the true pinnacle of excellence" and "the highest realization of warfare is to attack the enemy's plan."[7] Finally, Chapters 4 to 6 of *The Art of War*, in which the focus moves to operations and battles, can be seen as corresponding to the third element in the trinity, namely "chance" (non-rationality). More precisely, these chapters are concerned with the management of chance and probability as well as the general uncertainty generated in war.

Trinitarian Analysis: Sun Tzu's Version

Clausewitz's intention when establishing the trinity was to create an analytical framework. Yet *On War* also contains a number of practical, if slightly ambiguous, means for dealing with the complexities of war, particularly with regard to uncertainty and chance. In defining the trinity of war, Clausewitz emphasizes the role of uncertainty as one of the three elements, with "the play of chance and probability within which the creative spirit is free to roam"[8] having an impact on the conduct and outcome of warfare. The "creative spirit" to which Clausewitz refers is effectively a phrase that can be used synonymously with "genius." When discussing the practical means to achieve a degree of balance between the three elements that comprise the trinity, Clausewitz states that "[w]hat lines might best be followed to achieve this difficult task [of maintaining the balance between the three elements] will be explored in the book on the theory of war [Book Two]."[9] As the primary focus of Book Two, or Clausewitz's theory of war, is "genius," it is clear that Clausewitz views chance and probability—and in a broader sense, "friction"—as of paramount concern when confronted with the complexities of war. Clausewitz thus introduces the concept of genius as a theoretical complement to friction, since genius is the intelligence and willpower of the commander that moves the machinery of war forward, despite the friction that impedes it.[10] This focus on reducing friction and uncertainty in war undoubtedly has relevance with regard to the conduct of war. However, his introduction of an external concept (genius), which lies outside the original trinity, has only limited efficacy because Clausewitz effectively assumes that the concept of "genius" has some kind of intrinsic quality that can be readily understood and applied in various contexts. Unfortunately, for most students of war and strategy, precisely what Clausewitz means by "genius" is largely a question of interpretation. In the words of Daniel Moran, "the sources of that motive energy were mysterious, and could not be prescribed systematically."[11]

Like Clausewitz, Sun Tzu also views uncertainty and the ways in which it can be managed as the primary concern when seeking to cope with the complexities of war. However, in contrast to Clausewitz, Sun Tzu is able to find answers to this problem through the use of terms inside Clausewitz's trinity without employing extraneous concepts like "genius." To some extent, this is because Sun Tzu did not set up a trinitarian concept to begin with, and which comes along with a physical metaphor as Clausewitz did, he is therefore free from its constraints. He does not need to deal with the phenomenon that exhibits "an object suspended between three magnets."[12] As a result, he is free from the presumption that the "three magnets" have to be three separate entities. This is a serious limitation in the Clausewitzian trinity because war is now depicted in an idealized manner, and this aspect alone would have prevented Clausewitz from making much progress in his trinitarian analysis. Sun Tzu, on the other hand, has the freedom to interpret the three tendencies according to his own understanding of the complexities of war. Bassford remarks on these differences:

[T]wo of the trinity's elements—emotion and reason—are forces *internal* to the human mind, while the third—chance/probability—is *external* to the human mind. The point is that emotion and reason [i.e. irrationality and rationality] are both a matter of human intent, whereas chance/probability represents concrete reality—the [non-rational] real world, upon which our intentions must be forcibly imposed and which often makes those intentions unrealizable and/or irrelevant.[13]

Although war is ultimately a realm of chance, the so-called "chaos" of war (i.e. the phenomenon which displays "an object suspended between three magnets") is not a random phenomenon. Instead, the chaos of war can be viewed as "deterministic chaos"—a form of chaos determined by various inputs into the system. In the case of Clausewitz's trinity, the chaos of war is determined by the three elements, and as two of these are "forces *internal* to the human mind," it could be concluded that control over the human dimension would enable control of the system (i.e. war) as a whole. Following the same logic, we can consider that *war is not entirely a complex system, but a complex system with a dominant human dimension.* Whereas Chinese and Western strategists recognize the inherent complexity of the human dimension, Chinese strategic thought differs from its Western counterpart due to its long-standing and highly developed understanding of the speed with which war taps into irrational forces.[14] As a result of his understanding of the way rational and irrational forces operate in war, Sun Tzu tends to view war as being less unpredictable than Clausewitz, while he is also able to avoid introducing the external concept of genius to cope with friction or the general uncertainty (more than chance and probability alone) of war. Sun Tzu's discussion of this issue, which serves as the spine to his broader strategic thought as a whole, has the potential to revolutionize existing approaches to friction and uncertainty in war. In essence, Sun Tzu's system is not only designed to reduce uncertainty for his side, but also to magnify his adversary's uncertainty—only in this contextual framework can the work of Sun Tzu be fully understood.

Certain to Win

The first method Sun Tzu proposes to suppress uncertainty in war displays his tendency to promote the use of all possible means to achieve victory. Sun Tzu states that "a victory that is long in coming will blunt [the army's] weapons and dampen their ardor. If you attack cities, their strength will be exhausted. If you expose the army to a prolonged campaign, the state's resources will be inadequate" (Chapter 2).[15] Given that war will always incur some degree of economic cost, Sun Tzu's warning appears to be little more than common sense. However, as he later states: "Those who do not thoroughly comprehend the dangers inherent in employing the army are incapable of truly knowing the potential advantages of military actions" (Chapter 2). In other words, the economic cost of war can be used in an advantageous way as part of a strategy aimed at draining the resources of an adversary in a war of attrition.[16] It was this idea that Sun Tzu recommended to the king of Wu (the state where Sun Tzu served as a general) in his conflict with the state of Ch'u (Chu), Wu's nemesis, and a state about three times the size of Wu. Sun Tzu asked the king to divide his forces into three field armies, each of which was dispatched to engage the enemy in turn, but which were always directed to avoid becoming involved in protracted battles or decisive confrontations. This long-term campaign of harassment not only had physical objectives; it also sought to disrupt the enemy's chain of command, thereby sowing doubt and dissension, and making Ch'u's leadership feel incapable of coping with the threat that Wu posed.[17]

There are least two reasons why Sun Tzu's strategy with regard to exhausting the enemy is remarkable. First, it highlights the way in which the West's overemphasis on decisive battles, or the "militarization" of strategy, has led to a decline in the use of stratagems and other non-military means in Western strategic thinking and warfare (although the United States, whether intentionally or not, may have practiced an "exhausting" strategy against the Soviet Union, which led to that country's economic breakdown and demise). This lack of attention on non-military means to achieve the ends of war has arguably led to armed conflicts that could have been avoided, as well as the escalating use of violence to achieve aims that could have been achieved through less violent means.

Second, Sun Tzu's strategy shows a strong tendency to "linearize" the so-called "nonlinearity" (friction, chaos) in war by all possible means. Most nonlinearities in war are generated in battles, where all sorts of moral forces, dangers, and uncertainties play a much bigger role than they do in other occasions in war. "Intermixed and turbulent," says Sun Tzu, "the fighting appears chaotic, but they cannot be made disordered. In turmoil and confusion, their deployment is circular, and they cannot be defeated." (Chapter 5)[18] The passage further stresses the degree of complexity in war and the importance of bringing it under control. Even so, under such conditions no leader can ever guarantee that his army will stay ordered and remain undefeated, hence control needs to be exerted over other dimensions before a war turns "intermixed and turbulent." In this case, Sun Tzu spots the opportunity to make full use of the often-downplayed material dimension and to use it decisively against the adversary. This is one of Sun Tzu's preferred strategies for achieving two ideals of victory: "conquering the enemy and growing stronger" (Chapter 2) and "subjugating the enemy's army without fighting is the true pinnacle of excellence." (Chapter 3)[19]

After moving from the grand-strategic phase of "Waging War" (Chapter 2) to the strategic phase of "Planning Offensives" (Chapter 3), Sun Tzu specifies and evaluates a range of strategic actions employed in the conduct of war: "[T]he highest realization of warfare is to attack the enemy's plans; next is to attack their alliances; next to attack their army; and the lowest is to attack their fortified cities" (Chapter 3).[20] Among these four options, however, Sun Tzu only later explains why attacking fortified cities is the most costly and time-consuming option.[21] This gives the impression that the ranking is based on the cost of the attack alone. However, while such an interpretation no doubt accounts for the ranking of the last two options (attacking the enemy's army and fortified cities), it can hardly explain why "attacking plans and alliances," which does not belong among military actions, are preferred options. In fact, as Sun Tzu has already made clear in Chapter 2, his definition of victory is "conquering the enemy and growing stronger." The four options, therefore, should not be interpreted in terms of cost alone, as cost has already been taken into account. By putting the four different kinds of attack on the same plane, Sun Tzu is actually comparing the four in terms of their efficacy in leading to victory. Through this approach, he emphasizes that "subjugating the enemy's army without fighting" should not be viewed as an ideal; rather, it is the key premise for attaining certain victory.

While the meaning of "attack the enemy's alliances" is easy to grasp, the way in which it is possible to "attack the enemy's plans" is harder to understand. After all, attacking alliances or armies or fortified cities could be regarded as a "plan." While all English translations provide more or less the same interpretation, the original Chinese includes the meaning of "attacking by stratagem" as part of "attacking the enemy's plans." This interpretation is in accordance with the chapter's title, "Planning Offensives" (*mou gong* 謀攻), which in Chinese also contains the meaning of "attacking by stratagem." Regardless of which interpretation is correct, it is clear that stratagem is central to Sun Tzu's thought. Stratagems "are the ways military strategists are victorious. They cannot be spoken of in advance" (Chapter 1). However, by contrasting stratagem with the three other modes of attack, we should be better able to understand the nature of stratagem and why it is a preferred mode of attack.[22]

Liddell Hart, a "successor" to Sun Tzu, best articulates the basis for the assertion that "the highest realization of warfare is to attack the enemy's plans [attack by stratagem]." He states:

the true aim in war is the mind of the hostile rulers, not the bodies of their troops; that the balance between victory and defeat turns on mental impressions and only indirectly on physical blow.[23]

true victory lay in compelling one's opponent to abandon his purpose, with the least possible loss to oneself. If such result was obtained, there was no real advantage to be gained by winning a battle ... while the attempt would incur *a needless risk of defeat* ...[24]

War is essentially won by influencing the minds of hostile rulers; military actions have only an indirect effect on this goal. "If such result was obtained, there was no real advantage to be gained by winning a battle." The orientations of the two different approaches (i.e. influencing the minds of hostile rulers and employing military actions alone) have great impact upon the nature of a conflict since "attacking the enemy's plans" is very much a matter of individual perception while "attacking the army or fortified cities" has lots to do with mass psychology. Not only does the individual perception of the hostile leader carry more weight, but it is also pointless to risk meddling with the relatively less controllable mass psychology of combatants and masses if focused effort can change the minds of the leaders.

Thus Chinese strategy thought has long featured a highly developed understanding of the speed with which war creates irrational forces, as well as the consequences stemming from this. While an opponent may deviate from rational conduct during a war, rationality and irrationality are internal to a human mind or a relatively small number of minds; it is still largely predictable. However, when it involves the collective level (the army, the people), the irrational force will become external to the human mind and begin developing a character more similar to chance and probability. This is much less decipherable than the irrational force on the individual level. Once chance and probability (non-rationality) have superseded rationality and irrationality as the dominant tendency of the trinity, war again becomes highly complex, and thus less predictable, as Clausewitz depicts in his trinitarian analysis, and Sun Tzu's scheme of controlling the system through the human dimension will be far less effective. From this illustration, we can understand why Sun Tzu considers military actions a primary source of uncertainty in war, and why Sun Tzu always attempts to maintain war as a mind-game rather than letting it turn into a bloodbath.

The second quotation from Liddell Hart provides another perspective that explains Sun Tzu's preference for "attacking the enemy's plans and alliances" over "attacking their army and fortified cities." As "attacking the enemy's plans and alliances" can result in "compelling one's opponent to abandon his purpose, with the least possible loss to oneself," it is pointless to "incur a needless risk of defeat" by engaging one's army in battle or siege—the first step towards control is to avoid unnecessary risk of defeat. To engage an army in battle, one automatically confronts with the uncertainty generated by the terrain and the collective irrational force mentioned before. To lay a siege, one has to cope with additional risks that result from fortifications and the hardened resistance of both the enemy's troops and people. Sun Tzu states that "it is the nature of the army to defend when encircled; to fight fervently when unavoidable; and to follow orders when compelled [by circumstances]" (Chapter 11).[25] This highlights the paradoxical logic of military action, whereby the more aggressive or destructive an army is, the more resistance it will face, and hence, such actions can ultimately be counterproductive. Sun Tzu, however, focuses on consequences, not intentions, as other Chinese philosophers do.[26] This explains why he states: "Thus one who excels at warfare seeks [victory] through the strategic configuration of power (shih), not from reliance on men" (Chapter 5).[27] Men will act without being forced if the strategic configuration permits; hence a skillful defender always tries to create a strategic configuration that consolidates his army and people behind him, while a skillful attacker makes every effort to prevent the defender from achieving such a configuration.

In addition, since "attacking the enemy's plans and alliances" are a non-military means, they can be practiced in both peacetime and wartime. The implication behind this is that the "attacker" has more freedom of action if the implementation of strategy is no longer confined to wartime. Yet what ultimately distinguishes "attacking plans" from "attacking alliances" is that the former can effectively make full use of the whole spectrum of war. It is the processes of "militarization of war" and "tacticization of strategy" that have blinded us from identifying and rediscovering the countless opportunities in the non-military spheres of war. If the whole spectrum of war can be utilized, the chance that a stratagem or strategy can come into effect without being noticed or checked will greatly increase. By the same token, we would be able to find the course of least resistance more easily since there would now be more blind spots and gaps to exploit. Although literally, strategy is something to be countered, Sun Tzu suggests that a good strategy will remain undetected and thus not countered.

Sun Tzu consistently favored the use of non-military means, such as stratagem and diplomacy, for achieving victory. But his scheme for maximizing the certainty of victory does not stop here. One important point in this regard has often gone unnoticed, presumably because the line in which it appears seems slightly unremarkable:

One who cannot be victorious assumes a defensive posture; one who can be victorious attacks. In these circumstances by assuming a defensive posture, strength will be more than adequate, whereas in offensive actions it would be inadequate. (Chapter 4)[28]

This commonsensical line contains an important lesson that is also part of Sun Tzu's strategy for maximizing certainty in war. The concept is discussed in *Questions and Replies between T'ang T'ai-tsung and Li Wei-kung*, a work that records dialogues between one of China's greatest emperors (T'ang T'ai-tsung) and his best general (Li Wei-kung or Li Ching) on issues of war and strategy and on *The Art of War*:

[T]he essence of defensive strategy is to show the enemy an inadequacy. The essence of aggressive strategy lies in showing the enemy that you have a surplus. If you show the enemy an insufficiency, then they will certainly advance and attack. In this case "enemy does not know where to attack." If you show the enemy a surplus, then they will certainly take up defensive positions. In this case "the enemy does not know where to mount his defense."[29]

Although it is often assumed that Sun Tzu's original passage is nothing more than a truism, T'ang and Li read it from an entirely different angle in which the strategist utilizes "frozen" mindsets concerning attack and defense. It is important to note that "inadequacy" and "surplus," as discussed in the above passage, have little to do with the real strength of a force. They are just postures for shaping the enemy's perception, so that the enemy will stick with conventional norms that "one who cannot be victorious assumes a defensive posture; one who can be victorious attacks," and will deviate from his original plan. In other words, this stratagem can be regarded as "attacking the enemy's plans" at the operational/tactical level. This is one of Sun Tzu's methods for "controlling" the adversary and making his moves more predictable. At a higher level, the example manifests the workings of yin–yang, the dialectical engine of Chinese strategic thought, which suggests that any concept proposed without considering its opposite is only half a concept.

"Know thy Self, Know thy Enemy"

"One who knows the enemy and knows himself will not be endangered in a hundred engagements" (Chapter 3) is one of Sun Tzu's most well-known sayings: it was even used to provide a theoretical foundation for Information Warfare (IW), a key component of the Revolution in Military Affairs (RMA). However, the apparent association between the maxim and the concept of information superiority or dominance is indicative of the kind of serious misreading that Sun Tzu's ideas have thus far experienced in the West. Though the maxim certainly has something to say about intelligence, it would be misguided to view it through the lens of Information Warfare without first understanding its true meaning. If it were simply the case that the maxim notes the importance of intelligence and the collection of information about an opponent, then it would amount to nothing more than a self-evident truism. Moreover, Sun Tzu's thoughts on intelligence are elaborated at length in Chapter 13, entitled "Employing Spies."

Although Sun Tzu identifies various forms of intelligence, he places a particular emphasis on the role of cultural intelligence in war:

Of old the rise of the Yin (Shang) dynasty was because of Yi Yin who served the house Hsia; the rise of the Chou dynasty was because of Lu Ya [the Ta'i Kung/ Tai Gong] who served in the house of Shang. Thus only those farsighted rulers and their superior commanders who can get the most intelligent people as their spies are destined to accomplish great things. (Chapter 13)[30]

Yi Yin was a leading official in the Yin (Shang) dynasty, while Lu Ya, now commonly known as Ta'i Kung/Tai Gong (*Ta'i Kung's Six Secret Teachings* alludes to him), was the supreme commander of the Chou dynasty. Each had first served in the house of the enemy before changing sides, and the information they brought with them contributed to the fall of the houses of Hsia and Shang. Despite the fact that Sun Tzu's discussion of intelligence encompasses cultural intelligence, his statement that "[i]ntelligence is of the essence in warfare—it is what the armies depend upon in their every move" (Chapter 13)[31] is actually limited. Good intelligence alone is still not enough to avoid being "endangered in a hundred engagements." But "know thy self and know thy enemy" will prevent this.

The line that points to the real meaning of this maxim does not appear until Chapter 7:

The *ch'i* [i.e. morale, spirit, energy, etc.] of the Three Armies can be snatched away, the commanding general's mind can be seized. (Chapter 7)[32]

Here we get some idea as to what Sun Tzu considers the most important aspect of an army and a commander—its *ch'i* (*qi* 氣) and his mind, respectively. Though intangible, *ch'i* and mind constitute the "information" or "intelligence" that Sun Tzu deems most important. In *Questions and Replies between T'ang T'ai-tsung and Li Wei-kung* "know thy enemy and know thy self" is given its most clear annotation:

[A]ttacking their minds is what is referred to as "knowing them." Preserving one's *ch'i* [spirit] is what is meant by "knowing yourself."[33]

T'ai-tsung, the emperor of T'ang, further elaborates on this idea:

When I was about to engage in battle, I first evaluated the enemy's mind by comparing it with my mind to determine who was more thoroughly prepared. Only after that could I know his situation. To evaluate the enemy's *ch'i* I compared it with our own to determine who was more controlled. Only then could I know myself. For this reason, "know them and know yourself" is the great essence of the military strategists.[34]

The importance of "know thy self and know thy enemy" does not merely reside in self-knowledge and the collection of facts about an opponent. Instead of mere "knowing," it emphasizes the importance of interpreting and evaluating the intentions, traits, and thought patterns of the enemy as well as the mental condition of an opponent's troops. As with many of Sun Tzu's other maxims, this again highlights the way in which Sun Tzu viewed war as a mind-game, where attacking the enemy's mind is vastly more preferable to other forms of offense.

"Know thy self and know thy enemy" was never intended to be used in isolation, and explicating its true meaning also helps to unravel other misunderstandings. The dictum below, for example, invites misinterpretation if it is not seen as an extension of "know thy self and know thy enemy":

Of old the expert in battle would first make himself invincible and then wait for the enemy to expose his vulnerability. Invincibility depends on oneself; vulnerability lies with the enemy ... Being invincible lies with defense; the vulnerability of the enemy comes with the attack. (Chapter 4)[35]

As Sun Tzu is telling his readers to "wait for the enemy to expose his vulnerability," and that "being invincible lies with defense," a literal interpretation of this passage is likely to lead to the impression that the Chinese have a propensity to take a passive, defensive stance in war. But when the passage is considered in the psychological context of the maxim "know thy self and know thy enemy," it is possible to arrive at a completely different conclusion. As there is a strong psychological, non-military foundation to Sun Tzu's analysis of attack and defense, the assertion that "being invincible lies with defense; the vulnerability of the enemy comes with the attack" speaks to the psychological dimension of war rather than more physical forms of attack and defense. As Li Ching says:

For attacking does not stop with just attacking their cities or attacking their formations. One must have techniques for attacking their minds. Defense does not end with just the completion of the walls and the realization of sold formations. One must also preserve spirit and be prepared to await the enemy.[36]

And Tai-tsung concludes:

What Sun-tzu meant by "first make yourself unconquerable" is "know yourself" [preserving our *ch'i*]. "Waiting until the enemy can be conquered" is "knowing them" [attacking their minds].[37]

When read in this way, "invincibility depends on oneself; vulnerability lies with the enemy" is simply a variant of "know thy self and know thy enemy." As a result, the "waiting" that is required "for the enemy to expose its vulnerability" has more to do with grasping the enemy's mind than merely waiting for opportunities to launch a physical, military attack. If a leader can effectively manage his own army's *ch'i* and evade the enemy's attempt to decipher him, he will always have the chance to "attack" the enemy's mind and wait for conditions to ripen. "Thus one who excels at warfare first establishes himself in a position where he cannot be defeated while not losing [any opportunity] to defeat the enemy."[38] This also explains why Sun Tzu holds that "the victorious army first realizes the conditions for victory, and then seeks to engage in battle. The vanquished army fights first, and then seeks victory" (Chapter 4).[39]

"Know thy self, know thy enemy" and its related concepts

Know thy self	Know thy enemy
Preserving one's *ch'i* [spirit]	Attacking the enemy's mind
First make oneself invincible	Wait for the enemy to expose his vulnerability
Invincibility depends on oneself	Vulnerability lies with the enemy
Being invincible lies with defense	The vulnerability of the enemy comes with the attack

John Boyd fully understood this point, which in turn led him to identify two major differences between Sun Tzu and Clausewitz. First, whereas Clausewitz argues that the enemy should be led into a "decisive battle," Sun Tzu argues that the enemy should be unraveled before a battle has even taken place. Secondly, unlike Sun Tzu, Clausewitz focuses on how a commander can minimize friction (the equivalent of "being invincible"), but he does not explore the ways in which the enemy's friction can be maximized (exploring and exploiting "the vulnerability of the enemy").[40] In other words, while Clausewitz may know himself, he does not know his enemy. Thus he inevitably needs to demand a lot from his conception of genius to make up for missing the part about "know thy enemy" in his theory. While Boyd asserts that "Sun Tzu tried to drive his adversary bananas while Clausewitz tried to keep himself from being driven bananas," Sun Tzu's maxim of "know thy self and know thy enemy" effectively sought to achieve both.[41]

"Master of the Enemy's Fate"

Sun Tzu does not limit himself to specifying the mental and physical (battle) phases of war. He has determined that "attacking the enemy's mind" or "shaping the adversary's perception" is of higher importance than the actual battle, and these activities can be conducted both prior to and during battle. A leader can still mount his psychological "attacks," even if he is in a defensive position or if the war has reached a stalemate, in order to strengthen his "control" over the enemy's mind and create better battle conditions. The division of war into mental and physical phases allows a leader the luxury of establishing himself "in a position where he cannot be defeated while not losing [any opportunity] to defeat the enemy."

Such practice, however, is not entirely an Eastern concept and is not, in fact, new to the West. Napoleon's moves in the Battle of Austerlitz in 1805, the German breakthrough at Sedan in 1940, and even the Americans' "left hook" in the First Gulf War in 1991 all exhibited a distinct "attacking the mind" or "perception-shaping" phase prior to the battle. The success achieved in the last two examples in particular has often been attributed to the so-called "indirect approach," and this gives a false impression that one should search for the "indirect approach" vis-à-vis the conventional, direct approach. This is just the same as people placing more importance on *ch'i* (the unorthodox) than *cheng* (the orthodox).

But as we have already noted, it takes both *ch'i* and *cheng* to form a whole concept; they should never be considered individually (see Chapter 5). The essence of *ch'i* and *cheng* does not lie in seeking *ch'i* out of *cheng*, but rather in reaching a realm where "there are none that are not orthodox, none that are not unorthodox, so they cause the enemy never to be able to fathom them. Thus with the orthodox they are victorious, with the unorthodox they are also victorious."[42] The heart of *ch'i-cheng*, as Sun Tzu always emphasizes, is to "attack the enemy's mind." The activity is always psychological in nature. If a leader can successfully shape the adversary's perception and conceal his own intentions, then whatever sensible course the leader chooses will naturally become an "indirect approach."

Sun Tzu's emphasis on the mental phase prior to actual battle may appear to suggest that he had a strong, philosophical preference for psychology and mind-games, rather than real, violent conflict in order to achieve victory. However, Sun Tzu's emphasis on these factors should also be understood in the context of the time in which he lived. As technological breakthroughs were relatively rare and belligerents in conflict shared broadly similar technology, Sun Tzu's preference was entirely understandable: in the absence of new weapons and tactics that would ensure victory in each and every battle, there were only a small number of tactical options available to strategists, and such that there were would hardly be able to secure an advantage in the period preceding a battle. Entering a battle under such conditions left far too much to chance, and the battle could also easily develop into an indecisive bloodbath that helped neither side. This is what Sun Tzu regarded as "the vanquished army fights first, and then seeks victory." And this is why he recognized the real need to create advantageous conditions prior to battle or outside the battlefield. Although the army might still be employing ordinary tactical means in combat, the leader who had put the adversary under his "control" could expect an easy victory.

The substantial advantage to be gained in battle from "attacking the enemy's mind" is far from the full meaning behind the concept. To grasp it entirely, we must first revisit Sun Tzu's view of war's ultimate goal. Contrary to popular belief, Sun Tzu's primary concern was not to win battles and wars, but to put "All under Heaven" (i.e. to put all under the rule of one state, namely China). This involved winning successive battles and wars against multiple opponents until the objective was attained. Although Sun Tzu certainly recognized the importance of winning specific wars, he also sought to consider the impact that winning a specific war would have on the course of subsequent wars, and hence in achieving his long-term aim. In other words, Sun Tzu sought to ensure that any advantage enjoyed from a single war would not prove to be a disadvantage in another war, thereby preventing 'All under Heaven' from being realized. It is with this principal concern in mind that Sun Tzu says:

To anticipate the victory is not going beyond the understanding of the common run; it is not the highest excellence. To win in battle so that the whole world says "Excellent!" is not the highest excellence. Hence, to lift an autumn hair is no mark of strength; to see the sun and moon is no mark of clear-sightedness; to hear a thunder clap is no mark of keen hearing. He whom the ancients called an expert in battle gained victory where victory was easily gained. Thus the battle of the expert is never an exceptional victory, nor does it win him reputation for wisdom or credit for courage. His victories in battle are unerring. Unerring means that he acts where victory is certain, and conquers an enemy that has already lost. (Chapter 4)[43]

This passage appears to run contrary to traditional beliefs about victory in almost every sense: Sun Tzu argues that a "good" victory should be easy and unexceptional, like "lifting an autumn hair," "seeing the sun and moon," and "hearing a thunder clap." It should be so prosaic that everyone expects it, and nobody will think it is so extraordinary as to be "excellent." But how can this be possible? We can find a clue in the assertions: "His victories in battle are unerring. Unerring means that he acts where victory is certain, and conquers an enemy that has already lost." The concepts of certain victory and "conquer an enemy that has already lost" clearly refer to Sun Tzu's "attacking the enemy's mind." By dividing war into mental and physical phases, and by viewing the mental phase as the place where victory should be decided, one can act whenever "victory is certain" and "conquer an enemy that has already lost." Since the result of battle has already been decided in the mental phase, one can then employ ordinary tactical or strategic means (such as numerical superiority). This does not go "beyond the understanding of the common run" and nobody thinks such a victory is "excellent."

Controlling the Negative Feedback

One of the most important advantages to result from making victories appear easy is that potential enemies will gain the false impression that victory was gained because it was easy. This is likely to discourage opponents from learning anything significant from the conflict (or will slow down their learning or "orientation" process), so that the chance of winning does not diminish even after a number of engagements. Here again, Sun Tzu alludes to the fact that any tangible advantage has a limited shelf-life and will be countered sooner or later: the more frequently the advantage is put to use, the sooner it will cease to be effective. As a result, one must draw on mental efforts, which are intangible and are applicable to any conflict situation, at any time and any place, in order to secure victory in battle.

To borrow the language of cybernetics, Sun Tzu's strategy for winning an easy and unexceptional victory centers on controlling the enemy's negative feedback loop, or the "steering" mechanism of a machine or system. A negative feedback loop provides information to the machine on its performance and enables it to close the gap between its actions and what is expected of it.[44] Creating an impression of an easy and unexceptional victory, while winning the war/battle in the mental phase, requires delaying, distorting, or depriving the adversary of negative feedback so that the gap between what it does and what is expected of it will remain open throughout and subsequent to the course of war. As a result, the enemy will be left with limited material to use in terms of planning. In short, it is a measure for controlling the enemy's evolution. Although it is impossible to impede an enemy's evolution indefinitely, it is possible to control the pace at which this occurs.

However, repeatedly using the same tactic, or using unnecessary means (or more than what is needed) to subdue the enemy is no different from overusing antibiotics. To extend the analogy further, it simply hastens the evolution through the mutation of resistant bacteria. It is not only current enemies that are able to learn—potential enemies can learn as well (given that bacteria that have never been exposed to the pressure mutate as well). History is replete with examples of this: Napoleon was defeated when his enemies learned his tricks. The US demonstration of its advanced weaponry in the First Gulf War resulted in its opponents rapidly adapting to its technological superiority. And the relentless US pursuit of Al-Qaeda is forcing that terrorist group to disperse and evolve at a faster rate. Although Sun Tzu's dictum was developed in the context of ancient warfare, it still applies equally well in today's world, particularly as many contemporary conflicts, such as the "Global War on Terror" (GWOT), are long-term struggles. As military engagements are only brief episodes within a wider, protracted struggle, achieving victory in the long run requires that the use of strength is limited and properly concealed.

Of course, "winning easy and unexceptional victory" serves only as a grand principle on the strategic level. Not all adversaries can be defeated easily in an unexceptional manner. It was for this reason that Sun Tzu developed another concept for operational and tactical use—the concept of formlessness (Chapter 6).

Hsing (form 形) lies at the heart of the concept of formlessness. *Hsing* is of crucial importance in battle because it is this abstract representation of one's "form" that provides an ability to read an opponent's intentions and plans. *Hsing* and *shih* ("force," "momentum," "strategic configuration of power"—the word has no precise English translation) are the two most important abstractions that, if correctly grasped, contain almost the complete knowledge of a particular force vis-à-vis its opponent. Consequently, one of the most important tasks for those engaged in the battlefield involves evaluating the enemy's *hsing*, while concealing one's own or making it unfathomable: "I determine the enemy's disposition of forces (*hsing*) while I have no perceptible form" (Chapter 6).[45]

There have been a number of attempts to provide an accurate English-language translation of "*hsing*." Sawyer's translation of *The Art of War*, for example, employs various terms ranging from form, shape, military deployment, and disposition of force to configuration.[46] However, the translation that best conveys the meaning of *hsing* is "pattern" or "system." This translation would be consonant with Sun Tzu's repeated emphasis in *The Art of War* on the idea that the larger or stronger are not always victorious. Thus there must be another indicator or element at a higher plane that determines the ultimate result of battles and wars. Sun Tzu states:

As I analyze it, even though Yueh's army is numerous, of what great advantage is it to them for attaining victory? Thus I say victory can be achieved. Even though the enemy is more numerous, they can be forced not to fight. (Chapter 6)[47]

The Mongols, who in most cases were numerically inferior to their enemies, achieved a series of overwhelming victories against their opponents. This was because the Mongols constituted a better "system" than their enemy, and the underlying pattern of their system was beyond the understanding of the latter. Andrew Ilichinski offers us an explanation that fully corresponds with this phenomenon. Those who consider numerical superiority to be the main determinant of victory and defeat view "quantities" as the basic elements that explain matters in the world. But those like Sun Tzu and the Mongols see "patterns" as the basic elements. Ilichinski believes that we are now experiencing a shift from the former worldview to the latter one.[48]

Over 2,500 years ago Sun Tzu fully articulated such a worldview in his concept of formlessness. Boyd, Sun Tzu's best "successor" in the West, elucidates the phenomenon and Sun Tzu's concept of formlessness in modern Western terms:

The reason for [the reversal appears to be that] these smaller organizations were able to avoid or negate the larger's advantages in size and strength. Somehow they had managed *not* to become systems in the eyes of their larger opponents. *This might lead one to suspect that in any competitive endeavor, if you can be modeled ["sand-tabled," is how Boyd refers to it] you aren't using strategy at all, and you can be defeated.*[49]

Due to the terminology brought to us by the "new sciences," the real face of Sun Tzu's concept of formlessness is finally being unveiled in the West. To be "formless," one has to manage "*not* to become systems in the eyes of their larger opponents" or to make the underlying pattern exhibited by his system imperceptible. This, however, by no means implies that everything has to be hidden from the enemy. As Sun Tzu states:

In accord with the enemy's disposition [*hsing*] we impose measures on the masses that produce victory, but the masses are unable to fathom them. Men all know the disposition [*hsing*] by which we attain victory, but no one knows the configuration [*hsing*] through which we control the victory. (Chapter 6)[50]

119

This passage refers to two different kinds of *hsing* (forms): one is tangible ("Men all know the disposition [*hsing*] by which we attain victory") and the other intangible ("but no one knows the configuration [*hsing*] through which we control the victory"). The translations that are traditionally used, such as form, shape, military deployment, disposition of force, and configuration, belong to the first, tangible category of *hsing*. These are the factors that an enemy will always be able to detect or learn. The second, intangible type of *hsing* refers to the "form" at the systemic level that serves to dictate flexibility and adaptability, and thus the competitiveness of a system or an organization (e.g. the army). More flexible or adaptable armies are harder for the enemy to "model" and understand as they will not behave in the way expected of an ordinary army ("not becoming systems in the eyes of the opponent"). In order to illustrate why an army with no constant *hsing* is stronger and less likely to be deciphered by the adversary, Sun Tzu again uses a water analogy:

[T]he army's disposition of force [*hsing*] is like water ... Water configures [*hsing*] its flow in accord with the terrain; the army controls its victory in accord with the enemy. Thus the army does not maintain any constant strategic configuration of power [*shih*], water has no constant shape [*hsing*]. (Chapter 6)[51]

As Sun Tzu's concept of formlessness points at "form" at the systemic level, rather than a physical "form," it is futile to counter a "formless" army with better intelligence or technological superiority, as these will only deal with its physical "form":

Thus the pinnacle of military deployment [*hsing*] approaches the formless. If it is formless, then even the deepest spy cannot discern it or the wise make plans against it. (Chapter 6)[52]

In addition, expending effort trying to identify the enemy's real "form" by focusing on the physical "form" simply makes it easier for the enemy to confuse and deceive, as there may be no correlation between the physical "form" and the real "form," and on most occasions it is only for the enemy's consumption. Even if the same military deployment is used twice, it should never be assumed that the real "form" of a "formless" army will always be the same: "Thus a victorious battle [strategy] is not repeated, the configurations [*hsing*] of response [to the enemy] are inexhaustible" (Chapter 6).[53]

At first glance, the concept of formlessness does not appear to have any relationship with the goal of "winning easy and unexceptional victory." However, both require that the enemy's negative feedback loop is brought under control. The strategy of "winning easy and unexceptional victory" involves controlling an enemy's (and potential enemies') negative feedback by leaving them with nothing or very little to learn, thereby delaying their orientation and learning processes on the strategic level. The concept of formlessness, on the other hand, controls the negative feedback by preventing the opponent from modelling one's pattern of actions. As "the configurations [hsing] of response [to the enemy] are inexhaustible," by the time the opponent believes he has managed to understand the situation (i.e. has received the negative feedback), the feedback is already outdated and no longer of any constructive use. In Boyd's words, the concept of formlessness is an idea that involves magnifying the friction/uncertainty of an opponent and paralyzing him by denying him the opportunity to expend effort.[54] It is a measure that can directly, if not completely, disorganize an adversary.

"Winning easy and unexceptional victory" and the concept of formlessness form a twofold approach that is able to nullify almost any strategic advantage the enemy enjoys, regardless of whether one has gained the initiative in the first place. In other words, Sun Tzu's overall strategy is designed to be applicable in all conflict situations as long as the conflict retains its dialectical nature, which involves negative feedback. Sun Tzu states:

Thus one who excels at warfare first establishes himself in a position where he cannot be defeated while not losing [any opportunity] to defeat the enemy. (Chapter 4)[55]

Sun Tzu's emphasis on controlling the enemy's negative feedback informed Boyd's famous OODA loop, which claims that the key to success in conflict is to get inside an adversary's mind and decision-making process, which in effect embodies Sun Tzu's "attacking the enemy's mind." notions such as "[t]he most amazing aspect of the OODA loop is that the losing side rarely understands what happened" and "the adversary is dealing with outdated or irrelevant information and thus becomes confused and disoriented and can't function" strikingly manifest Sun Tzu's scheme of controlling the enemy's negative feedback.[56]

Controlling the Positive Feedback

Sun Tzu's understanding of "attacking" the enemy's negative feedback loop informs some of his most renowned maxims. Yet Sun Tzu also emphasizes the role that positive feedback can play in war. As the negative feedback loop tends to bring a system to equilibrium, Sun Tzu's practice of controlling the flow of information in the enemy's negative feedback loop ("winning easy and unexceptional victory" and "being formless") can delay or prevent the enemy from ever establishing that equilibrium. The positive feedback loop, on the other hand, tends to push a system out of equilibrium. As a consequence, if the negative feedback loop is disrupted or manipulated, the positive feedback loop can run out of control, resulting in the collapse of the system, and thereby creating a vicious circle.[57] Sun Tzu, of course, would not let the enemy (system) crumble on its own simply by controlling the negative feedback. He would "start" and accelerate the vicious cycle himself by controlling the positive feedback. As Sun Tzu explains:

So the task of a military operation is to accord deceptively with the intentions of the enemy. If you concentrate totally on the enemy, you can kill its military leadership a thousand miles away. This is skillful accomplishment of the task. (Chapter 11)[58]

"To accord deceptively with the intentions of the enemy" is Sun Tzu's primary means of controlling the enemy's positive feedback. By acting as if the enemy's plan is working effectively, the enemy can be led to believe that everything is working according to the plan and the enemy will become more and more willing to deceive himself in the subsequent course of the war. When the enemy becomes the prisoner of his own wishful thinking to the extent that he no longer can readjust himself to the true "reality," it is the time to stop pretending and to "concentrate totally on the enemy." In so doing, it is possible to "kill its military leadership a thousand miles away" in one shot.

Sun Tzu's emphasis on controlling the enemy's positive feedback is based on the idea that "we are never deceived. We only deceive ourselves."[59] This can clearly be applied to numerous, catastrophic failures of intelligence, ranging from Stalin's refusal to believe that the Nazi's would invade the USSR to the 9/11 terrorist attacks. Real success in war is often based on the opponent's willingness to deceive himself. Perception is everything; manipulating perception is consequently the essence of strategy.[60] To this, Boyd adds: "The real impact of such a strategy is the dissipation of resources, *the creation of both self-fulfilling and suicidal prophecies*, and the destruction of truth and trust. It maximizes confusion and disorder and destroys the organization's resilience, adaptability, core values, and ability to respond."[61] The key to the strategy, Sun Tzu points out, is:

Do not fix any time for battle, assess and react to the enemy in order to determine the strategy of battle. (Chapter 11)[62]

Sun Tzu's approach differs substantively from conventional practice, according to which gaining the initiative is among the most important tasks in war. Indeed, his observation questions the validity of the concept of initiative in war and strategy, which most modern (and particularly Western) armies still view as a fundamental principle of war, if not an eternal truth. If we follow Sun Tzu's logic, however, we see that if one side "instinctively" strives for the initiative, the other side will "accord deceptively with the intentions of the enemy" by giving up the initiative (temporarily). And in the process of gaining the initiative, that side will have already revealed much of their intentions and other information to the enemy. Therefore, armies that unthinkingly accept "taking the initiative" as a principle of war will easily fall prey to opponents who practice Sun Tzu's strategy; this partly explains the "helplessness" of modern armies in the face of guerrillas and insurgents. To Sun Tzu, control over the enemy is the purpose. Any measure that can help achieve this purpose (including giving up the initiative) should be seen as valid. When control over an enemy has been secured, all that is left is to seek a chance to finish him off. "At first be like a virgin; later—when the enemy opens the door—be like a fleeing rabbit. The enemy will be unable to withstand you" (Chapter 11).[63]

Controlling the enemy's positive feedback leads to another valuable lesson in Sun Tzu's thought: "The army values compelling men [controlling the enemy] and does not want to resist [confront] them."[64] Here, "compelling the enemy (men)" fails to reflect Sun Tzu's original meaning in full, and it should be replaced by "controlling the enemy," for compelling the enemy is only a subsidiary effect that derives from effective control or manipulation of the enemy. Moreover, if Sun Tzu's purpose is to avoid resisting (confronting) the enemy, compelling the enemy would be counterproductive. Sun Tzu emphasizes control over the enemy because such control can significantly reduce the need to confront the enemy directly; it is an important measure that makes "subjugating the enemy's army without fighting" possible. Behind his principle of controlling the enemy, Sun Tzu is putting across one of the most essential facts regarding the conduct of war: though the nature of war is confrontational, the means employed in war are not necessarily so.

A Theory of Control

"One thousand essays, ten thousand sections do not go beyond 'compel [control] others, do not be compelled [controlled] by them.'" Li Ching, one of the best-known commentators on and practitioners of Sun Tzu's thought, regards this as a central organizing idea of *The Art of War*.[65] Among Sun Tzu's "successors" in the West, Boyd has undoubtedly comprehended most of Sun Tzu's thought. But his understanding seldom goes beyond the scope of confusing the enemy. It is Wylie who correctly identifies that "*the aim of war is some measure of control over the enemy*."[66] Wylie argues that this is a more universal, inclusive assertion than the Clausewitzian dictum that the aim of the army in war is the defeat of the enemy's army. He also realizes that Liddell Hart (another "successor" of Sun Tzu) has used this theme as the basis for his theory of the indirect approach.[67] However, Wylie never recognizes that he is reproducing Sun Tzu's idea, although this is largely the fault of the translators of *The Art of War*.

To summarize, Sun Tzu's theory is a general theory of control. It consists of two parts: the first examines control over the complexities of war as a whole, whereas the second deals with control over the enemy. Sun

Tzu recognizes that war is a complex system with a dominant human dimension; by controlling the human dimension, it is possible to achieve control over the system (i.e. war). This view is remarkably similar to Wylie's: *"The ultimate determinant in war is the man on the scene with a gun. This man is the final power in war. He is control."*[68]

With respect to control over the enemy, Sun Tzu stresses the need to "know thy self and know thy enemy," or more precisely, "attacking the enemy's mind." "Attacking the enemy's plan" and "subjugating the enemy's army without fighting" are the two highest realizations of controlling the enemy. Again, there is a similar emphasis in Wylie's work:

[A] fairly careful scrutiny of the opponent's thought pattern and their underlying assumptions should be an early component of our own planning process. *If we could deliberately make his theory invalid, we have gone a long way toward making his actions ineffective.* An examination of this type might uncover something crucial in reaching toward establishment of control.[69]

In this passage, "careful scrutiny of the opponent's thought pattern and their underlying assumptions" is clearly analogous with "attacking the enemy's mind," and "making his theory invalid" is equivalent to "attacking the enemy's plan."

In order to retain control over an opponent when a war develops into armed conflict, Sun Tzu emphasizes the need to target the opponent's negative and positive feedback. In this sense, it is Boyd who best captures the essence of Sun Tzu's thought. The fact that Wylie and Boyd arrive independently at conclusions which are similar to those of Sun Tzu thus serves to confirm Handel's proposition that the basic logic of strategy is universal—there is no such thing as an exclusively "Western" or "Eastern" approach to strategy.[70] One of the most important tasks of a general theory of strategy is to elucidate this unarticulated universal logic of strategy.

Ultimately, control brings certainty; certainty means victory. Humans are at the center of war, and their minds are the subjects of control—war can be controlled by controlling humans.

In the following chapter, we will have a closer look of how a number of Western strategic thinkers rediscover and reproduce Sun Tzu's thought and further integrate his ideas into the Western strategic framework.

5

THE SUCCESSORS OF SUN TZU IN THE WEST

The previous chapter identified a number of "successors" to Sun Tzu in the West, including Basil H. Liddell Hart, J.C. Wylie, and John Boyd. These strategic thinkers are being called Sun Tzu's successors, not only because their ideas contain certain elements of Sun Tzu's thought, but also for the reason that their attempts to redefine and re-theorize Western strategy have made Western strategic thought more attuned to Sun Tzu's thought as well as Chinese strategic thought as a whole. In this chapter, we focus on and reexamine the thought of two successors of Sun Tzu—Liddell Hart and Boyd—through a Chinese lens. By looking more closely at the development of their thought, it is easier to note that their integration of some Chinese elements, whether knowingly or unknowingly, into the mainstream Western strategic thought has indeed opened new avenues for the development and self-rectification of Western strategy. It also suggests a new way of approaching and understanding Chinese strategic thought for the Western world.

The Art of War first appeared in the West in 1772. However, over the course of the 150 years that followed, the text attracted little by way of attention, even after a more precise, English-language translation by Lionel Giles was published in 1910. It was only due to the work of Liddell Hart that *The Art of War* finally started to have an impact on Western strategic thought. Liddell Hart first read Sun Tzu in the spring of 1927;[1] two years later, some of Sun Tzu's ideas featured in Liddell Hart's "strategy of the indirect approach," which was set out in *The Decisive Wars of History: A Study in History* (the earliest version of Liddell Hart's best-seller, *Strategy*). Liddell Hart's work paved the way for the further incorporation of Chinese and Eastern strategic thought into its Western counterpart.[2] Subsequently, a number of influential strategic thinkers, including Beaufre, Wylie, and Boyd, embraced and further developed Liddell Hart's theory. It should be noted that these developments with regard to Sun Tzu's ideas coincided with two significant processes in China and the international arena: namely, the rise of Mao Zedong and the onset of the cold war, the latter of which rendered classical strategic thought obsolete, and led to a search for new paradigms through which to understand security and strategy. It was within this context that the thought of Sun Tzu, as well as Chinese strategic thought more generally, began to grow in influence in the West.

Basil H. Liddell Hart: Rediscovering Sun Tzu

"The Indirect Approach"

Liddell Hart was one of the first in the West to rediscover Sun Tzu, and it is easy to see why he was so receptive to Sun Tzu's ideas.[3] Before he had even read Sun Tzu, Liddell Hart had formulated his "Expanding Torrent" system of attack—the aim of which is to obtain in the attack an automatic and continuous progressive infiltration by combat units[4]—which clearly echoes Sun Tzu's "Water Metaphor." The idea for which he is most well known, "the strategy of the indirect approach," emerged in 1928, about a year after his first reading of Sun Tzu, and was put to wider application in *The Decisive Wars of History* (1929)[5]—it is notable that the later versions of the book begin with thirteen quotes from *The Art of War*. As a result, "the indirect approach" can be seen as a milestone in the development of Western strategic thought—it represents the first systematic effort to synthesize Chinese and Western strategic thought. Contrary to the claims of some critics that "The Indirect approach" is oversimplified or even a tautology, the concept itself is not a single concept as the term suggests. Rather, it contains a series of related concepts, or more precisely, a series of related concepts borrowed from Sun Tzu.

THE SUCCESSORS OF SUN TZU IN THE WEST

At the beginning of his book, Liddell Hart states that the indirect approach has both physical and psychological dimensions, although it is believed that Liddell Hart derives the concept from the physical/geographic realm in the first place:

[T]hroughout the ages, effective results in war have rarely been attained unless the approach has had such indirectness as to ensure the opponent's unreadiness to meet it. The indirectness has usually been physical, and always psychological. In strategy, the longest way round is often the shortest way home.[6]

Liddell Hart's juxtaposition of indirect and direct approaches replicates Sun Tzu's dual-concept, *ch'i* and *cheng* (the unorthodox and orthodox). However, the juxtaposition is likely to have been informed by the so-called "tactics of the circuitous (indirect) and the direct":

In military combat what is most difficult is turning the circuitous into the straight, turning adversity into advantage. Thus if you make the enemy's path circuitous and entice them with profit, although you set out after them you will arrive before them. This results from knowing the tactics of the circuitous and the direct ... The one who first understands the tactics of the circuitous and the direct will be victorious. (Chapter 7)[7]

"The tactics of the circuitous and the direct" can be seen as the indirect approach for military operations and for that purpose only, with the theoretical aspect of the concept that is difficult to understand being largely removed. However, Liddell Hart then goes on to set out the theoretical basis for the indirect approach—and this leads him to Sun Tzu's dual-concept of *ch'i* and *cheng*.

As was discussed in the previous chapter, Liddell Hart's indirect approach can give the impression that the "indirect approach" should be actively searched for vis-à-vis the conventional, direct approach. This is equivalent to placing more importance on *ch'i* (the unorthodox) than *cheng* (the orthodox). But in Chinese strategic thought *ch'i* and *cheng* should form a single concept; they should never be considered individually. Such a misconception can be explained by returning to the original text in *The Art of War*: "In general, in battle one engages with the orthodox [*cheng*] and gains victory through the unorthodox [*ch'i*]" (Chapter 5).[8] By reading this line individually, it is not hard to image why Liddell Hart would choose to ignore the first half, given that it says the orthodox is for engaging and fixing the enemy and that it is through the unorthodox that victory can be gained—"clearly enough," it is the unorthodox that matters. And as we look at Liddell Hart's selection of Sun Tzu quotes in the beginning of his book, we can notice that Liddell Hart might have dropped the important lines behind "in battle one engages with the orthodox and gains victory through the unorthodox" that stress the true essence of *ch'i* and *cheng*:

In warfare the strategic configurations of power (*shih*) do not exceed the unorthodox and orthodox, but the changes of the unorthodox and orthodox can never be completely exhausted. The unorthodox and orthodox mutually produce each other, just like an endless cycle. Who can exhaust them? (Chapter 5)[9]

Liddell Hart clearly chose to leave out the lines that emphasize the complementarity of *ch'i* and *cheng*. One possible reason for this is because he is not equipped with the Chinese logic of yin–yang. The direct result of this, however, is that the indirect approach is merely employed as a means to create surprise and identify the enemy's gaps. This departs from Sun Tzu's idea that one should make use of his form/pattern (*hsing*) to create a state where "there are none that are not orthodox, none that are not unorthodox, so they cause the enemy never to be able to fathom them. Thus with the orthodox they are victorious, with the unorthodox they are also victorious."[10] In addition, other sayings of Sun Tzu, such as "[t]he army's disposition of force (*hsing*) avoids the substantial and strikes the vacuous" (Chapter 6)[11] and "[d]o not intercept well-ordered flags; do not attack well-regulated formations," (Chapter 7)[12] all play a part in strengthening the impression that one should seek *ch'i* out of *cheng*. This misreading of Liddell Hart constitutes the primary reason why many people find the indirect approach tautological in nature.

Fortunately, there are other elements from Sun Tzu which Liddell Hart has got right that help remedy his misinterpretation of *ch'i* and *cheng*. As Liddell Hart emphasizes, the indirect approach "has usually been physical, and always psychological." The identification of the two kinds of indirectness, and maintaining that the psychological aspect is always the key, have greatly augmented the theoretical potential of the indirect approach and draw it closer to Sun Tzu's original idea. Among Liddell

Hart's quotations of Sun Tzu's dictums, it is believed that Liddell Hart is inspired by the saying: "Men all know the disposition (*hsing*) by which we attain victory, but no one know the configuration (*hsing*) through which we control the victory" (Chapter 6).[13] As discussed in the previous chapter, the first and second *hsing*(s) (form/pattern) in the saying are two different kinds of *hsing*. The first kind will be known or exposed once it is employed in battle ("Men all know the disposition [*hsing*] by which we attain victory"), and the second kind may not be known or deciphered even after the war ("but no one knows the configuration [*hsing*] through which we control the victory"). The second kind can be attained by not getting modelled or becoming systems in the eyes of the opponent—that is the essence of Sun Tzu's concept of formlessness. From these two kinds of *hsing*, Liddell Hart perceives the first tangible kind as physical and the second invisible kind as psychological. As a result, although Liddell Hart has largely omitted the circularity and complementarity of *ch'i* and *cheng*, which is one of the key theoretical underpinnings of the concept of formlessness, he simplifies the concept by attributing one's success mostly to the psychological aspect of the indirect approach. This, however, cannot be seen as a self-creation of Liddell Hart entirely, for shaping the adversary's perception and concealing one's own intentions—attacking the enemy's mind—has always been the main theme of Sun Tzu's thesis.

As Richard Swain puts it, "[a]t the end of the day one must admit that the idea of the indirect approach is a tautology."[14] It is very disappointing that an author who studies and writes on Liddell Hart's continuing value as a military theorist would give such a partial evaluation. Yet from my analysis above, one should realize that this evaluation arises mainly because the philosophical underpinning behind *ch'i* and *cheng*, which is equivalent to that of yin–yang, is missing in the West. Owing to this cultural barrier, Liddell Hart fails to realize the full potential behind the dual-concept of *ch'i* and *cheng*, and can never effectively convey the idea to his Western audiences. Nevertheless, there are a number of signs showing that Liddell Hart was not totally unaware of the dynamics and interactions behind the yin–yang (or *ch'i–cheng*) which are at once opposed and complementary. For example, from the case which Liddell Hart criticizes that Clausewitz and his disciples have got the concept of concentration completely wrong, he demonstrates some true understanding of the basis of strategy:

A deeper truth to which Foch and other disciples of Clausewitz did not penetrate fully is that *in war every problem, and every principle, is a duality*. Like a coin, it has two faces. Hence the need for a well-calculated compromise as a means to reconciliation. This is the inevitable consequence of the fact that war is a two-party affair, so imposing the need that while hitting one must guard. Its corollary is that, in order to hit with effect, the enemy must be taken off his guard. Effective concentration can only be obtained when the opposing forces are dispensed; and, usually, in order to ensure this, one's own forces must be widely distributed. Thus, *by an outward paradox, true concentration is the product of dispersion.*[15]

Even such understanding is still far from reproducing the dialectical monism or dualistic monism (i.e. the premise of yin–yang) in Chinese strategic thought, but at least, unlike many Western strategic thinkers, Liddell Hart does not find this paradoxical at all but rather as a matter of course. This no doubt was highly remarkable in Liddell Hart's time and remains a rarity in today's Western world. We can find another example in Liddell Hart's *Strategy* that seems commonsensical, yet demonstrates quite precisely that he himself indeed understands the "circularity" of the direct and indirect approach. In his discussion of Hitler's open self-revelation of his plans and methods to fulfill his goals in *Mein Kampf* and his speeches, Liddell Hart deems Hitler had realized that:

men easily miss what is right under their eye, that concealment can often be found in the obvious, and that *in some cases the most direct approach can become the least expected*—just as the art of secrecy lies in being so open about most things that the few things that matter are not even suspected to exist.[16]

It is never easy to judge from a handful of examples the degree of Liddell Hart's understanding of *ch'i* and *cheng*, and whether his understanding is a result of Sun Tzu's influence. Yet what one can be sure about is that the indirect approach just cannot be a tautology—this can be justified by the fact that Liddell Hart is one of the most well-known Western strategic thinkers in China. How would the Chinese, the originators of *ch'i* and *cheng*, possibly read Liddell Hart and take the indirect approach seriously if it is a tautology? They probably see Liddell Hart's

Strategy as a simplified, yet updated version of Sun Tzu that interprets Western and modern military history. The difference in the reception of the indirect approach in the West and China may well suggest that it is the West that lacks the philosophical framework and language necessary for the proper understanding of the concept. Paraphrasing Wylie, the incomplete vocabulary of strategy as an intellectual discipline limits the communication of the central concept of indirectness.[17]

The Condition–Consequence Approach[18]

For a strategic thinker like Liddell Hart, who "never missed an opportunity to criticize Clausewitz," and was deeply hostile to the Clausewitzian ideas of "decisive battle,"[19] it is not that hard for him to strike a chord with an important teaching of Sun Tzu: "the victorious army first realizes the conditions for victory, and then seeks to engage in battle. The vanquished army fights first, and then seeks victory" (Chapter 4)[20] What is striking about the maxim is that its first and second halves constitute one of the most defining characteristics of Chinese and Western military thought respectively, and to both sides, oddly enough, the practice of the other side seems unthinkable. Nevertheless, after the bloodbaths in the First World War, it became apparent that the West was urgently in need of an alternative strategic model that offered better prospects of attaining more certain, and less costly, victories—in the case of Liddell Hart, such could most likely be found in Chinese strategic thought which advocated a fundamentally different concept of efficacy. So it happens that the personal preference or hatred of Liddell Hart toward Clausewitz indeed has helped the West discover the condition–consequence approach vis-à-vis the mean-ends rational approach that is commonly employed by the West (see Chapter 3).

The condition–consequence approach, according to François Jullien, is a Chinese concept of efficacy that teaches one to learn how to allow an effect to come about: not to aim for it directly but to implicate it as a consequence.[21] Hence one has to create the suitable conditions to allow things to happen, rather than through a goal that leads directly to action to achieve an effect. Put in strategic terms, the Western practice that the destruction of the enemy's armed forces and battle are conceived as the only sound aim in war and the only goal of strategy, respectively, which Liddell Hart himself strongly opposes, is a prime example of the means–end approach. Its main drawback is that "it incited generals to seek battle at the *first* opportunity, instead of creating an advantageous opportunity," and the condition–consequence approach of the Chinese shows that it can be done otherwise.[22] As Liddell Hart realizes:

battle is the only one of the means to the end of strategy. If the conditions are suitable, it is usually the quickest in effect, but if the conditions are unfavorable it is folly to use it.[23]

For even if a decisive battle be the goal, the aim of strategy must be to bring about this battle under the most advantageous circumstances. And the more advantageous the circumstances, the less, proportionately, will be the fighting.[24]

Albeit logical and sensible as they are, Liddell Hart's statements mark a breakaway from the Western norm, as Philip Windsor suggests, that Western strategic thinking "does still depend largely on the assumption that strategic considerations are *causal* rather than *consequential* in nature."[25] In fact, what Liddell Hart has discovered is a new paradigm that employs battle in a completely different manner, yet most people fail to notice the difference:

[The] *true aim is not so much to seek battle as to seek a strategic situation so advantageous that if it does not of itself produce the decision, its continuation by a battle is sure to achieve this. In other words, dislocation is the aim of strategy; its sequel may be either the enemy's dissolution or his easier disruption in battle. Dissolution may involve some partial measure of fighting, but this has not the character of a battle.*[26]

As opposed to the destruction of the enemy's forces through a decisive battle, Liddell Hart's paradigm does not effectively share "the character of a battle." Its essences are—"*dislocation* and *exploitation*. One precedes and one follows the actual blow—which in comparison is a simple act. You cannot hit the enemy with effect unless you have first created the opportunity; you cannot make that effect decisive unless you exploit the second opportunity that comes before he can recover."[27] These schemes, apparently derived from the condition-consequence approach, have formed an integral part of the indirect approach and eventually became the foundation of so-called maneuver warfare. Through the condition-consequence approach, Liddell Hart has realized the possibility of fulfilling the national object by "pure" strategy only, without any physical action at all being required[28]—"Subjugating the enemy's army without fighting is the true pinnacle of excellence" (Sun Tzu).[29] This leads him to the understanding that the military means is only one of the means to the end of grand strategy and guides him the way to a new intellectual endeavor to explore the subject matter of grand strategy.

Grand Strategy

Needless to say, grand strategy, even before the concept itself has been founded, has long been formulated and practiced by rulers and leaders of all times. However, prior to Liddell Hart, the systematic study of grand strategy was virtually nonexistent in the West, while even the study contributed by Liddell Hart was far from being comprehensive and remained underdeveloped until his death in 1970. The long-delayed examination of the subject matter, and indeed the long-term absence of the concept in the West, really baffle the Chinese, for Chinese strategy has always had a grand-strategic orientation and they take to heart that military strategy should always be guided by politics and grand strategy. Through the lens of Chinese strategy, ideas such as total war or viewing battle as the only goal of strategy are close to the point of absurdity. Even though time had ripened for the development of the concept of grand strategy during the time of Liddell Hart, and that the theories of sea power should have inspired Liddell Hart, there are substantial reasons to believe that Sun Tzu remains a main source of inspiration for Liddell Hart's study of grand strategy.

Liddell Hart's concept of grand strategy is distinctively Chinese in at least three ways. First, the concept is the extension of the indirect approach from the tactical level to the level of grand strategy. Second, the concept draws heavily upon Sun Tzu's "subjugating the enemy's army without fighting is the true pinnacle of excellence" for its theoretical basis. And third, the peace-oriented thinking in the concept is almost perfectly in line with that in *The Art of War*.

DECIPHERING SUN TZU

As noted by Tony Corn, by 1934 Liddell Hart had managed to study the application of the indirect approach at all levels of war, including the tactical level (*Lawrence of Arabia*), the operational level (*The Ghost of Napoleon*), the strategic level (*The Decisive Wars of History*), and the level of grand strategy (*The British Way in Warfare*).[30] In a nutshell, the indirect approach is the cornerstone of Liddell Hart's strategic thought. As it extends to other levels, the influence from Sun Tzu permeates into these levels accordingly. There are signs from Liddell Hart's works that he is simply reapplying his thought from one level to another, for instance:

It should be the aim of grand strategy to discover and pierce the Achilles' heel of the opposing government's power to make war. And strategy, in turn, should seek to penetrate a joint in the harness of the opposing forces. To apply one's strength where the opponent is strong weakens oneself disproportionately to the effect attained. To strike with strong effect, one must strike at weakness.[31]

Clearly, Liddell Hart is sharing the same principle at the levels of grand strategy and strategy. And the principle is Sun Tzu's concept of "vacuity and substance" (Chapter 6)—"the army's disposition of force (*hsing*) avoids the substantial and strikes the vacuous"—a theoretical underpinning of the indirect approach.

The catalyst for the transformative outgrowth of Liddell Hart's indirect approach to the grand-strategic level could well be Sun Tzu's maxim: "subjugating the enemy's army without fighting is the true pinnacle of excellence" (Chapter 3). Liddell Hart's open acceptance of the maxim can be clearly seen as he maintains: "The perfection of strategy would be, therefore, to produce a decision without any serious fighting"—an outright adoption of Sun Tzu's maxim.[32] What is so special about this maxim is that it has inspired Liddell Hart in two respects across two levels of war. First of which is that it helps Liddell Hart recognize that, in the realm of *warfare*, decision can be achieved by military strategy alone without any serious fighting. Having realized the new possibilities created out of this maxim, Liddell Hart begins to explore its applications in grand strategy:

While such bloodless victories have been exceptional, their rarity enhances rather than detracts from their value—as an indication of latent potentialities, in strategy and grand strategy.[33]

136

This then leads us to the second interpretation of Sun Tzu's maxim that "subjugating the enemy's army without fighting" could also denote the use of non-military means to achieve the aim of *war*, so that at once Liddell Hart has taken Western strategy to the height of grand strategy:

Just as the military means is only one of the means to the end of grand strategy—one of the instruments in the surgeon's case—so battle is only one of the means to the end of strategy.[34]

fighting power is but one of the instruments of grand strategy—which should take account of and apply the power of financial pressure, of diplomatic pressure, of commercial pressure, and, not least of ethical pressure, to weaken the opponent's will.[35]

Hence, even though Liddell Hart's study of grand strategy is far from complete, it has facilitated the "demilitarization of strategy" and fundamentally changed Western strategic thought. The trigger of this could possibly be Sun Tzu's famous saying, "subjugating the enemy's army without fighting is the true pinnacle of excellence." It has provided the West with much-needed inspiration and impetus to find its way out of its overly military-oriented strategic thought.

While Liddell Hart completes the leap from strategy to grand strategy by extending his ideas from the one level to another, he never reapplies them blindly. He considers that "for while grand strategy should control strategy, its principles often run *counter* to those which prevail in the field of strategy."[36] As Western strategic thought, which originated from tactics in a bottom-up manner, progresses to the level of grand strategy, two issues arise—one of them is the issue of peace, and the other is that of morality, though they are indeed the two sides of the same coin:

Whereas strategy is only concerned with the problem of winning military victory, grand strategy must take the longer view—for its problem is the winning of the peace."[37]

While strategy is the very opposite of morality, as it is largely concerned with the art of deception, grand strategy tends to coincide with morality: through having always to keep in view the ultimate goal of the efforts it is directing.[38]

The long-term absence of the concept of grand strategy in the West before Liddell Hart has resulted in a misunderstanding that strategic thought should be military-centered, and thus amoral in nature. For this reason, a principle of reconciliation between military strategy and grand strategy fails to take root. It has been a long delay before Liddell Hart finally identifies that grand strategy "should not only combine the various instruments, but so *regulate their use as to avoid damage to the future state of peace*–for its security and prosperity."[39] Such principle of regulation or reconciliation is being called the principle of "preservation" (*quan* 全) in *The Art of War*:

Thus one who excels at employing the military subjugates other people's armies without engaging in battle, captures other people's fortified cities without attacking them, and destroys other people's states without prolonged fighting. He must fight under Heaven with the paramount aim of "preservation." Thus his weapons will not become dull, and the gains can be preserved. This is the strategy for planning offensives. (Chapter 3)[40]

The above calls attention to an important lesson that it is essential to limit the damage caused in order to preserve the gains won in the war—this is the key of winning the peace. And Liddell Hart repeats the lesson by putting it in modern context:

Still clearer is the extremely detrimental effect of industrial bombing on the post-war situation. Beyond the immense scale of devastation, hard to repair, are the less obvious but probably more lasting social and moral effects.[41]

How Liddell Hart manages to go beyond Sun Tzu, is that he clearly states that: "The object in war is to attain a better peace—even if only from your own point of view. Hence it is essential to conduct war with constant regard of peace you desire."[42] Yet when he comes to define the meaning of victory, that "[v]ictory in the true sense implies that the state of peace, and of one's people, is better after the war than before,"[43] it only reminds us of Sun Tzu's saying: "conquering the enemy and growing stronger." (Chapter 2)[44]

After all, it could be a difficult task to distinguish Liddell Hart's thought from Sun Tzu's in a black-and-white manner, for Liddell Hart himself admits that "in that one short book [*The Art of War*] was embodied almost as much about the fundamentals of strategy and tactics as I had covered in more than twenty books."[45] But in spite of everything, his rediscovery of Sun Tzu and extensive adoption of his ideas has forever changed the scene of Western strategic thought, and influenced Beaufre, Wylie, and Boyd, whose works are less Western-centered and had a higher degree of universal applicability.

John Boyd: The American Sun Tzu

While Liddell Hart's attempt to encapsulate Sun Tzu's teachings into the scheme of "The Indirect Approach" is, on balance, no more than a marginal success and is often being criticized as oversimplified and tautological, John Boyd, who is heavily influenced by Liddell Hart and, above all, Sun Tzu, follows Liddell Hart's footsteps but not his strategy. Like Liddell Hart, Boyd writes to convince people that the military doctrine and practice of his day were fundamentally flawed, and aims for an almost full adoption of Sun Tzu's thought into the Western strategic framework. Yet he repackages, rationalizes and modernizes the Eastern thought using various scientific theories from the West.

In *Patterns of Conflict*, a 193-page presentation that contains Boyd's core ideas on conflict and warfare, Boyd starts with Sun Tzu, then takes the readers to the twentieth century, and finally ends with Sun Tzu.[46] In a nutshell, it is to a large extent Boyd's reading of military history (though highly biased) through the lens of Sun Tzu. And Boyd makes it clear in the beginning the themes and strategies from Sun Tzu to which he attaches great importance:

Theme

- Harmony and trust
- Justice and well being
- Inscrutability and enigma
- Deception and subversion
- Rapidity and fluidity
- Dispersion and concentration
- Surprise and shock

Strategy

- Probe enemy's organization and dispositions to unmask his strengths, weaknesses, patterns of movement and intentions.
- "Shape" enemy's perception of world to manipulate his plans and actions.
- Attack enemy's plans as best policy. Next best disrupt his alliances. Next best attack his army. Attack cities only when there is no alternative.
- Employ *cheng* and *ch'i* maneuvers to quickly and unexpectedly hurl strength against weaknesses.

And the desired outcome, as Boyd identifies, is to "subdue the enemy without fighting" and "avoid protracted war."[47] It should not be questionable that such a condensed form of Sun Tzu's teachings can only be arrived at by a true disciple of Sun Tzu. Boyd is more than qualified to be one as, according to Robert Coram, Boyd's biographer, he eventually owned *seven* translations of *The Art of War*, each with long passages underlined and with copious marginalia. The translations of Samuel Griffith and, later, Thomas Cleary were his favorites. *The Art of War* became Boyd's Rosetta stone, the work he returned to again and again. *It is the only theoretical book on war that Boyd did not find fundamentally flawed.*[48] His strong attachment for Sun Tzu has even resulted in a farfetched claim that early commanders such as Alexander, Hannibal, Belisarius, Genghis Khan, and Tamerlane, who seem consistent with the ideas of Sun Tzu, especially the principles of *ch'i* and *cheng* and shattering adversary prior to battle, are to be identified as "Eastern commanders" vis-à-vis "Western commanders" who have been more directly concerned with winning the battle, in order to highlight the superiority of Sun Tzu's approach to that of the West.[49]

It is also Sun Tzu who provides Boyd with the theoretical underpinning to bridge the impossible gap between the two new and powerful forms of warfare in the twentieth century at the two extremes of the spectrum—*Blitzkrieg* and *guerilla warfare*. Blitz and guerillas, said Boyd, infiltrate a nation or regime at all level to soften and shatter the moral fiber of the political, economic and social structure. Simultaneously, via diplomatic, psychological, and various sub-rosa or other activities, they strip-away potential allies thereby isolating intended victim(s) for forthcoming blows. To carry out this program, a la Sun Tzu, blitz, and guerillas:

- Probe and test adversary, and any allies that may rally to his side, in order to unmask strengths, weaknesses, maneuvers, and intentions.
- Exploit critical differences of opinion, internal contradictions, frictions, obsessions, etc., in order to foment mistrust, sow discord and shape both adversary's and allies' perception of the world thereby:
- Create atmosphere of "mental confusion, contradiction of feeling, indecisiveness, panic"...
- Manipulate or undermine adversary's plans and actions.
- Make it difficult, if not impossible, for allies to aid adversary during his time of trial.

The purpose of this is either to "force capitulation when combined with external political, economic, and military pressures" or to "weaken foe to minimize his resistance against military blows that will follow."[50] It is only through the lens of Sun Tzu that the mutual conceptual foundation between these two contrasting ways of warfare can be discovered, and the basis for Boyd's moral-mental-physical conflict be established.

Although it is Sun Tzu, "who must be considered the true conceptual, albeit ancient, father of Boyd's work,"[51] it is Mao Zedong who acts as the "conceptual midwife" who plays an important part in transforming and validating Sun Tzu so that his teachings remain relevant in modern time. Yet his role in Boyd's thought has been almost completely overlooked, as Mao has only been mentioned *once* in A *Discourse of Winning and Losing*:

Mao Tse-tung synthesized Sun Tzu's ideas, classic guerilla strategy and tactics, and Napoleonic style mobile operations under an umbrella of Soviet revolutionary ideas to create a powerful way for waging modern (guerilla) war.

And the result is:

Modern guerilla warfare has become an overall political, economic, social and military framework for "total war."[52]

From Mao's way of war, Boyd not only sees a new way for waging guerilla warfare but also a new way for waging modern war, a new and different kind of "total war." This is why the proponents of Fourth Generation Warfare (4GW) regard Mao as the first practitioner or the father of 4GW.[53] It is particularly evident given the definition of 4GW: 4GW uses all available networks—political, economic, social, and military—to convince the enemy's political decision makers that their strategic goals are either unachievable or too costly for the perceived benefit.[54] This is central to Boyd's thought, for he emphasizes the employment of simultaneous menaces and attacks at multiple levels, which is exactly the way addressed by Sun Tzu 2,500 years ago. More importantly, Mao's way of war is one of Boyd's very few sources of idea that offers truly grand-strategic and effect-based orientations—it forms the backbone for both moral-mental-physical conflict and grand strategy in Boyd's thesis.

The under-recognition of Mao's way of war could well be an indication of Boyd's ongoing, yet incomplete, transition from the Western strategic framework to that of Sun Tzu. As Frans Osinga, a major interpreter of Boyd's theory, notices, Sun Tzu offers a myriad of strategic and tactical factors which span the mental, the moral and the physical dimensions, that, together with the grand strategic factors such as the quality of the alliances of the opponent, combine to get the enemy off balance.[55] Nevertheless, it is J. F. C. Fuller who, after observing the impact of Ludendorff's infiltration tactics in 1918, provides Boyd with a *definite* concept of the three spheres of war—the physical, the mental, and the moral dimension, with which Boyd structures his argument and develops three modes of conflict in *Patterns of Conflict*.[56] Respectively, these three spheres deal with the destruction of the enemy's physical strength (fighting power), disorganization of his mental processes (thinking power), and disintegration of his moral will to resist (staying power). Fuller adds that forces operating within these spheres do so in synergistic, not isolated, ways.[57] Fuller's concept of the three spheres of war almost fully resembles Sun Tzu's scheme but there is one fundamental difference: Fuller's concept is operational, at most strategic, in nature, while Sun Tzu's is grand-strategic and systemic. Hence, also given the focus of Boyd's study which is largely military-based, even though Boyd realizes that Mao's way of war constitutes a powerful way for waging modern war, he has to revert to military operations and warfare that effectively follows Fuller's concept.

He seems not fully able to grasp that Mao's way of war is essentially the modern variant of Sun Tzu's thought. As a consequence, despite that Boyd attempts to extend his scheme of moral-mental-physical conflict to the realm of grand strategy in *The Strategic Game of ? and ?*, another briefing/presentation of Boyd, the result is far from satisfactory, and he is nowhere close to recreating the grand-strategic orientation of Sun Tzu and Chinese strategic thought.[58]

This "unfinished business" of Boyd, however, is done by his 4GW disciples who view war from the angle of Sun Tzu and Mao. Instead of seeing Boyd's scheme as applying multiple methods simultaneously at several levels, they consider Boyd has proposed three new levels of war that supersedes the classical levels of war—tactical, operational and strategic:

Colonel Boyd identified these three new levels as the *physical*, the *mental* and the *moral*. Further, he argued that the physical level—killing people and breaking things—is the least powerful, the moral level is the most powerful and the mental level lies between the other two.[59]

This leads to the central dilemma of Fourth Generation war: what works for you on the physical (and sometimes mental) level often works against you at the moral level. It is therefore very easy in a Fourth Generation conflict to win all the tactical engagements yet lose the war. To the degree you win at the physical level by pouring on firepower that causes casualties and property damage to the local population, every physical victory may move you closer to moral defeat. And the moral level is decisive.[60]

The contradiction between the physical and moral levels of war in Fourth Generation conflicts is similar to the contradiction between the tactical and strategic levels, but the two are not identical. The physical, mental and moral levels all play at each of the other levels—tactical, operational and strategic. Any disharmony among levels creates openings which Fourth Generation opponents will be quick to exploit.[61]

The introduction of new levels of war is revolutionary since they are made for the conduct of war (i.e. strategy) and for that purpose only. They consider all the classical levels of war together and focus solely on strategic effects. Consequently, this has at the outset to a large extent precluded disharmonies among the levels. Moreover, the new levels of war are sufficiently "demilitarized" so they can be used in all conflict situations, and in both wartime and peacetime. This brings about a major advancement in the explanatory power of the new scheme over the old one. In any case, the new levels of war mark an important step in progressing toward effect-based war/strategy and a grand-strategy-centered way of war proposed by Sun Tzu and Mao.

Boyd is just one step away from fully grasping this essence of Chinese strategic thought, as his new levels of war resemble remarkably what is suggested in an ancient Chinese strategic text called *Wei Liao-tzu*, a work that was included in the *Seven Military Classics of Ancient China* together with Sun Tzu and other strategic volumes. Wei Liao-tzu states:

In general, [in employing] the military there are those who gain victory through the Tao; those that gain victory through awesomeness; and those that gain victory through strength.[62]

It is not difficult to notice that the moral, mental, and physical levels of war resemble the Tao, awesomeness, and strength. Wei Liao-tzu's text does not arrange the three means according to their effectiveness, but as in Boyd's work all three means are considered important and are meant to be used jointly. Boyd believes, however, that moral leverage and authority have a special role in grand strategy.[63] Nevertheless, Boyd's emphasis on the moral level of war finds a parallel in Sun Tzu's work. Sun Tzu recognizes the contradiction between the physical and moral levels of war, and he maintains that the physical level should give way to the moral level:

The general rule for use of the military is that it is better to keep a nation intact than to destroy it. It is better to keep an army intact than to destroy it, better to keep division intact than to destroy it, better to keep a battalion intact than to destroy it, better to keep a unit intact than to destroy it. (Chapter 3)[64]

This coincides with Boyd's "moral design for grand strategy," which aims to:

Preserve or build-up our moral authority while compromising that of our adversaries' in order to pump-up our resolve, drain-away adversaries' resolve, and attract them as well as others to our cause and way of life.[65]

It takes a long way for Boyd to realize moral-mental-physical conflict at the operational level, extend it all the way to the level of grand strategy, and finally return to Sun Tzu's philosophy of war, yet one would realise that all of these never go beyond the scope of Sun Tzu's maxim: "subjugating the enemy without fighting is the true pinnacle of excellence."

The above shows the elements that Boyd has directly inherited from Sun Tzu, which are apparent to those who have read the works of Boyd and Sun Tzu. But the legacies of Boyd that are crucial to the transformation of Western strategic thought and its further synthesis with its Chinese counterpart, in fact, rest in a number of aspects that are hard to discern by Western people. This is because these aspects are, on one hand, missing not only in Western strategic thought, but in the Western cultural and philosophical frameworks as well, and, on the other hand, they are *inherent* to Chinese strategic thought and philosophy, so they are seldom being adequately elucidated in the Chinese works—this poses a real challenge for Westerners to approach them. Yet without these aspects or premises, the Western understanding of Chinese strategic thought will be like building on quicksand. Therefore it takes someone like Boyd who is at the same time familiar with Sun Tzu, Taoism, and Miyamoto Musashi (a famous Japanese swordsman who practiced Samurai Zen or Zen Buddhism) to identify these aspects in order to re-lay the ground for Chinese strategy to take root in Western strategic thought.

For Boyd whose thought is so heavily indebted to the ideas of Sun Tzu, it is not hard to notice that Western strategic theories are fundamentally different from their Chinese counterparts—*Western strategic theories are basically theories of war, not strategy.* Western strategic thinkers concentrate most of their effort on finding out what war is and how it has changed, but do little to understand how strategy (or the "art" of strategy) should be practiced. This has been hindering the West from establishing sound strategic theories for action. From the Chinese angle, a strategic theory should focus on how to think about war and warfare, and how to wage them. Unlike Chinese strategic thought that offers Sun Tzu and Lao Tzu's military and strategic dialectics (see Chapter 3), this cognitive dimension is nonexistent in Western strategic thought, hence Boyd needs to build them from scratch.

Boyd's OODA loop has effectively filled this vacuum. It provides Western strategic thought with a method of thought. While most commentators may question whether the OODA loop originated from Boyd's fighter pilot experience or Sun Tzu's scheme of "attacking the enemy's mind," *the real significance of the OODA loop to Western strategic thought is that it reconstructs the mental operations that are pivotal to strategy and strategic thinking per se.* Ultimately, Boyd's aim was not to convince people about the validity of this or that doctrine, but instead to create among his audience a way of thinking; a thought process.[66] And as Boyd himself puts it:

Without OODA loops...and without the ability to get inside other OODA loops (or other environments), we will find it impossible to comprehend, shape, adapt to, and in turn be shaped by an unfolding, evolving reality that is uncertain, everchanging, unpredictable.[67]

The OODA loop itself indeed is *an epistemological statement.* It is an abstract and theoretical model of the way we derive knowledge from our environment.[68] This is a major step forward toward reinstating Western strategic thought to its original "strategic" form.

From the OODA loop (particularly its final, graphical representation in *The Essence of Winning and Losing,* Boyd's final briefing, see below), we can also note *Boyd's intention of bringing back intuitive thinking and judgment to the framework of Western strategy.* Even though the four-phase OODA loop is composed of Observation, Orientation, Decision, and Action, it is almost entirely driven by Orientation: "The second O, orientation...is the most important part of the O-O-D-A loop since it shapes the way we observe, the way we decide, the way we act."[69] And Boyd's definition of Orientation implicates intuitive thinking:

Orientation is an interactive process of many-sided implicit cross-referencing projections, empathies, correlations, and rejections that is shaped by and shapes the interplay of genetic heritage, cultural tradition, previous experiences, and unfolding circumstances.[70]

Moreover, as indicated in the graphical representation of the OODA loop, we can notice that Boyd includes the "Implicit Guidance and Control" from "Orientation" with both "Observations" and "Action." This is his way of pointing out that when one has developed the proper *Fingerspitzengefuhl* ("finger tips feeling") for a changing situation, the tempo picks up and it seems one is then able to bypass the explicit

"Orientation" and "Decision" part of the loop, to "Observe" and "Act" almost simultaneously. The speed must come from a deep intuitive understanding of one's relationship to the rapidly changing environment. This is what enables a commander seemingly to bypass parts of the loop.[71] No matter how hard Boyd has tried to repackage all these with scientific language and models, it is impossible to conceal that he is trying to convince his Western audiences of something alien to their way of thinking—intuitive thinking. Such is nonetheless revealed by Coram, Boyd's biographer, that "the orientation phase is a nonlinear feedback system, which, by its nature, means this is a pathway into the unknown."[72]

It is easy to come to a conclusion that the whole notion of rapid OODA loops is *coup d'oeil* in action, and Clausewitz would have no trouble recognizing the capacity for *coup d'oeil* in Boyd.[73] However, the notion of OODA loop carries more than making quick decisions alone. Another important aspect is pattern recognition, a crucial process responsible for synthesizing isolated bits of data and experience into an integrated picture, which is of even higher importance in the realm of strategy. With regard to this aspect of the OODA loop, and Boyd's conceptual and intellectual proximity to Sun Tzu, one should revisit the whole concept of OODA loop from the orientation of Sun Tzu. As mentioned in the previous chapter, given that intuition was the dominant mode of thinking for the Chinese and the practice of *coup d'oeil* in war is already inherent in *The Art of War*, it is unnecessary for Sun Tzu to highlight them, not to mention that Sun Tzu has as well developed concepts like *hsing* and *shih* to capture two different kinds of highly abstract pattern in wars and battles. There is no way that Boyd could have omitted this important Chinese school of pattern recognition, and the OODA loop is where the incorporation takes place. According to Boyd, "[p]atterns (hence, orientation), right or wrong or lack thereof, suggest ability or inability to conduct many-sided implicit cross-references.[74] The passage suggests that creating the correct pattern or mental image is likely to be a reason why Boyd attached so much importance to Orientation (or intuitive thinking) in the first place. This view is in line with the reexamination of Boyd's thought by Osinga, who considers Sun Tzu the conceptual father of Boyd's work and read Sun Tzu from a Boydian perspective in his work:

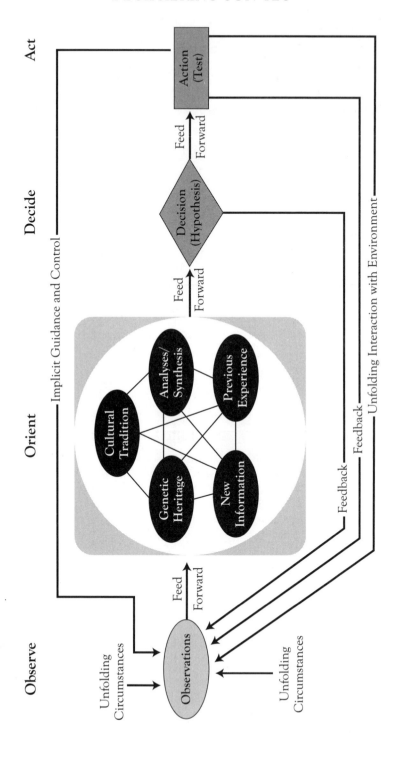

THE SUCCESSORS OF SUN TZU IN THE WEST

Sun Tzu's work implies that it is possible to have complete knowledge, but it emanates not from the attainment of absolute certainty, but from the formation of a correct interpretation of the situation, a very important theme in Boyd's work. *Foreknowledge springs from the ability to discern patterns and relations, implying that it derives from a holistic view of an object.* Even if one has perfect information it is of no value if it is not coupled to a penetrating understanding of its meaning, if one does not see the patterns. Judgment is key. Without judgment, data means nothing. *It is not necessary the one with more information who will come out victorious, it is the one with better judgment, the one who is better at discerning patterns.* Moreover, it is a judgment of highly dynamic situation. Sun Tzu only claims that one who excels at warfare can tell when a situation will offer chances for victory or defeat, realizing that this particular impression of *shih* is a snapshot from a distance at a particular time.[75]

What is more remarkable about Boyd's adoption and re-formation of Chinese strategy is his insistence on capturing the philosophical basis of Chinese strategic thought. He understands he can get nowhere closer to the heart of Chinese strategy without first getting this right. And a major hurdle to cross is the principle of yin-yang—unlike other Chinese philosophical concepts discovered by Boyd, yin-yang does not have any Western scientific parallel and is contradictory to the logic of the West. Therefore, Boyd has to realize it very much by himself. Once he masters the concept, nevertheless, he infuses it right into his way of thinking, and it soon becomes a constant theme in Boyd's thought:

He looked at terms of their opposites, both ends of the continuum, and trade-offs between the extremes. Black-white, on-off, up-down, slow-fast, and countless other pairings dot his thinking routinely. Boyd could not deal with only a half a concept. He had to explore its opposite, an alternative, and, more important, the relationship between the two. Examining the grey area between came naturally. It was his way of thinking. This led him with greater frequency than most to challenge the so-called conventional wisdom and to assess the opposite interpretation.[76]

There are signs of the Chinese logical and dialectic engine throughout Boyd's work, in the form of analysis-synthesis, destruction-creation, open-closed, living-non-living, isolate-interact, implicit-explicit, etc. As Boyd has grasped the idea, he is on the same wavelength with Sun Tzu, since almost all important concepts of Chinese strategic thought, such as *ch'i* and *cheng* as well as vacuity and substance, are expressed in the form of correlating pairs on the basis of yin-yang. And just like the Chinese, Boyd never sees yin-yang as paradoxical but, on the contrary, actively uses it to resolve contradictions and paradoxes. While the absence of the notion of yin-yang in Western strategy marks a fundamental difference between Chinese and Western strategic thought, Boyd's insistence on reestablishing it in the Western strategic framework not only has bridged the gap, but his extensive use of yin-yang on all levels of war also shows the West that the Chinese logical engine indeed is an indispensable element in the general theory of strategy.

Unlike the concept of yin-yang that has a clear Chinese origin, Boyd's systemic orientation, which is displayed by his understanding and applications of chaos and complexity theories, and the concept of complex adaptive systems in his strategic thinking, can be obtained from the insights of the new sciences of the West or the teachings of Sun Tzu and Taoism, or both. It is never my intention to demonstrate that the influence comes solely from the East, or that the Eastern influence exceeds that that of the West—these are merely impossible. However, given Boyd's extensive knowledge of Eastern thought as well as his theoretical proximity with Sun Tzu, it is meaningful to examine whether Boyd's application of scientific developments throughout his work is an end in itself or a means to the goal of re-manifesting the Chinese strategic worldview.

Even though the answer to the inquiry above could be no more than a matter of judgment and probably no one can prove it, it is worthwhile to compare the case of Clausewitz with Boyd's, for they both incorporated scientific developments of their times into their theories. The Clausewitzian conceptions of friction and center of gravity are clearly derived from Newtonian science, while Boyd draws very extensively from the insights of the new sciences.[77] The case of Clausewitz makes us understand the importance of vocabulary, model, metaphor, and imagery in the communication of strategic concepts. Only with the availability of appropriate vocabulary, model, metaphor, and imagery can the concepts be properly conveyed. Without the Newtonian scientific framework, the Clausewitzian conceptions of friction and center of gravity may probably be dismissed as some formless ideas. But in any case, what can be sure, is that Clausewitz used Newtonian science to explain some phenomena in war or perceptions *already in his mind*. The same is likely to hold true in Boyd's case—he exploited the new sciences to *explain* his thought. But this time, apart from explaining Boyd's own thought, it is equally possible that Boyd intended to make use of the scientific developments offered by the new sciences to illuminate what the West had been unable to illuminate before—Chinese strategic thought and its cognitive and philosophical foundations behind. This window of opportunity had been closed to the strategic thinkers before his time.

What is even more special about the case of Clausewitz is that, *without the appropriate vocabulary, model, metaphor, or imagery, Clausewitz's recognition of the nonlinearity of war can only be unveiled toward the end of the twentieth century, 160 years after the publication of On War*.[78] This makes a strong case that, on one hand, the vocabulary, model, metaphor, and imagery are the vital enablers and, on the other, even more importantly, it always requires one's own thought to allow them to enable. According to Alan D. Beyerchen:

Yet another reason Clausewitz relied upon metaphorical imagery was that *he did not trust the established jargon of his day*, which was full of rigid (and French!) geometric principles and models. He preferred the new sciences of his time— chemistry, thermodynamics, magnetism, electricity, embryology. These offered novel, high-tech, research-forefront terms for the dynamic phenomena he wanted to discuss.[79]

What Boyd was facing in his days was almost identical to what Clausewitz had experienced. They both had to make use of the new sciences of his time to break away from the old, established system, or otherwise their ideas can never be adequately explained. Even so, there was an added dimension in Boyd's case in which he had to deal with cross-cultural matters between Chinese and Western thought. But Boyd was lucky—he lived in a time never short of scientific developments, and work such as Fritjof Capra's *The Tao of Physics* had helped him a great deal in bridging the enormous gap between Western science and Eastern mysticism.[80]

In *Science, Strategy and War*, Osinga notes that Boyd's thesis is not as a general theory of war but *a general theory of the strategic behavior of complex adaptive systems in adversarial conditions*.[81] He is right—not only about Boyd but also about Sun Tzu. *The Art of War* is never intended to be a general theory of war, but a general theory of strategy that teaches one how to win wars in a systemic manner. The organic metaphors, which Boyd considers armed forces as complex adaptive systems and war as the non-linear clash of two complex adaptive systems, may possibly originate from Sun Tzu.[82] Even the terminology of complex adaptive systems and non-linearity did not exist back in the age of Sun Tzu. Just as the above case of Clausewitz, Sun Tzu could discern them by himself, not to mention systemic thinking had long rooted in Chinese thinking and philosophy prior to Sun Tzu. Therefore, when Osinga lists out Robert Jervis' three suggestions for strategies when acting in a system in which interconnections are prevalent and powerful,[83] the strategies do more to associate Sun Tzu with chaos and complexity theories than to show the applications of insights of these theories to the social realm. Below are Jervis' three suggestions for strategies:

- Constraining the opponents' options;
- Understanding the non-linearity of the environment;
- Aim for indirect effects and apply multiple strategies.[84]

The first method can be noticed in Sun Tzu's schemes of controlling the enemy. The second is inherent in the Chinese worldview, and the third not only is manifested in the condition-consequence approach, but the method is indeed the signature tunes of Sun Tzu repeatedly borrowed by Liddell Hart and Boyd—Sun Tzu's thought truly makes sense in terms of systems thinking! And at this point, it is clearer than ever that Boyd's application of scientific developments throughout his work just cannot be an end in itself—it essentially carries the purpose of *reintroducing Chinese strategic thought to the West by using Western scientific theories* as well.

In *The John Boyd Roundtable*, there is a diagram showing the primary sources for *Discourse on Winning and Losing*.[85] It has divided the primary sources into three "zones": the first zone is military history and strategy, the second, science and mathematics, and the third, Eastern philosophy. As mentioned earlier, Boyd's overview to military history and strategy in *Patterns of Conflict* is a biased one—it is to a large extent Boyd's reinterpretation of military history through the lens of Sun Tzu that reflects his own proposal. Even so, together with Eastern philosophy, two out of three main areas (zones) of Boyd's primary sources are in fact closely associated with Sun Tzu and Eastern thought, let alone Sun Tzu is considered the true conceptual father of Boyd's work. A re-reading of Boyd's thesis through the lens of Sun Tzu and Eastern thought is long overdue. However, due to the limited knowledge of the West on these areas, this has resulted in a shift, if not distortion, of the orientation and purpose of Boyd's work. If this is not to be corrected, Boyd's effort to reorient Western strategic thought and prepare the ground for further incorporation of Chinese strategic thought will be wasted altogether.

Conclusion

Liddell Hart and Boyd are the "nonlinear changes" in the evolution of Western strategic thought. They both looked toward Sun Tzu at times when Western strategy was in need of change. Liddell Hart borrowed from Sun Tzu an alternative strategic model contrasting that of Clausewitz, as well as much-needed principles and orientation of grand strategy (and peace), while Boyd learnt from the master that a much belated transformation of Western strategic thought from the nature of theory of war toward that of strategy was needed. Even so, their ways of dealing with Chinese/Eastern thought are fundamentally different, as are their degree of understanding about the subject. Despite that Liddell Hart is among the first Westerners to rediscover Sun Tzu, his adoption of Sun Tzu's ideas is, unsurprisingly, piecemeal and incomplete. Nor did he have any intention to grasp the underlying basis of Chinese strategy. As a result, his indirect approach lacks a solid theoretical foundation, and is often being dismissed as tautological. This in turn limits the communication of his concept and even puts his entire thesis in jeopardy. On the other hand, Boyd realized the Western military doctrine and practice was fundamentally flawed, thus a full swing of the development of Western strategic thought toward the Chinese side was necessary. He tried to (quietly) import a number of aspects from Chinese and Eastern thought to Western strategic thought by reproducing them in Western terms using its scientific language and theories. Notwithstanding his attempt is far from being successful and many of his proposals have gone unnoticed, Boyd has indeed opened a crucial window of opportunity for Western strategic thought. By repackaging and rationalizing the Eastern thought using Western scientific theories, Boyd has made very significant progress in "synchronizing" Chinese and Western strategic thought. In other words, *Boyd has laid a foundation for Western strategy to directly absorb and adopt elements of Chinese strategic thought.* Once the Western strategic community grasps the significant meaning behind this unprecedented opportunity, it will open many new avenues for the development and self-rectification of Western strategic thought, the (re)understanding of Chinese strategic thought, and the establishment of a general theory of strategy.

6

ON CHINESE STRATEGIC CULTURE

The role played by Chinese strategic culture in China's international behavior has been the subject of extensive research. This chapter consequently presents an overview of Chinese strategic culture and the ways in which the analysis of previous chapters can enhance our understanding of this culture in the West. Given the emphasis on a specifically "Chinese" strategic culture, this chapter follows Ken Booth in defining strategic culture as a "nation's traditions, value, attitudes, patterns of behavior, habits, symbols, achievements and particular ways of adapting to the environment and solving problems with respect to the threat or use of force."[1]

Chinese Strategic Culture as a Western Construct

What is Chinese strategic culture? "Strategic culture" is a Western concept. As a result, Chinese strategic culture, as currently understood in the West, was determined by the West and Western interpretations and understanding of China, including Chinese political and military thought, as well as its national culture. Ever since the publication of Alastair Iain Johnston's *Cultural Realism* (1995), most Western scholars have postulated the existence of two competing strategic cultures in China, each of which is based on distinct cultural values. The first of these, the Confucian-Mencian strategic culture, is based on the philosophy of Confucius (551–479 BC), which was in turn partly filtered through his interpreter Mencius (390?–305? BC). This culture reflects idealistic, pacifist and defensive sentiments. The second, the parabellum or realpolitik strategic culture, views the world in realist terms and believes that the offensive use of force is not only legitimate but also desirable.[2] Although Johnston argues that these two strategic cultures exist in China, he contends that only one—the parabellum paradigm—is operative, while the other is purely for "idealized discourse."[3] Andrew Scobell, in contrast, argues that both the realpolitik and Confucian–Mencian strands are operative and that the two strands interact in a dialectic fashion to produce a distinctive "Chinese Cult of Defense."[4] As a result, this twofold framework, though not unchallenged, has become the established paradigm for research on Chinese strategic culture. Yet the existing research tends towards silence when explaining why these strands of Chinese strategic culture were identified, and, moreover, why there are only two of them.

However, notwithstanding the above, the two existing models of Chinese strategic culture can still serve an important function in terms of research. Whereas the Confucian–Mencian model can be seen as applicable to China's national strategic culture, the parabellum model can be used to understand China's military strategic culture. Moreover, as many Western analysts tend to have a limited knowledge of the Chinese classics, Western scholars often rely on well-known Confucian–Mencian works (e.g. *The Analects*) and the *Seven Military Classics* (which includes *Sun Tzu: The Art of War*) to explain Chinese strategic culture.

Lastly, it is essentially Johnston's purpose to look for Confucian-Mencian pacifist elements in the *Seven Military Classics*, hence it becomes necessary for him to "identify" the two strands of Chinese strategic culture and to dismiss the Confucian-Mencian strand thereafter.

As a result, not only is the idea of Chinese strategic culture a Western construct, but the ways in which it is understood in the West has largely been defined by Western authors as comprising Chinese political culture (i.e. the Confucian–Mencian tradition) and military/strategic thought (e.g. Sun Tzu). For the Chinese, however, there is no such thing as a Confucian-Mencian strategic culture: while China recognizes that both models are fundamental to its political–strategic decision-making, Confucianism is nothing more than a tradition of political thought and culture. The *Seven Military Classics*, on the other hand, merely represent Chinese military and strategic thought; it undoubtedly belongs to the realist tradition, but it is seldom viewed as a parabellum strategic culture. In short, given the extensive efforts to "crowbar" Chinese elements into the Western concept of strategic culture, the extent to which Chinese strategic culture can actually be viewed as "Chinese" is open to question. However, a close examination of the original Western concept of strategic culture, as below, reveals that the existing framework for understanding Chinese strategic culture, despite its shortcomings, can still serve a useful explanatory function.

The concept of "strategic culture" was first developed by Jack Snyder in order to explain Soviet strategic thought with regard to its nuclear missiles. The use of the concept was subsequently expanded to a nation's decision-making process and behavior regarding the use of force.[5] Scobell defines the use of force as the employment of overt military power, including explicit, credible threats of military action backed by troop movements, military exercises, missile or artillery tests, or the construction or expansion of military installations in a border area.[6] Thus the primary concern of strategic culture is the threat and use of force. However, while this framework was certainly useful for explaining Soviet behavior, it is inherently incompatible with Chinese strategic thought as Chinese strategy is grand-strategic in nature and stresses the use of non-military means. Even so, since the primary concern of Chinese strategic culture is the threat and use of force, all it needs to discern are under what circumstances and how would the Chinese use force or go to war—this is much more attainable than grasping Chinese strategic theory and practice as a whole. Furthermore, as Confucian-Mencian tradition was brought into the picture, the Western scholarship on Chinese strategic culture indeed has discovered an important control mechanism of Chinese strategic behavior. The study of Chinese strategic culture has achieved a major goal due to the fact that this mechanism has been discovered.

DECIPHERING SUN TZU

On "War Should Only Be Used in Unavoidable Circumstances"

Johnston, as we saw above, dismisses the Confucian–Mencian strategic culture as an idealized discourse, and argues that only the parabellum strategic culture is operative in China. However, he has identified the roles played by the two strategic cultures and under what circumstances would the Confucian-Mencian strategic culture give way to the parabellum strategic culture—Johnston has got lots of things right, yet he simply jumped to his conclusion too quickly. As Johnston notes, the Confucian-Mencian paradigm emphasizes the use of non-violent, accommodative grand strategies over violent defensive or offensive strategies in terms of strategic choices. The paradigm thus stresses "benevolent," "righteous," and "virtuous" government as the basis for security.[7] The model is based on the so-called concept of righteous war (*yi zhan* 義戰) through which the Chinese define the nature of the adversary and the role of violence in state security.[8] From a Chinese perspective, force can only be legitimately employed when fighting a "righteous war" against those who have created the conditions for war to take place.[9] According to Johnston, this reluctance to resort to force is embodied in one of the sayings contained in the Chinese classics: "war and weaponry is an inauspicious tool, and should only be used in unavoidable circumstances" (兵者凶器也不得已而用之). Johnston maintains that this demonstrates an inherent disdain of violence in the Confucian moral order.[10] Yet he dismisses the notion of "using force under unavoidable circumstances" as a mere linguistic construct. This, Johnston concludes, indicates that the Confucian–Mencian paradigm is purely for idealized discourse, as the notion that war can be both an inauspicious, immoral instrument and an instrument of righteousness is contradictory:

How can war be both an inauspicious, immoral instrument *and* an instrument of righteousness? The resolution lies in the fact that the *Seven Military Classics* see the nature of the military (*bing* 兵) in relative terms. The military is not an inauspicious instrument in an absolute sense, only in a relative one. Some uses are more inauspicious and immoral than others. Some uses are more righteous than others. This implies that the military, weapons, or war are themselves neutral tools of policy. What gives them moral content is who uses them for what purpose. What makes the use of force legitimate as a tool of state policy, then, is its use for the purposes of upholding righteousness.[11]

158

From the passage, obviously Johnston does not recognize that in the Chinese intellectual tradition, there is no necessary incompatibility between the belief that A is the case and the belief that not-A is the case, as mentioned earlier in Chapter 1, let alone that the Chinese are particularly fond of seeing things in relative terms. Why do the Chinese have to see the military as an inauspicious instrument in an absolute sense anyway? This is an unreasonable threshold which Johnston has placed upon Chinese strategic theory and practice, and ironically, it should be the purpose of the study of strategic culture to identify such differences between Western and Chinese norms. In addition, it makes little sense to dismiss the Chinese just war (righteous war) theory as a linguistic construct on a basis that a nation should not prepare for war or contain any parabellum element or tendency in its strategic culture as it disfavors the use of force—the Confucian-Mencian and parabellum strategic cultures are not mutually exclusive; it would be idealistic and oversimplistic to view that the Confucian-Mencian strategic culture can work and stand totally on its own. As Scobell puts it, we are presented with something of a false Confucian–Realpolitik dichotomy.[12] Furthermore, why couldn't the military, weapons, or war be neutral tools of policy in the case of China? Why couldn't intention and purpose for the sake of upholding righteousness be of importance and a justified cause? It would just be idealistic to view that a nation could perform its strategic decision-making totally on a moral basis. Johnston in particular has already noted that "Confucius did not oppose military preparations, though he downplayed their role in the security of the state" and rationalized the Confucian–Realpolitik dichotomy by arguing that it is "probably true that most societies have a need to make external strategic behavior a seemingly natural or legitimate extension of the state's internal activities."[13]

Johnston places a great deal of emphasis on the saying that "war and weaponry is an inauspicious tool, and should only be used in unavoidable circumstances" in order to represent the inherent disdain of violence in the Confucian moral order. However, it should be noted that this saying actually originated either from Lao Tzu or *Tao Te Ching*: "Military weapons are inauspicious instruments [and should only be used in unavoidable circumstances], and so when you have no choice but to use them, it is best to do so coolly and without enthusiasm. Do not glorify weapons, for to do so is to delight in killing people, and anyone who delights in killing people will come up short in the world" (Chapter 31). The first part of this saying can also be found in a range of classics in the Confucian, Taoist, Legalist (Realist), and Military School traditions.[14] It is customary that when the Chinese mention the first part of the saying, it also implies the latter part without saying it. However, Johnston, whether deliberately or not, chooses to omit the lines beginning from "it is best to do so coolly and without enthusiasm" and uses only the first part as the basis for his analysis. The omission is crucial to his claim that only the parabellum strategic culture was operative and the Confucian–Mencian one was for idealized discourse only. By doing so, he gives his readers a false impression that, once the ends of war are deemed righteous by the Chinese, then any and all means become righteous by themselves, including using force in an unrestrained manner.[15] He further asserts that the Confucian–Mencian tradition was used as precepts to mask the advocacy of the extermination of the adversary.[16] Under this pretext, "[t]he enemy is irredeemably an enemy, one who cannot be won over but must be destroyed," and "any and all means of eliminating this enemy are legitimate."[17] Even the limit on the application of violence is lifted, it does not necessarily mean the enemy has to be "destroyed," "eliminated," or "exterminated." And from Lao Tzu's saying we come to know that it is in Chinese tradition that restraint is still exercised when using force.

Sun Tzu's principle of "not fighting and subduing the enemy" is apparently a substantial rebuttal to Johnston's claim that the Chinese application of force after the moral and political limits are lifted is unrestrained in nature. Johnston again presents us with a false dichotomy like the Confucian-Realpolitik dichotomy, trying to use the same trick to deal with what he needs to explain away—this time he tries to dismiss "not fighting and subduing the enemy" by putting it up against the notion of absolute flexibility (*quan bian* 權變):

Whereas "not fighting and subduing the enemy" as a decision rule implies an a priori strategic-preference ranking in which nonviolent methods are preferred, the notion of *quan bian* lifts this restriction, since the nature of conflict requires an ability to transcend fixed responses to particular contingencies. *Quan bian* in effect states that when facing a contingency, choose any and all actions that will achieve one's goals. One could argue, then, that the essence of strategic choice in the military texts is not "not fighting and subduing the enemy" but "respond flexibly to the enemy and thus create conditions for victory" (*yin die er zhi sheng* 因敵而制勝)[18]

First of all, even though "not fighting and subduing the enemy" may carry more grand-strategic or strategic implications, it does not mean that it has no operational importance. This suggests that there is no need to presume that there is only one essence of strategic choice in *The Art of War*, not to mention "not fighting and subduing the enemy" and *quan bian* are highly compatible with each other at the operational level. In fact, the purpose of "respond flexibly to the enemy and thus create conditions for victory" or *quan bian* is to create conditions for easy or even bloodless victories, and through this, "not fighting and subduing the enemy" is made possible. Therefore Sun Tzu says:

the victorious army first realizes the conditions for victory, and then seeks to engage in battle. The vanquished army fights first, and then seeks victory.[19] (Chapter 4)

One who is free from errors directs his measure toward [certain] victory, conquering those who are already defeated.[20] (Chapter 4)

The working together of "not fighting and subduing the enemy" and *quan bian* could allow one side "first realizes the conditions for victory" and conquer "those who are already defeated."

Second, does *quan bian* really state that when facing a contingency, one could choose any and all actions that will achieve one's goals, resulting in that the strategist "cannot be restricted, constrained by, or wedded to self-imposed a priori political, military, or moral limits on strategic choices" as Johnston suggests?[21] It seems nothing is more direct than revisiting the notion of "respond flexibly to the enemy and thus create conditions for victory" in *The Art of War*. Following is the excerpt containing the notion:

Now the army's disposition of force (*hsing*) is like water. Water's configuration (*hsing*) avoids heights and races downward. The army's disposition of force (*hsing*) avoids the substantial and strikes the vacuous. Water configures (*hsing*) its flow in accord with the terrain; *the army controls its victory in accord with the enemy* [i.e. "respond flexibly to the enemy and thus create conditions for victory"]. Thus the army does not maintain any constant strategic configuration of power (*shih*), water has no constant shape (*hsing*). One who is able to change and transform in accord with the enemy and wrest victory is termed spiritual.[22] (Chapter 6)

The water metaphor above emphasizes the property of water: it has no form and constantly adapts, suggesting that prescribed plan and action are the last things a general should seek in warfare. And François Jullien adds that:

For, as it is recognized in warfare, nothing is more dangerous than immobilizing yourself within one particular case; and nothing is more worse than setting up rules and imperatives for yourself, for these make your conduct inflexible and prevent you from the variation from which all potential stems (and the same applies to morality).[23]

This explains why the notion of "respond flexibly to the enemy and thus create conditions for victory" was needed in the first place. It is more about *the attainment of the mindset* of absolute flexibility that prevents one from "immobilizing yourself within one particular case." Johnston may be right stating that the flexibility axiom (*quan bian*) found in the operational strategic culture allows for a wide range of strategic behaviors aimed at increasing the efficacy of the military instrument.[24] But by no means does it contain Johnston's proposition that, when practiced, the strategist "cannot be restricted, constrained by, or wedded to self-imposed a priori political, military, or moral limits on strategic choices"—it is just impossible that the strategist or general is being "hijacked" by the notion altogether. Also, by suggesting that what Mao clearly borrowed from Sun Tzu and traditional strategic thought was the notion of absolute flexibility (Johnston's version), Johnston attempts to force through his claim that "China has historically exhibited a relatively consistent hard realpolitik or *parabellum* strategic culture that has persisted across different structural contexts into the Maoist period (and beyond)."[25] But in fact Johnston himself also states that: "Flexibility is essential because the constant process of change in conflict situations requires a constant awareness of the appearance and disappearance of opportunity."[26] This attainment of a

162

mindset is what the original purpose of the notion of absolute flexibility is supposed to be. In essence, *quan bian* is just *not* the notion for which Johnston has been looking to show that the Chinese would use whatever action it takes to destroy the enemy, something that would help promote his proposition that only the parabellum strategic culture, which considers the offensive use of force not only legitimate but desirable, was operative in Chinese strategic culture.

"The Big Red Button"

The above examples show how Johnston has gone too far and ended up turning many of his correct observations into inaccurate, and even extreme, propositions, but after all he has got many things right about Chinese strategic culture. He has identified the roles played by the two strategic cultures, and under what circumstances would the Confucian-Mencian strategic culture give way to the parabellum strategic culture. This constitutes an important control mechanism of Chinese strategic behavior. Johnston is no doubt right that the concept of righteous war is effectively what is connecting the political (or idealized as he calls it) and operational strategic cultures. The Confucian-Mencian strategic culture seems idealized in the eyes of Westerners because it denounces war, is reluctant to use force, and has little strategic and military considerations—to its advocators, only morality and the popular support from which it derives matters. Therefore, in real-world scenarios, the Chinese had little choice but to rely on Chinese strategic thought when dealing with military and strategic affairs. And there is no surprise that "Chinese strategic thought shares many of the same assumptions as *parabellum* or hard real-politik worldviews found in some variants of Western realism" as Johnston sees it, because it is not the military branch of the Confucian-Mencian thought and, more importantly, it is built precisely for that purpose and in accordance with that kind of worldview—we should not expect having military/strategic thought entirely based on morality after all. Chinese strategic thought simply takes up the job where the Confucian-Mencian strategic culture leaves off. And again, it would be an oversimplification if we assume that the operational strategic culture stands *in contrast with* the Confucian-Mencian strategic culture.

As a result, the interplay between the two strategic cultures by the righteous-war doctrine could easily give an impression that righteousness "does not constrain one's options, but rather opens them up" and "the idealized [Confucian-Mencian] strategic culture lifts any moral or political limits on the application of violence."[27] Despite that it is untrue that "once the ends of war are deemed righteous, then any and all means become righteous by themselves" as discussed earlier, once the nature of the enemy is defined as unrighteous by the concept of righteous war, it "opens up" the use-of-force options. In other words, the Confucian-Mencian strategic culture has been acting as a power limiter in Chinese strategic theory and practice—it is the "big red button" (carrying no nuclear sense here). When the "button" is pressed, it marks the setting in of the operational strategic culture on top of the Confucian-Mencian strategic culture. This "red button" mechanism is also applicable to the Chinese view of war as the last resort. As the Confucian-Mencian political culture requires the righteous-war doctrine to open up its use-of-force options and the setting in of Chinese strategic thought to cope with such issues, war is in most cases the last resort given all these limitations. Yet "war as the last resort" is merely the result, the main determinant is still the definition of the nature of the enemy by the righteous-war doctrine. Very often, it implies that the enemy has created and fulfilled the conditions for war, so that force can then be legitimately employed to fight a "righteous war." The same logic applies to Mao's admonition, "If someone doesn't attack us, we won't attack them, however if someone does attack us, we will definitely [counter] attack." The quote indicates the condition for which China would go to war, and it essentially involves the interplay of the two sets of strategic cultures as shown in the righteous-war doctrine. In sum, in a use-of-force context, the righteous-war doctrine has offered valid explanations and been quite a good predictor of Chinese strategic behavior, for it is capable of signaling the change of the pattern of behavior.

From Mao's Way of War to the Taoist Way of War

Yet what could be more significant than Johnston's overall conclusion that there is only a single operative parabellum strategic culture in China is that he has come very close to uncovering an alternative way of dealing with Chinese strategic culture. Such a tendency is unclear or even nonexistent in *Cultural Realism* (1995), but has become increasingly prominent in the article "Cultural Realism and Strategy in Maoist China" (1996). In his analysis of Mao's doctrine of "active defense" in the article, Johnston, albeit focusing on examining its offensive nature, starts realizing that the doctrine has political, operational, and military designs at once—it is designed to bring about effects across these aspects:

For one thing the term *active defense* was more politically palatable; it could be used in arousing righteous indignation among masses and soldiers or to attract sympathetic support from external sources.[28]

Mao evidently preferred an offensive "second strike" (*hou fa zhi ren*). Again, the reasoning was both political and military. To strike the enemy, particularly its territory, first, without specific provocation would be to give it the sympathy of world opinion and would tar the just side with the politically damaging label of *aggressor*.[29]

Militarily, Mao's version of a second strike offensive was designed to compel the enemy to move first, thus allowing an opportunity to gauge its intentions and capabilities. One could thereby ascertain the enemy's weak points, and attacks on these points, not first strike per se, were decisive in conflict.[30]

As Johnston puts it, active defense "is dictated by an instrumental need to frame one's own actions as entirely defensive and just, a position that is important for winning popular support and sympathy."[31] But it is not that hard to note that it is far more than mere propaganda, for Mao used active defense, "second strike", and the righteous-war doctrine in a highly integrated, coordinated, and instrumental manner. They all have their role to play in attaining the desired strategic effect. If Johnston was not so obsessed with proving his thesis right, he would have noticed that such instrumental use and extension of the righteous-war doctrine is very different from the way the doctrine is applied in the Confucian-Mencian paradigm.

Mao's active defense clearly lies outside the scope of Johnston's Confucian–Realipolitik dichotomy. As discussed earlier, the Confucian–Mencian strategic culture has few strategic and military considerations in itself. And once the nature of the enemy is defined as unrighteous and the use-of-force options are opened up as a result, Chinese strategic thought, or the operational strategic culture, has to step in to cope with the situation. In other words, according to the "standard" Confucian image of Chinese strategic thought, the Confucian-Mencian strategic culture and the parabellum strategic culture are largely separated and not always in harmony, thus any coordinated action or scheme, like Mao's active defense between the two strategic cultures, is not really possible. That is why Johnston observes that "the Confucian-Mencian paradigm is disconnected from the operational advice, axioms, and decision rules that derive from the *parabellum* paradigm" in the first place.[32]

Therefore, though Johnston has failed to notice this himself, *there are indeed two approaches regarding the use of morality in Chinese strategic theory and practice.* One is just as what is depicted in the standard Confucian image that the Confucian-Mencian strategic culture serves as the moral and political restraints and provides the conditions for which a nation would use force. Another approach is shown in Mao's doctrine of active defense in which morality is used in a completely instrumental and strategic manner. The existence of two approaches regarding the use of morality might have given Johnston a strong, but false, impression that "the idealized Confucian-Mencian strategic culture should not impose any a priori limits on strategic choice at the operational *parabellum* level," and that only the parabellum strategic culture was operative.[33] This particular way of war adopted by Mao has a predominantly Chinese origin, yet it cannot be fully explained by using the Confucian-Mencian and parabellum paradigms—*it belongs to the Taoist strategic tradition.*[34] As mentioned in Chapter 3, *Tao Te Ching,* the Taoist canon, has given Chinese strategic thought its final transformation by augmenting Sun Tzu's military and strategic thought, taking it further to the political and philosophical scenes and levels. It has incorporated numerous elements from the Chinese military school (*bing jia* 兵家) but has gone beyond it to the extent that *it can work on its own politically and grand-strategically and is predisposed to strategy.*[35] This explains why Johnston insists that only the parabellum strategic culture was operative, yet he has never managed to decipher the full picture. This is because he regards the *Seven Military Classics,* not *Tao Te Ching,* as the foundation of the Chinese parabellum strategic culture, and is dismissive of Taoism in his works. As a result, the parabel-

lum strategic culture upon which he draws his conclusion remains operational and military in nature, and is unable to offer explanation to anything beyond that level.

In what ways does Mao's doctrine of active defense (and his way of war)
resemble the Taoist way of war? In his examination of Lao Tzu's principle
of "taking the lower position" (Chapter 61),[36] Jullien emphasizes that this
"humility (literally, the choice to put oneself below) is neither moral nor
psychological; it is purely strategic."[37] The Taoist utilization of humility in
this case is similar to Mao's instrumental use of active defense, second
strike, and the righteous-war doctrine—they both are purely strategic and
instrumental, but not without moral or ethical considerations (and this
differs remarkably from the Western realpolitik tradition). This is the
true face of the notion of absolute flexibility (i.e. *quan bian*) put forward
by Johnston, and is what Mao had inherited from Sun Tzu and Lao Tzu.
However, the notion is incomplete and may not be practicable without
the prior attainment of so-called absolute objectivity developed by Sun
Tzu and the Taoists:

[A]mong the main points of emphasis in Sun Tzu's art of war is objectivity, and
his classic teaches how to assess situations in a dispassionate manner ... the
interior detachment cultivated by Taoists for attaining impersonal views of
objective reality.[38]

The ancient Taoist masters show how real ruthlessness, the coldness of complete
objectivity, always includes oneself in its cutting assessment of the real
situation.[39]

For strategic thought which stresses putting everything under cold
calculation, how would it possibly ignore moral and psychological factors
and effects at the operational level as Johnston suggests? Even the notion
of absolute flexibility (*quan bian*) could not affect this, not to mention
absolute flexibility and absolute objectivity are matching concepts. The
above illustration clearly demonstrates how seriously the real picture of
Chinese strategic culture and thought could be distorted and misread
without taking Taoism into consideration. Alas the strategic thought of
Taoism is precisely the blind spot of the Western strategic community.

DECIPHERING SUN TZU

Johnston and Scobell: One or Two Strategic Culture(s)?

As the Taoist way of war plays a dominant role in Chinese strategic behavior and Chinese strategic thought (in its most sophisticated form) must be understood through the lens of Taoism. The omission of Taoism in the studies of Chinese strategic culture by Johnston and Scobell is fatal. Even so, their findings and conclusions show that they are slowly progressing to the discovery of the Taoist paradigm and have important implications in the Western quest for demystifying Chinese strategic thought and culture. To recap, while Johnston has identified the existence of two strands of Chinese strategic culture (Confucian-Mencian and parabellum), he concludes that only the parabellum strand was operative. Unlike Johnston, Scobell argues that both the parabellum and Confucian-Mencian strands are operative, and contends that the two strands interact in a dialectic fashion to produce a distinctive "Chinese Cult of Defense." The two conclusions, however, are not as different as they seem: Given that the Chinese logic is dialectical/dualistic monist in nature—"a yin and a yang is what is called the Tao," the whole necessarily expresses itself in dualistic terms (i.e. yin and yang) (see Chapter 1). In short, it can be seen as monist (one), dualistic (two) or dialectical monist (two in one), depending on where one stands. Therefore, the conclusions of Johnston and Scobell are only different in a matter of degree that Johnston presumes monism and Scobell embraces dualism and dialectical monism.

Nevertheless, it would be untrue to say that Johnston is completely unaware of the dialectic nature of Chinese strategic thought. He probably just considers contradiction problematic rather than useful, like most Westerners do:

The *parabellum* paradigm appears to pervade the causal relationships and argument structures in the *Seven Military Classics*. But a perplexing problem is how or if Chinese strategic thought resolves the apparent tension between this paradigm and the more benign Confucian-Mencian one.[40]

Clearly, Johnston is more toward the Western practice of "obliterating the contradiction rather than accepting it or transcending it or using it to understand some state of affairs better."[41] This predominantly Western practice may explain why Johnston insists that only the parabellum paradigm was operative in Chinese strategic culture—he simply sees the interplay of the two strategic cultures as "tension" rather than transcendence. Furthermore, his presumption of monism seems to not really affect his assessment of the intrinsic nature of Chinese strategic culture:

Chinese strategic culture—with its stress on the overall efficacy of force for achieving state security, and on careful, capabilities-based assessments of opportunities for applying force—arguably predisposes those socialized in it to make strategic decisions roughly along realpolitik expected-utility lines.[42]

It is hard to deny that Chinese strategic culture does involve the making of "strategic decisions roughly along realpolitik expected-utility lines," given that Sun Tzu and the Taoists emphasize the attainment of impersonal views of objective reality in the assessment of the real situation (i.e. absolute objectivity). However, with the presence of the Taoist element, one should not easily put the Chinese realpolitik strategic culture on a par with the Western realpolitik tradition.

In comparison, despite that he contends that the two strands of Chinese strategic culture interact in a dialectic fashion to produce a distinctive "Chinese Cult of Defense," Scobell does not seem to understand the role and nature of dialectical monism in Chinese strategic thought. And the so-called Chinese Cult of Defense which identifies six principles that influence Chinese strategists, namely (1) the primacy of national unification; (2) heightened threat perceptions; (3) the concept of active defense; (4) Chinese just war theory; (5) chaos phobia; and (6) an emphasis on the welfare of the community over that of the individual, is largely descriptive and unable to show the real working of Chinese strategic thought.[43] Even so, Scobell is successful in presenting a bigger and clearer picture regarding the Chinese use of force that can cut through the political and operational levels and their strategic cultures.

Chinese Strategic Culture and Chinese Strategic Thought

So here comes the question: is Chinese strategic culture a good approach or framework for understanding and analyzing Chinese strategic behavior? As a starting point for understanding Chinese strategic theory and practice, Chinese strategic culture, as a cultural approach, is useful in helping Westerners or non-Chinese familiarise with China's strategic preference and assumptions. That the approach focuses on Confucianism also hits on the right target, for Confucianism has been the most dominant culture in China. It has enormous influence on many aspects of Chinese lives and relations, both domestic and foreign, ranging from father-son and ruler-subject relations to the Tribute System. More importantly, the approach provides insight on Chinese political-strategic decision-making regarding the use of force, given that the Confucian-Mencian strategic culture could act as the "big red button", as discussed above. Chinese strategic culture, however, ceases to be effective beyond that very point, for the cultural approach is particularly inapt for deciphering Chinese strategic thought. It is not hard to notice by seeing that Johnston encapsulates the essence of Chinese strategic thought in the notion of absolute flexibility (*quan bian*) and nothing else, and that Scobell's Chinese Cult of Defense reveals little information about how the Chinese strategize and wage war.

Therefore, as long as the main goal of Chinese strategic culture is to understand China's use of military force, it is very likely the cultural approach will remain unable to capture the essence of Chinese strategic thought. The reason is twofold: first, Chinese strategic thought, in its more sophisticated form, is systemic and grand-strategic in nature—it is applicable both in peacetime and wartime. The current approach simply does not take this into consideration. Its focus on the use of force implies that the approach remains military-centered and is of limited value when the situation involves little or no employment of overt military power. And also, given the nature of Chinese strategic thought and the immense risk involved in using force nowadays, what if China chooses to use all other grand-strategic measures but warfare? Boyd indicates that Mao synthesized Sun Tzu's ideas, classic guerilla strategy and tactics, and Napoleonic style mobile operations under an umbrella of Soviet revolutionary ideas to create a powerful way for waging modern (guerilla) war. And modern guerilla warfare has become an overall political, economic, social, and military framework for "total war."[44] The West has been putting too much emphasis on guerilla warfare, while often ignoring the fact that Mao has created and waged a new kind of "total war." It is the Chinese strategic framework, which is highly grand-strategic thus flexible in nature, that enables Mao to synthesize different elements and turn them into "an overall political, economic, social, and military framework for 'total war.'" It would not surprise us at all if the same Chinese strategic framework could produce new systems of measures which the purpose is political and has less reliance on the use of force. Having seen that the current strategic culture approach is unable to provide an accurate reading of Mao's active defense (see above), it is not hard to expect that it will once again fail to encapsulate the essence of any new Chinese strategic framework or way of war.

The second reason why the cultural approach is unsuitable for the task is that it has little consideration for the Chinese philosophical tradition, particularly Taoism, that forms the philosophical basis of Chinese strategic thought, and constitutes the key factor for differentiating Chinese strategic thought from its Western counterpart. Chinese strategy is highly philosophy-driven and this is reflected in the Chinese dialectical logic, the Taoist worldview, epistemology, and methodology, and the condition-consequence approach that forms the main pillars of Chinese strategic thought (see Chapters 1 & 3). These aspects all have Taoist root and are, unfortunately, least comprehensible by Westerners. As Jullien notes:

[*Tao Te Ching* or *Lao Tzu/Laozi*] is the briefest of the great Chinese classics—barely five thousand words in all—and is also the Chinese text most translated into European languages, no doubt because it seems to be at once the most revealing and the least translatable (the one perhaps implies the other), the most crucial yet also the most disconcerting. It carries a message that is the more precious because it has never quite got through to us Europeans and because we suspect that it has been more or less lost (so we are now forced to interpret it as best we can).[45]

Based on this incomplete understanding of Chinese strategic thought, Johnston is dubious about that:

there is also a generally accepted view that these characteristics [of Chinese strategic culture] have changed little from Sun Zi through Mao Zedong. Though there is not much explanation of why the evolution of China's alleged strategic culture has been so exceptionally slow. The tendency in the literature is to focus almost exclusively on Sun Zi, compare him with Mao, and assume that an unbroken strategic-cultural chain links the two.[46]

Unable to grasp the Taoist root behind the key premises of Chinese strategy, Johnston can only look at the change and continuity of Chinese strategy from a number of relatively superficial characteristics of Chinese strategic culture, such as preference for strategic defense and limited war, and an apparently low estimation of the efficacy of violence. Using a lens of strategic culture, he cannot explain why "the evolution of China's alleged strategic culture has been so exceptionally slow," because the "unbroken chain" linking Sun Tzu and Mao is more than strategic-cultural in nature—it is *strategic-philosophical*. What have really been passed on to Mao from ancient/traditional Chinese strategic thought are the philosophy-driven aspects such as the Chinese dialectical logic, the Taoist worldview, epistemology, and methodology, and the condition-consequence approach. And these aspects are inherently less subject to change.

Without managing to capture the essence of Chinese strategic thought, therefore, Scobell's concern that the scholarship on Chinese strategy "runs the risk of perpetuating a belief that China is unlike any other country in the world and can therefore only be on its own terms (i.e. a fortune cookie)" is not valid. Scobell is concerned that:

This is a particular danger for strategic culture analyses because of a tendency to highlight the unique or at least distinctive aspects of Chinese culture and traditions. The unfortunate result could be that we only succeed in making Chinese approaches to warfare and strategy appear more impenetrable and incomprehensible to outsiders, and decipherable only to those possessing extensive study, language training, and in-country experience. Only learned high priests can accurately interpret the oracle bone, or in this case, read the tea leaves. This outcome would retard rather than advance strategic culture scholarship.[47]

In the case of China, in which even its logic is so distinctive and fundamentally different from formal Western logic, there should be no question that "only learned high priests" who have overcome the language, cultural, and philosophical barriers can accurately interpret Chinese strategy. I do not see why such is not the case or why the task should be left to those who are not equipped with the right qualities. It is precisely the failure of the current approach in exploring the philosophical basis of Chinese strategy that retards advance strategic culture scholarship; it has nothing to do with understanding Chinese strategy on its own terms. From the analysis above, it is apparent that the strategic culture approach has reached its limit. As the readers might have noticed in the course of reading this book, I am trying to advocate the return to the historical and philosophical approach (vis-à-vis the current strategic culture approach) as an alternative way of studying Chinese strategy. I start adopting the approach in this book by incorporating a historical analysis of *The Art of War* (Chapter 2) and an examination of the strategic-philosophical thought of Sun Tzu and Lao Tzu (Chapter 3).

The two approaches are not mutually exclusive but vary greatly in terms of depth. The strategic culture approach not only is ineffective in dealing with the philosophical aspect of Chinese strategy, it also has a weak historical foundation as there has been no systematic study of Chinese military and strategic history in the West so far. If the scholarship on Chinese strategy wants to make further study possible, the return to the historical and philosophical approach will be an obvious, if not the only promising, option. In addition, there is no doubt that the strategic culture approach is capable of identifying lots of important characteristics of Chinese strategic culture. However, the characteristics identified tend to be easily discernible. They just represent the tip of the iceberg when considering the essence of Chinese strategy failed to be captured by the strategic culture approach. This is a particular danger for analyses of Chinese strategy because the approach gives those who study Chinese strategic culture a false impression, if not a false sense of security, that they have already demystified Chinese strategic thinking and behavior. In the same way, the strategic culture approach runs the risk of becoming a lazy man's approach of studying Chinese strategy, given that "outsiders" think now they can now get the (incomplete) picture of Chinese strategy without needing to go into the historical and philosophical aspects. This again shows that it is the strategic culture approach itself that actually hinders the West's exploration of Chinese strategic thought and history.

Even though the philosophical aspect of Chinese strategy pose a barrier to the West in understanding Chinese strategy, to some extent this could be remedied by a more extensive study of Chinese military and strategic history. China's long history, and rich military and strategic history that comes with it, are indispensable for the study of Chinese strategic thought and culture. They serve as the common language and knowledge of Chinese strategists of all times. For example, in "On Protracted War," Mao uses the Battle of Chengpu (632 BC, 城濮之戰) as an example to illustrate how victories were won by small and weak armies against big and powerful armies in Chinese history.[48] Chinese strategists like Mao could frequently and easily draw on military and strategic lessons from cases from over 2,500 years ago, with no further explanation at all in most of the cases. Moreover, much of China's military and strategic wisdom was distilled into novels and literary classics such as *Romance of the Three Kingdoms*, *The Water Margin*, and *The Romance of the Eastern Zhou*. In Henry Kissinger's words:

In no other country is it conceivable that a modern leader would initiate a major national undertaking by invoking strategic principles from a millennium-old event—nor that he could confidently expect his colleagues to understand the significance of his allusions. Yet China is singular. No other country can claim so long a continuous civilization, or such an intimate link to its ancient past and classical principles of strategy and statesmanship.[49]

Plainly, without incorporating these elements, the current Western way of studying Chinese strategy can never be on the same wavelength with Chinese strategic thought.

As a student of both Chinese and Western strategic thought, I do not understand why the West deems it does not have to do it the hard way—examining the history and philosophy in addition to culture—when studying Chinese strategy. The Chinese have gone through the same processes when studying Western strategic theory and practice. And clearly they have a better understanding of Western strategic thought than vice versa. Even Chinese strategic culture as an approach could be a good start for understanding Chinese strategic behavior, the historical and philosophical approach can offer more precise conclusions with respect to how the Chinese strategize and wage war because it looks directly at the Chinese strategic mindset and thinking, not just its cultural settings. I hope this work will help ignite the historical and philosophical analyses of Chinese strategy in the West.

CONCLUSION

As a Chinese, I always wonder why there is no one questioning why both Liddell Hart and Boyd, the two most important Western strategic thinkers of the twentieth century, had to look East for ideas. Oddly enough, despite that Liddell Hart's Indirect Approach has been criticized as oversimplified and tautological, Boyd still insisted upon incorporating Chinese strategic thought into the Western strategic framework to an even fuller extent. This, however, should not surprise us, for that Liddell Hart's Indirect Approach is considered the only strategic theory that has a general validity by J. C. Wylie, and that *The Art of War* is the only theoretical book on war that Boyd did not find fundamentally flawed, all point toward the fact that Chinese strategic thought contains certain key aspects which are much needed by the Western strategic framework, yet can only be imported from the Chinese source.[1]

Theorizing War: Chinese and Western Thought

If the attainment of "absolute flexibility" and "absolute objectivity" is the ultimate object of Chinese strategic thought which form its very basis for producing a sound strategic theory for action, it is clear that Western strategic thought has been unable to develop anything as such. This is mainly because the West has been having problems theorizing war by conceiving it according to a "model" form. Since, in war, the opponent is a reacting, animate entity, Western thought has been essentially trying to "make a model of something that could not be modeled."[2] According to François Jullien:

The subject of warfare provides evidence of how difficult it is to theorize how to act. Given that warfare, as action, is radical and leads to extremes, it is particularly well suited to reveal the dead-ends into which any concept of efficacious action will lead us if it proceeds from model-making or limit itself to a technical view.[3]

From the Ancient Greek treatises on warfare to Clausewitz's On War, the West had been charging up the hill of strategy and action through model-building and "limiting itself to a technical view" but they all ended up in vain. This is bound to happen, as Jullien notes:

The West, with its own kind of theoretical equipment, which is of a formalizing and technical nature, has proved itself to be singularly inept at thinking about the conduct of warfare, taking account only of secondary matters (preparations and material data) and failing to consider the phenomenon itself (although Clausewitz himself identified it as "something that lives and reacts"). That being so, only one option was left—one that even Clausewitz was unable to reject entirely—namely, to involve pure chance and genius. In contrast, the intelligence developed by Chinese thought is, manifestly, eminently strategic.[4]

It is precisely the "non-formalizing" and "non-technical" nature of Chinese strategic thought that differs itself so much from its Western counterpart and attracted the attention of Liddell Hart and Boyd. Taking yin-yang as an example, both Liddell Hart and Boyd have incorporated the Chinese logic into their theories, for it at once resolves an age-old problem of Western strategic thought—its incapability of dealing with an object that lives and reacts and keeps betraying its model. Given that, in warfare, the polarity of the situation stems from the antagonism between the forces involved, it is clear that Chinese thought, which conceived of reality in terms of polarity, was predisposed to strategy.[5]

Toward a General Theory of Strategy: Cases of Mao and Boyd

Therefore, the success and ascendency of Mao's way of war is no accident. As Boyd indicates, Mao synthesized Sun Tzu's ideas, classic guerilla strategy and tactics, and Napoleonic style mobile operations under an umbrella of Soviet revolutionary ideas to create a powerful way for waging modern (guerilla) war.[6] On surface, Mao's way of war demonstrates a successful synthesis of Chinese and Western strategic thought. Yet if we take a closer look, we would notice it is far more significant than that—it is Chinese strategic thought offering the overall strategy, grand-strategic orientation, worldview, and epistemology (they are to some extent "reconditioned" by Marxism), implemented by modern and Western operational and tactical means. The "division of labor" involved clearly shows the indispensable qualities of Chinese strategic thought—its timelessness and compatibility even with non-Chinese operational and tactical ways and means. These are the stringent requirements a general theory of strategy has to meet. In Wylie's words:

The Mao theory of political warfare is by far the most sophisticated of the current theories of war. It, more clearly than any other, states its purpose and sets forth the systems of measures for its accomplishment. That its purpose is political, and that its systems of measures include political, social, and economic as well as military measures is an indication of both the scope and the realism of the theory in practice.[7]

The case of Mao is a substantial one to reveal that Chinese strategic thought could be the most qualified candidate for being the core of a single, universal general theory of strategy. As discussed earlier and in Chapter 1, the orientation and way of Chinese thought are predisposed to strategy, while in the area of operations and tactics, as well as in technology and its applications, the West clearly has an edge over the Chinese. And Mao's case illustrates exactly how the scheme for a general theory of strategy, which takes into consideration the strengths and weaknesses of both Chinese and Western strategic thought, was put into action and prevailed.

Nevertheless, Mao's model might have given the West some not-so-realistic hope. For Mao was a Chinese and, to a certain extent, he could think in a Western way as well. He could cope with the synthesis of Chinese and Western strategic thought with ease, particularly as the Chinese part, which was supposed to be tough for Westerners, was a no-brainer to him. As a result, Mao faced little problem when employing this cross-cultural scheme. However, when Boyd tried to emulate the models of Mao and Sun Tzu in a Western setting, problems arose right away, given the incompatibility of Chinese ideas with Western thought. This is the fault of the Chinese though—as shown in the Chinese use of paradox, Chinese thought is "never bothering to investigate it but always treating it as an underlying assumption. It never wastes time in setting it up as a principle. This being so, and given that it is so implicit in the entire treatise, but always deeply so rather than in an eye-catching way, the danger is that we may overlook it or fail to appreciate its importance."[8] And the same largely applies to other Chinese principles as well. That could well explain why Boyd was trying so hard to capture the cognitive and philosophical bases of Chinese strategic thought and to prepare the ground for further incorporation of Chinese strategic thought into the Western framework. He was well aware that Chinese strategic thought, which is eminently strategic in nature, carries the answers to many Western strategic questions, which can only be attained by taking the hard way of exploring Chinese strategic thought in a more exhaustive manner. Hence even though both Chinese and Western strategic thought will certainly play a part in the formation of a single, universal general theory of strategy, its forthcoming development will necessarily be moving more toward the Chinese side, given that the existing theories are simply not "Chinese" enough, as we have learnt from the cases of Mao and Boyd. This makes breaking the philosophical and cultural barrier the first and foremost assignment of the Western strategic community.

Understanding Chinese Strategic Thought as a Philosophical and Cultural Undertaking

I do not deny that the historical-theoretical-philosophical and cross-cultural analyses of Sun Tzu in this book are not easy to digest, especially for the readers who are unfamiliar with *The Art of War* in the first place. Yet without these aspects being discussed, one will never get a fuller picture of Chinese strategic thought, which also means the West could hardly escape from the current impasse of the study of Sun Tzu, in which most people reduce the text to short and decontextualized axioms, aphorisms, and phrases.

The grasping of Chinese philosophy, especially Taoism, remains the key to understanding Sun Tzu and Chinese strategic thought. As indicated in Chapter 1, even though the Four Schools (horizontal dimension) and the Three Levels (vertical dimension) of Chinese strategic thought were developed after Sun Tzu's time, they are essentially modeled on *The Art of War*. And if one does not have the basic understanding of the concepts of yin-yang and Tao, as well as the relationship between the two, he might already have problems comprehending the two dimensions that constitute the system of Chinese strategic thought. Hence, when we examine Sun Tzu's philosophy of war, we should not focus solely on the schemes such as "subjugating the enemy's army without fighting" and "the victorious army first realizes the conditions for victory, and then seeks to engage in battle," but also on the condition-consequence approach, the systemic orientation, and the yin-yang logical and dialectic engine embedded in the work.

Moreover, the Chinese use a philosophical work—*Tao Te Ching*—as their strategic text. The schemes and stratagem offered by Taoist text is fully compatible with the Taoist philosophy. The coming together of philosophical and strategic thought has greatly enriched Chinese strategic thought as a whole, hence it is known to many Chinese that *Tao Te Ching* is far more "lethal" than *The Art of War*. As a result, even though *The Art of War* precedes *Tao Te Ching*, a circular and seemingly paradoxical relationship has developed between the two texts—*The Art of War* has provided *Tao Te Ching* with original thought for development, while the latter perfects the former with more substantial Taoist schemes, worldview, and epistemology in return. That is why the claim that Taoist thought forms the philosophical basis of *The Art of War* is still valid nowadays, despite that we have discovered that *The Art of War* precedes *Tao Te Ching*. Furthermore, without seeing Chinese strategic thought from a Taoist (philosophical) lens, one could easily arrive at some simplistic, one-sided perceptions, such as that Chinese strategy is anti-militaristic or defensive in nature. I do not imply that these are totally untrue, but considering the dialectical nature of Chinese thought, it is just unwise to make such hasty and over-simplistic generalizations. The contrasting treatment of protracted war between Sun Tzu and Mao Tse-tung makes a good case in point that the same set of principles can lead to completely different strategic options. Even though Sun Tzu emphasizes that "in military campaign I have heard of awkward speed but have never seen any skill in lengthy campaigns,"[9] he also addresses guerrilla war indirectly, discussing principles and stratagems that one can easily apply to that form of conflict.[10] And Mao chose to follow the latter interpretation of Sun Tzu's thought. By the same token, only with Sun Tzu's principles as Boyd's theoretical foundation can he bridge the gap between blitzkrieg and guerilla warfare by discovering the mutual conceptual foundation between these two seemingly contrasting forms of warfare.

Examination of Sun Tzu from whichever perspective always stems from historical analysis. As shown in Chapter 2, an effective analysis has to practically cover almost the entire Spring and Autumn Period (771–403 BC), and this is something many Westerners do not bother to conduct, not to mention they generally lack the materials and cultural knowledge of China for the task. In the case of Sun Tzu, for example, at least one has to first recognize the state of Qi (Sun Tzu's home country) and differentiate it from other states in the period. Despite the difficulties, the examination of the culture of Qi and its impact on Sun Tzu's thought is remarkably fruitful. We can find the origins of *The Art of War* from the military traditions, economic activities, and cultural traits of Qi. It is fascinating to see how these extraordinary qualities of the Qi culture manifested in *The Art of War* eventually, and how they acted as the fertile soil for Sun Tzu's ideas to flourish.

The statecraft and diplomacy of Guan Zhong, and its crucial role played in Qi's rise to hegemony, allow us to make more specific attribution of Sun Tzu's ideas on those aspects. It is believed that Guan Zhong and his statecraft not only had influenced Sun Tzu, but the Confucian, Taoist, and Legalist (Realist) schools of thought that emerged at a later time as well. Some Chinese even consider Guan Zhong the godfather of China's Legalist school of thought. It is a serious omission of the West, who wants to understand Chinese international mindset and behavior, yet fails to notice or study Guan Zhong. Guan Zhong had set the precedents for many premises and schemes in Chinese statecraft and diplomacy. He was probably one of the first proponents of soft power in the world. And it is quite unimaginable that he practiced economic warfare through the means of trade, currency, pricing of economic goods, and increasing economic dependence of other states upon Qi in 7th century BC.[11] From above, it is not hard to discern how Guan Zhong had influenced the key schemes of Sun Tzu, such as "subjugating the enemy's army without fighting," "the highest realization of warfare is to attack the enemy's plans; next is to attack their alliances...army...fortified cities," and the use of all available means to attain victory. In the same way, Guan Zhong's emphasis of gaining supremacy not by sheer force, but by changing and winning the hearts and minds of other international actors, had set the tone for Chinese strategic and diplomatic thought thereafter.

It is important to note that, with the exception of deception as the key principle of warfare, almost all aspects of *The Art of War* we find useful nowadays or having continuing relevance, including its grand-strategic orientation and the teachings on the conduct of war, *did not originate in Sun Tzu's time* (i.e. middle to late Spring and Autumn Period) but in early Spring and Autumn Period. This is closely related to the fact that Sun Tzu was living in a transitional period that allowed elements from different periods to appear in his thesis. And quite obviously, the focus and orientation of a general (i.e. Sun Tzu's post in the State of Wu), which was a new military title created in Sun Tzu's time as a consequence of the bifurcation of officials and generals in the state, were gradually shifting from a strategic nature to a military one. In other words, we are able to learn from the important lessons of Sun Tzu today largely because strategic treatises back then had not yet been fully transformed and systematized into military texts. Yet this was not the only occasion that Chinese strategic thought was benefited from a period of tremendous change and the unfinished transformation it brought. *Tao Te Ching* originally positioned itself as a book of statecraft for rulers. However, as the text was written and compiled by a number of Taoists across a long period of time, there came a shift in the trend of thought, just as it happened to *The Art of War*, but this time it was philosophy that was getting in fashion. Hence finally, *Tao Te Ching* essentially contains both aspects on statecraft and philosophy, resulting in people debating on whether the treatise is a strategic or philosophical text. And just as the case of Sun Tzu, it is again the untransformed part of *Tao Te Ching* that carries most of the strategic lessons. This leads to a rather baffling view that Chinese strategic thought remains useful throughout times because its core texts had withstood systematizations and prevented themselves from being developed into purely military (*The Art of War*) or philosophical (*Tao Te Ching*) work. This very fact reminds us that a large part of the efficacy of Chinese strategic thought actually stems from ideas attained when they were not being heavily systematized. This suggests that any attempt to heavily systematize Chinese strategic thought could be counterproductive after all.

Such resistance to systematization is not a problem of Chinese strategic thought but possibly its built-in feature indeed. It constitutes part of an important quality of Chinese strategic thought that is too inherently Chinese to be effectively conveyed to the West. That is the traditional Chinese way of thought which emphasizes holistic and systemic thinking and encapsulation of the overall picture. As strategy requires its practitioners to come up with a holistic view of the situation, this way of thinking provides the Chinese with a significant edge as well as an alternative way to Western rational thinking when dealing with strategic issues. In *The Analysis of Chinese Strategic Principles* (a Chinese work), the author believes this trait of the Chinese way of thought is closely associated with Chinese characters. Chinese characters, which consist of pictograms, ideograms, and ideogrammic compounds, not only possess a much greater information-carrying capacity than English alphabet and word, but also enable the user's spontaneous perception of the information they contain and suggest. The coming together of the Chinese way of thought, characters, and metaphorical imagery helps bring the Chinese closer to the essence of strategy and strategic thinking, and allows Chinese strategic thought to better fulfill the requirements of strategy. Hence the author of that book even claims that the "real" strategic thought emerged from China, given its well-matchedness with Chinese traditional culture.[12] Nonetheless, Boyd had shown the West the possibility of adopting the Chinese way. Even though he did not know Chinese himself, he actively used changing metaphors, thought association, and forced analogies, which are commonly used in Eastern cultures, to make connections and explore for them in order to produce new ideas.[13] The excerpt below demonstrates Boyd's way and how it is different from the default mode of the West:

[Boyd] called the Acolytes to discuss the meaning of a word for hours. "What do you see when you hear the word?" he asked. "What picture comes to mind?"

CONCLUSION

It was an exasperating business. Boyd liked ambiguity, believing it opened new vistas and led in unexpected directions. Burton was uncomfortable with Boyd's lack of fix. "You are taking advantage of the fact words can have more than one meaning," Burton said. "You are using words and ideas and concepts in ways that people don't use those words and ideas and concepts."[14]

"Picture," "ambiguity," and "words can have more than one meaning" are all indicative of the Chinese/Eastern way in action in Boyd's mind. No one would bother to take this difficult, yet essential, step unless he aims to master Chinese strategic thought himself.

This book helps reveal to the West one of the most important findings in the study of Chinese strategic thought—that *The Art of War* precedes *Tao Te Ching*. The discovery has changed, and indeed reversed, the bearings in the study of the subject. It gives us a much clearer picture of the evolution of Chinese strategic thought and how it progressed and broke away from the military stream, enabling Chinese strategy to transcend scopes and areas. Moreover, *Tao Te Ching* had effectively redefined Chinese strategy as an art of the weak defeating the strong, thus making the Chinese way of war more "unrestricted" and lethal than ever.

Seeing from another angle, that *The Art of War* precedes *Tao Te Ching*, has greatly advanced the importance of Sun Tzu in Chinese thought (not just Chinese strategic thought). We realize that Sun Tzu's thesis contains the seeds of Chinese strategic thought, statecraft, and stratagem, Taoist thought, Chinese dialectics, and even the Legalist (Realist) school of thought. What is more fascinating is that *The Art of War* had inspired *Tao Te Ching*, not only in terms of strategic schemes, but philosophical notions as well. While we keep praising *The Art of War* as one of the greatest works on strategy ever, too often we fail to notice that Sun Tzu himself was a real genius, who performed marvellously both as a general and a thinker.

The enduring value of *The Art of War* stems from Sun Tzu's sound and sensible philosophy and a matching set of principles of war. In many ways, Mao's way of war and the so-called "Unrestricted Warfare" are modern and updated versions of Sun Tzu's ideas, but they seldom surpass the depth and scope of *The Art of War*.[15] These modern variants of *The Art of War* view the Western way of war from a critical lens. They have correctly envisioned and actively shaped modern war(fare), and have proven value—

they are of immense value to Western strategic thought if properly and adequately examined. However, it turns out that the West has been wrongly placing emphasis on Sun Tzu's axioms of war only, leading to a misinterpretation that the Chinese way of war stresses deception and cunning solely, and ruthlessly employs whatever means it takes to attain its goal. This utilitarian view takes no notice of Sun Tzu's philosophy of war at all. Yet there is no easy way to understand the Chinese philosophy of war unless one makes real effort to get himself familiar with Chinese history, philosophy, and culture. I believe this work has helped the West move a great leap forward into that direction.

NOTES

INTRODUCTION: SUN TZU IN THE WEST

1. Sun Tzu, Samuel B. Griffith, *Sun Tzu: The Art of War*, London: Oxford University Press, 1963, Appendix 3 (electronic version).
2. Ibid.
3. Ibid.
4. *Wu Bei Zhi* (武備志 *Treatise on Armament Technology* or *Records of Armaments and Military Provisions*), 1621.
5. Sun Tzu, *Sun-tzu: The Art of War*, trans. Ralph D. Sawyer, Boulder, CO: Westview, 1994.
6. Sun Tzu, *The Art of War*, trans. Thomas Cleary, Boston: Shambhala, 1988; Sun Tzu, *Sun-tzu: The Art of Warfare*, trans. Roger T. Ames, New York: Ballantine, 1994.

1. THE SYSTEM OF CHINESE STRATEGIC THOUGHT

1. An earlier version of this chapter appeared in *Comparative Strategy*, 29, 3 (July 2010), pp. 245–59.
2. François Jullien, *A Treatise on Efficacy: Between Western and Chinese Thinking*, Honolulu, HI: University of Hawai'i Press, 1996, p. 49.
3. See Richard E. Nisbett, *The Geography of Thought: How Asians and Westerns Think Differently ... and Why*, New York: Free Press, 2003.
4. See Qiao Liang and Wang Xiangsui, *Unrestricted Warfare*, Beijing: PLA Literature and Arts Publishing House, 1999.
5. Nisbett, *The Geography of Thought*, p. 176.
6. Ibid., p. 27.
7. Ibid., pp. 176–7.
8. Jullien, *A Treatise on Efficacy*, p. 189.
9. Nisbett, *The Geography of Thought*, p. 27 (my emphasis).

10. Jullien, *A Treatise on Efficacy*, p. 194.
11. Ibid., p. 85. Another translation, "when one does nothing at all there is nothing that is undone," is being used in other chapters in this book.
12. Ibid., p. 81.
13. *Questions and Replies between T'ang T'ai-tsung and Li Wei-kung*, in *The Seven Military Classics of Ancient China*, trans. Ralph D. Sawyer, Boulder, CO: Westview Press, 1993, p. 330.
14. *The Seven Military Classics of Ancient China*, trans. Sawyer, p. 506.
15. *Questions and Replies*, in *The Seven Military Classics*, trans. Sawyer, pp. 356–7.
16. Sun Tzu, *Sun-tzu*, trans. Sawyer, p. 222.
17. See Li Ling, *Sun Zi Shi San Pian Zong He Yan Jiu* 《孫子》十三篇綜合研究 [A Comprehensive Study of Sun Tzu's Thirteen Chapters], Beijing: Zhonghua Book Company, 2006, pp. 421–3.
18. Li Ling, *Bing Yi Zha Li: Wo Dou Sun Zi* 兵以詐立：我讀《孫子》 [Strategy is Based on Deception: How I Read Sun Tzu], Beijing: Zhonghua Book Company, 2006, pp. 55–6.
19. See Sun Tzu, *Sun-tzu*, trans. Ames.
20. There is no doubt that the first edition of *Sun Tzu: The Art of War* (the one that Sun Tzu presented to King Wu) had thirteen chapters. It was later expanded to eighty-two chapters with nine scrolls of diagrams as mentioned in the "Record of Literary Works." It is believed that Cao Cao (AD 155–220) cut it down to thirteen chapters, the form that the existing edition of *The Art of War* has today.
21. Sun Bin, *Sun Bin: The Art of Warfare*, trans. D.C. Lau and Roger T. Ames, Albany, NY: State University of New York Press, 2003, p. 120.
22. Ibid., p. 119.
23. Sun Tzu, *Sun-tzu*, trans. Sawyer, p. 167.
24. Sun Bin, *Sun Bin*, trans. Lau and Ames, p. 123.
25. Ibid., p. 8.
26. Ibid., p. 73.
27. Sun Tzu, *The Art of War*, trans. Cleary, p. 13.
28. Mao, Tse-tung, "On Protracted War," in *Selected Works of Mao Tse-tung*, <http://www.marxists.org/reference/archive/mao/selected-works/volume-2/mswv2_09.htm>
29. Ibid.
30. Ibid.
31. Ibid.
32. Edward N. Luttwak, *Strategy: The Logic of War and Peace*, Rev. and enl. edn, Cambridge, MA: Belknap Press, 2001, pp. 2, 16.
33. Sun Tzu, *The Art of War*, trans. Cleary, pp. 13, 30.
34. Jullien, *A Treatise on Efficacy*, p. 114.
35. Nisbett, *The Geography of Thought*, p. 177.

36. See Thomas X. Hammes, *The Sling and the Stone: On War in the 21st Century*, St. Paul, MN: Zenith, 2004; and Antoine Bousquet, *The Scientific Way of Warfare: Order and Chaos on the Battlefields of Modernity*, New York: Columbia University Press, 2009.

37. *Questions and Replies*, in *The Seven Military Classics*, trans. Sawyer, pp. 359–60 (my emphasis).

38. Sun Tzu, *The Art of War*, trans. Sawyer, p. 167.

39. *Questions and Replies*, in *The Seven Military Classics*, trans. Sawyer, p. 344.

40. Sun Tzu, *Sun-tzu*, trans. Sawyer, p. 187.

41. *Questions and Replies*, in *The Seven Military Classics*, trans. Sawyer, p. 336.

42. Ibid., pp. 324–5.

43. Ibid., p. 353.

44. Ibid. (my emphasis).

45. Jullien, *A Treatise on Efficacy*, p. 188.

46. *Wu-tzu*, in *The Seven Military Classics*, trans. Sawyer, p. 207.

47. Edmund S.J. Ryden, *Philosophy of Peace in Han China: A Study of the Huainanzi, Ch. 15 on Military Strategy*, Taipei: Taipei Ricci Institute, 1998, p. 23 (my emphasis).

48. Jullien, *A Treatise on Efficacy*, pp. 72–3.

2. THE GENESIS OF *THE ART OF WAR*

1. Known as the Yin-ch'ueh-shan Texts or the bamboo strips of Yin-ch'ueh-shan.

2. See Sun Tzu, *Sun-tzu*, trans. Ames.

3. Its last record is in "The Record of Literary Works" (Yi Wen Chih 藝文志) in the *History of the Han Dynasty* (*Han Shu* 漢書) (c.AD 100).

4. Sun Tzu, *Sun-tzu*, trans. Ames, p. 22.

5. See Ho Ping-ti, *Three Studies on Suntzu and Laotzu*, Taipei: Institute of Modern History, Academia Sinica, 2002; Li Zehou, *Zhong Guo Gu Dai Si Xiang Shi Lun* 中國古代思想史論 [On the History of Chinese Ancient Thought], Taipei: San Min Book Co., 2000.

6. Since modern historians believe that *Six Secret Strategic Teachings*, though it may possibly contain Tai Gong's original thought, is not written by Tai Gong himself and nominally date its final composition to the Warring States Period (403–221 BC), it is not used as a source of Tai Gong's thought in this book.

7. See *Questions and Replies*, in *The Seven Military Classics*, trans. Sawyer, p. 330.

8. Qiu Wen-shan, *Qi Wen Hua Yu Zhong Hua Wen Ming* 齊文化與中華文明 [The Culture of Qi and Chinese Civilization], Jinan: Qi Lu Shu She, 2006. The remaining trait is romanticism.

9. See *The Record of the Grand Historian*—"House of Qi Taigong."

10. Li Ling, *Bing Yi Zha Li*, p. 8

11. See *Sun-tzu: The Art of War*, Chapter 2.

12. Qiu, *Qi Wen Hua Yu Zhong Guo Wen Ming*, p. 42.

13. Feng Zhen Hao, *Qi Lu Wen Hua Yan Jiu*, 齊魯文化研究 [A Study on the Cultures of Qi and Lu], Jinan: Qi Lu Shu She, 2010, p. 384.

14. Sun Tzu, *Sun-tzu*, trans. Ames, p. 120.

15. See *The Record of the Grand Historian*—"Biographies of Usurers."

16. Qiu, *Qi Wen Hua Yu Zhong Guo Wen Ming*, p. 85.

17. Sun Tzu, *Sun-tzu*, trans. Sawyer, p. 173.

18. Ibid., p. 203.

19. Ibid.

20. Ibid.

21. Ibid., p. 223.

22. Ibid., pp. 223–4 (my emphasis).

23. Cleary, pp. 159–60.

24. Sawyer, p. 177.

25. See Li Ling, *Bing Yi Zha Li*, pp. 308–9; Wei Ru-lin, *Sun Zi Jin Zhu Jin Yi* 孫子今註今譯 [The Modern Commentaries on and Translations of Sun Tzu], Taipei: The Commercial Press, 2001, pp. 216–20.

26. Sun Tzu, *Sun-tzu*, trans. Sawyer, p. 184.

27. Mao Tse-tung, "On Protracted War," in *Selected Works of Mao Tse-tung, Vol. II*, Peking: Foreign Languages Press, 1967, p. 166 (my emphasis).

28. Ibid.

29. *The Methods of the Ssu-ma*, in *The Seven Military Classics*, trans. Sawyer, p. 129.

30. Ibid., p. 127 (my emphasis).

31. Sun Tzu, *Shi Yi Jia Zhu Sun Zi Xiao Li* 十一家注孫子校理, ed. Yang Bing-an [The Collation of the Eleven Schools of The Art of War Annotations], Beijing: Zhonghua Book Company, 1999, p. 322.

32. Mi Zhen-yu (ed.), *Zhong Guo Jun Shi Xue Shu Shi, Vol. 1*, 中國軍事學術史 (上卷) [History of Chinese Military Scholarship, Vol. 1], Beijing: People's Liberation Army Publishing House, 2008, p. 92.

33. Ibid., p. 98.

34. Sun Tzu, *Sun-tzu*, trans. Sawyer, p. 231.

35. Ibid., p. 224.

36. Sun Tzu, *Sun-tzu*, trans. Sawyer, pp. 173–4.

37. Ibid.

38. Ibid., p. 198.

39. Ibid., p. 168.

40. Ibid., p. 184.

41. Ibid., p. 177.

42. Ibid.

43. Ibid., p. 167.

44. Ibid.
45. Ibid., pp. 179, 214–15.
46. See Ho, *Three Studies on Suntzu and Laotzu*.
47. Even though there are doubts concerning the historicity of Sun Tzu, Lao Tzu, and their works—Lao Tzu could be a myth and Sun Tzu might not be the author of *The Art of War*—I try not to question the existence of the two figures and their connections with the works named after them in this book, for that is not doing us any good to a better understanding of Sun Tzu and Chinese strategic thought. I believe at the current stage the West needs a fuller picture of Chinese strategic thought more than anything else. And a preoccupation with historical authenticity that is unlikely to achieve, if not impossible to prove, would deprive general Western readers of their chance to get acquainted with some generally accepted "facts" on the subject.

3. FROM SUN TZU AND LAO TZU: THE COMPLETION OF CHINESE STRATEGIC THOUGHT

1. Ralph D. Sawyer, (trans.), *The Tao of War: The Martial Tao Te Ching*, Boulder, CO: Westview Press, 2003.
2. *Questions and Replies*, in *The Seven Military Classics*, trans. Sawyer, p. 330.
3. Mi (ed.), *Zhong Guo Jun Shi Xue Shu Shi, Vol. 1*, p. 463.
4. See Ho, *Three Studies on Suntzu and Laotzu*.
5. Li Zehou, *Zhong Guo Gu Dai Si Xiang Shi Lun*, pp. 85–97.
6. Sun Tzu, *Sun-tzu*, trans. Sawyer, p. 168.
7. Ibid.
8. Michael I. Handel, *Masters of War: Classical Strategic Thought*, 3rd edn, London: Frank Cass, 2001, pp. 224–5.
9. Carl von Clausewitz, *On War*, ed. and trans. Michael Howard and Peter Paret, Princeton, NJ: Princeton University Press, 1984, pp. 202–3.
10. Li Zehou, *Zhong Guo Gu Dai Si Xiang Shi Lun*, p. 82.
11. Ibid., p. 83.
12. Ibid., p. 82.
13. Ibid., pp. 82–3.
14. Ibid., p. 83.
15. Ibid., pp. 83–4.
16. Sun Tzu, *Sun-tzu*, trans. Sawyer, p. 188.
17. Ibid., p. 168.
18. Ibid., p. 188.
19. Ibid., p. 187 (my emphasis).
20. Handel, *Masters of War*, p. 271 (emphasis original).
21. Sun Tzu, *Sun-tzu*, trans. Sawyer, p. 168; "If they are humble, encourage their

arrogance" is an alternative translation from Sun Tzu, *Sun-tzu*, trans. Ames, p. 105.

22. Sun Tzu, *Sun-tzu*, trans. Sawyer, p. 184.
23. *T'ai Kung's Six Secret Teachings*, in *The Seven Military Classics of Ancient China*, trans. Sawyer, p. 59 (my emphasis).
24. Lao Tzu, *Tao Te Ching*, in Thomas Cleary (ed.), *The Taoist Classics, Volume 1: The Collected Translations of Thomas Cleary*, Boston: Shambhala, 1994, p. 26.
25. Ibid.
26. Ibid., p. 24.
27. Jullien, *A Treatise on Efficacy*, p. 39.
28. Ibid., p. 90.
29. Lao Tzu, *Tao Te Ching*, in Cleary (ed.), *The Taoist Classics, Vol. 1*, p. 21.
30. Ibid., p. 28.
31. Ibid., p. 20.
32. Ibid., p. 29.
33. Colin S. Gray, *The Strategic Bridge: Theory for Practice*, New York: Oxford University Press, 2010, p. 18.
34. Philip Windsor, *Strategic Thinking: An Introduction and Farewell*, Boulder, CO: Lynne Rienner, 2002, p. 174 (my emphasis).
35. Jullien, *A Treatise on Efficacy*, p. 20.
36. Ibid., p. 40.
37. Ibid., p. vii.
38. Sun Tzu, *Sun-tzu*, trans. Ames, p. 120.
39. Ibid.
40. Sun Tzu, *Sun-tzu*, trans. Sawyer, p. 184.
41. Jullien, *A Treatise on Efficacy*, p. 177.
42. Ibid., p. 117 (my emphasis).
43. Ibid., p. 40.
44. Ibid. p. 42 (my emphasis).
45. Sun Tzu, *Sun-tzu*, trans. Sawyer, p. 193.
46. Jullien, *A Treatise on Efficacy*, p. 33.
47. Sun Tzu, *Sun-tzu*, trans. Sawyer, p. 193.
48. Jullien, *A Treatise on Efficacy*, p. 127.
49. Ibid., pp. 38-9.
50. Ibid., p. 135.
51. Ibid., pp. 174-5.
52. Sun Tzu, *Sun-tzu*, trans. Sawyer, p. 188.
53. Lao Tzu, *Tao Te Ching*, in Cleary (ed.), *The Taoist Classics, Vol. 1*, p. 46.
54. Ibid., p. 24.
55. Ibid., p. 45.
56. Sun Tzu, *Sun-tzu*, trans. Sawyer, p. 187 (my emphasis).

57. Lao Zi, *Dao De Jing: A Philosophical Translation*, trans. Roger T. Ames and David L. Hall, New York: Ballantine Books, 2003, p. 133.

58. Lao Tzu, *Tao Te Ching*, in Cleary (ed.), *The Taoist Classics, Vol. 1*, p. 46 (my emphasis).

59. Sun Tzu, *Sun-tzu*, trans. Sawyer, p. 193.

60. Lao Tzu, *Tao Te Ching*, trans. D.C. Lau, Hong Kong: The Chinese University Press, 2001, p. 3.

61. Ibid., p. 7.

62. Ibid., p. 20.

63. Ibid., p. 21.

64. Ibid., pp. 31–3.

65. Jullien, *A Treatise on Efficacy*, p. 182.

66. Li Zehou, *Zhong Guo Gu Dai Si Xiang Shi Lun*, p. 96.

67. Jullien, *A Treatise on Efficacy*, p. 192.

68. Lao Tzu, *Tao Te Ching*, in Cleary (ed.), *The Taoist Classics, Vol. 1*, pp. 21–2.

69. Ibid., p. 31.

70. Chen Ku-ying and Bai Xi, *Lao Zi Ping Zhuan* 老子評傳 [A Critical Biography of Lao Tzu], Nanjing: Nanjing University Press, p. 143.

71. Jullien, *A Treatise on Efficacy*, p. 11.

72. Ibid., p. 13.

73. Ibid., p. 180.

74. Lao Tzu, *Tao Te Ching*, in Cleary (ed.), *The Taoist Classics, Vol. 1*, p. 33.

75. Sun Tzu, *Sun-tzu*, trans. Sawyer, p. 197 (my emphasis).

76. Ibid., p. 183.

77. Ibid., p. 224.

78. Ibid.

79. Jullien, *A Treatise on Efficacy*, p. 72.

80. Lao Tzu, *Tao Te Ching*, trans. Lau, p. 83.

81. Sun Tzu, *Sun-tzu*, trans. Sawyer, p. 187.

82. Lao Tzu, *Tao Te Ching*, trans. Lau, p. 83.

83. Ibid., p. 85.

84. Ibid., pp. 69–71.

85. Jullien, *A Treatise on Efficacy*, p. 85.

86. Ibid., p. 86.

87. Ibid., p. 85.

88. Ibid., pp. 51, 54–5, 86.

89. Lao Tzu, *Tao Te Ching*, trans. Lau, p. 45.

90. Jullien, *A Treatise on Efficacy*, p. 88.

91. Sun Tzu, *Sun-tzu*, trans. Sawyer, p. 183.

92. Lao Tzu, *Tao Te Ching*, trans. Lau, p. 35.

93. Ibid., pp. 113–15.

94. Ibid., p. 87.
95. Ibid., p. 89.
96. Ibid., p. 41.
97. Ibid., p. 89.
98. *Bu zheteng* is an expression used by Northern Chinese. It was used by Hu Jintao when he delivered a speech during the conference to mark the thirtieth anniversary of the convening of the 3rd Plenary Session of the 11th CPC Central Committee on December 18, 2008. For the highlights of the speech, see http://news.xinhuanet.com/english/2008-12/18/content_10525417.htm
99. The translation of the expression has been problematic. The literal translation of *tao guang yang hui* is "hide brightness, nourish obscurity," but the Americans tend to use "hide our capabilities and bide our time" ever since the expression is translated that way in the Annual Report on the Military Power of the People's Republic of China 2002. It is questionable whether the expression carries the element of time, and some prefer using "hide its light" or "keep a low profile" instead.

4. DECIPHERING SUN TZU

1. An earlier version of this chapter appeared in *Comparative Strategy*, 27, 2, pp. 183–200.
2. Handel, *Masters of War*, p. 21.
3. Jeremy Black, *Rethinking Military History*, London: Routledge, 2004, p. 89.
4. Clausewitz, *On War*, p. 89.
5. Edward J. Villacres and Christopher Bassford, "Reclaiming the Clausewitzian Trinity," *Parameters* (Autumn 1995), pp. 9–19, <http://www.clausewitz.com/CWZHOME/Trinity/TRININTR.htm>
6. Ibid.
7. Sun Tzu, *Sun-tzu*, trans. Sawyer, p. 177; Clausewitz, *On War*, p. 89.
8. Clausewitz, *On War*, p. 89.
9. Ibid.
10. Daniel Moran, "Strategic Theory and the History of War," Paper (2001), p. 8. <http://www.clausewitz.com/CWZHOME/Bibl/Moran-StrategicTheory.pdf>
11. Ibid.
12. Clausewitz, *On War*, p. 89.
13. Christopher Bassford, "Teaching the Clausewitzian Trinity," Jan. 2003 (emphasis original) <http://www.clausewitz.com/CWZHOME/Trinity/TrinityTeaching Note.htm>
14. Christopher Coker, *Waging War without Warriors? The Changing Culture of Military Conflict*, London: Lynne Rienner, 2002, p. 115.
15. Sun Tzu, *Sun-tzu*, trans. Sawyer, p. 173.

16. Ibid.
17. Ibid., pp. 110–11.
18. Ibid., p. 188.
19. Ibid., pp. 174, 177.
20. Ibid., p. 177.
21. "Preparing large movable protective shields, armored assault wagons, and other equipment and devices will require three months ... This is the disaster that results from attacking [fortified cities]." Ibid.
22. Ibid., p. 168.
23. B.H. Liddell Hart, *Strategy*, 2nd rev. edn, New York: Meridian, 1991, p. 204.
24. Ibid., p. 43 (my emphasis).
25. Sun Tzu, *Sun-tzu*, trans. Sawyer, p. 223.
26. Coker, *Waging War without Warriors?* p. 115.
27. Sun Tzu, *Sun-tzu*, trans. Sawyer, p. 188.
28. Ibid., p. 183.
29. *Questions and Replies*, in *The Seven Military Classics*, trans. Sawyer, p. 352.
30. Sun Tzu, *Sun-tzu*, trans. Ames, p. 171.
31. Ibid.
32. Sun Tzu, *Sun-tzu*, trans. Sawyer, p. 198.
33. *Questions and Replies*, in *The Seven Military Classics*, trans. Sawyer, p. 353.
34. Ibid.
35. Sun Tzu, *Sun-tzu*, trans. Ames, p. 115.
36. *Questions and Replies*, in *The Seven Military Classics*, trans. Sawyer, p. 353.
37. Ibid.
38. Sun Tzu, *Sun-tzu*, trans. Sawyer, p. 184.
39. Ibid.
40. Robert Coram, *Boyd: The Fighter Pilot Who Changed the Art of War*, Boston, MA: Little, Brown & Co., 2002, p. 332.
41. Ibid.
42. *Questions and Replies*, in *The Seven Military Classics*, trans. Sawyer, pp. 324–5.
43. Sun Tzu, *Sun-tzu*, trans. Ames, pp. 115–16.
44. Christopher Coker, *The Future of War: The Re-Enchantment of War in the Twenty-First Century*, Oxford: Blackwell, 2004, p. 34.
45. Sun Tzu, *Sun-tzu*, trans. Sawyer, p. 192.
46. Ibid., pp. 192–3.
47. Ibid., p. 192.
48. Andrew Ilichinski, *Land Warfare and Complexity, Part II: An Assessment of the Applicability of Nonlinear Dynamic and Complex Systems Theory to the Study of Land Warfare (U)*, Alexandria, VA: Center for Naval Analyses, 1996, pp. 52–3.
49. Chet Richards, *Certain to Win: The Strategy of John Boyd, Applied to Business*, Philadelphia, PA: Xlibris, 2004, p. 48 (emphasis original).

50. Sun Tzu, *Sun-tzu*, trans. Sawyer, p. 193.
51. Ibid.
52. Ibid.
53. Ibid.
54. See Boyd, *Patterns of Conflict*.
55. Sun Tzu, *Sun-tzu*, trans. Sawyer, p. 184.
56. Coram, *Boyd*, pp. 334–5.
57. See http://en.wikipedia.org/wiki/Positive_feedback
58. Sun Tzu, *The Art of War*, trans. Cleary, p. 161.
59. Hammond, *The Mind of War*, p. 186.
60. Ibid., p. 181.
61. Ibid., p. 186 (my emphasis).
62. Sun Tzu, *Sun-tzu*, trans. Sawyer, p. 224.
63. Ibid.
64. *Questions and Replies*, in *The Seven Military Classics*, trans. Sawyer, p. 349.
65. Ibid., p. 337.
66. J.C. Wylie, *Military Strategy: A General Theory of Power Control*, New Brunswick, NJ: Rutgers University Press, 1967, p. 79 (emphasis original).
67. Ibid., p. 82.
68. Ibid., p. 85.
69. Ibid., p. 102 (my emphasis).
70. Handel, *Masters of War*, pp. xvii, 3.

5. THE SUCCESSORS OF SUN TZU IN THE WEST

1. Sun Tzu, *Sun Tzu*, trans. Griffith, pp. vi–vii.
2. B.H. Liddell Hart, *The Decisive Wars of History: A Study in History*, London: G. Bell & Sons, 1929.
3. Tony Corn, "From Mars to Minerva: Clausewitz, Liddell Hart, and the Two Western Ways of War," *Small Wars Journal* (21 May 2011), p. 29; <http://smallwarsjournal.com/blog/journal/docs-temp/767-corn.pdf>
4. Richard M. Swain, "B.H. Liddell Hart and the Creation of a Theory of War, 1919–1933," *Armed Forces & Society*, 17, 1 (Fall 1990), pp. 35–51 (electronic version).
5. Ibid.
6. Liddell Hart, *Strategy*, p. 5.
7. Sun Tzu, *Sun-tzu*, trans. Sawyer, pp. 197–8.
8. Ibid., p. 187.
9. Ibid.
10. *Questions and Replies*, in *The Seven Military Classics*, trans. Sawyer, pp. 324–5.
11. Sun Tzu, *Sun-tzu*, trans. Sawyer, p. 193.

12. Ibid., p. 199.
13. Sun Tzu, *Sun-tzu*, trans. Sawyer, p. 193.
14. Swain, "B.H. Liddell Hart and the Creation of a Theory of War, 1919-1933" (electronic version).
15. Liddell Hart, *Strategy*, p. 329 (my emphasis).
16. Ibid., p. 208 (my emphasis).
17. Wylie, *Military Strategy*, p. 70.
18. Please refer to Chapter 3 for a more detailed discussion of the condition-consequence approach.
19. Corn, "From Mars to Minerva," pp. 18, 20.
20. Sun Tzu, *Sun-tzu*, trans. Sawyer, p. 184.
21. Jullien, *A Treatise on Efficacy*, p. vii.
22. Liddell Hart, *Strategy*, p. 342 (emphasis original).
23. Ibid., p. 325.
24. Ibid., p. 324.
25. Windsor, *Strategic Thinking*, p. 174.
26. Liddell Hart, *Strategy*, pp. 325-6 (emphasis original).
27. Ibid., p. 336 (emphasis original).
28. Ibid., p. 325.
29. Sun Tzu, *Sun-tzu*, trans. Sawyer, p. 177.
30. Corn, "From Mars to Minerva," p. 27.
31. Liddell Hart, *Strategy*, p. 212.
32. Ibid., p. 324.
33. Ibid., p. 325.
34. Ibid.
35. Ibid., p. 322.
36. Ibid., p. 353 (my emphasis).
37. Ibid., pp. 349-50.
38. Ibid., p. 220.
39. Ibid., p. 322 (my emphasis).
40. Sun Tzu, *Sun-tzu*, trans. Sawyer, p. 177.
41. Liddell Hart, *Strategy*, p. 349.
42. Ibid., p. 353.
43. Ibid., p. 357.
44. Sun Tzu, *Sun-tzu*, trans. Sawyer, p. 174.
45. Sun Tzu, *Sun Tzu*, trans. Griffith, p. vii.
46. See Boyd, *Patterns of Conflict*.
47. Boyd, *Patterns of Conflict*, p. 13.
48. Coram, *Boyd*, p. 331 (my emphasis).
49. Boyd, *Patterns of Conflict*, p. 14.
50. Ibid., p. 69.

51. Frans P.B. Osinga, *Science, Strategy and War: The Strategic Theory of John Boyd*, New York: Routledge, 2007, p. 35.
52. Boyd, *Patterns of Conflict*, p. 66.
53. See Hammes, *The Sling and the Stone*, Chapter 5.
54. Ibid., p. 2.
55. Osinga, *Science, Strategy and War*, p. 37.
56. Ibid., p. 32; Hammond, *The Mind of War*, p. 148.
57. Osinga, *Science, Strategy and War*, p. 32.
58. See John Boyd, *The Strategic Game of ? and ?*, unpublished manuscript, 1987.
59. William S. Lind, "FMFM 1-A, Fourth Generation War," Paper 2005 (my emphasis) <http://www.d-n-i.net/lind/4gw_manual_draft_3_revised_10_june_05>
60. Ibid.
61. Ibid.
62. *Wei Liao-tzu*, in *The Seven Military Classics*, trans. Sawyer, p. 247.
63. Boyd, *The Strategic Game*, pp. 53–7.
64. Sun Tzu, *The Art of War*, trans. Cleary, p. 66.
65. Boyd, *The Strategic Game*, p. 54.
66. Osinga, *Science, Strategy and War*, p. 7.
67. John Boyd, *The Essence of Winning and Losing*, unpublished manuscript, 1995.
68. Osinga, *Science, Strategy and War*, p. 242.
69. John Boyd, *Organic Design for Command and Control*, unpublished manuscript, 1987, p. 26.
70. Ibid., p. 15.
71. Coram, *Boyd*, pp. 335–6.
72. Ibid., p. 335.
73. Hammond, *The Mind of War*, p. 198.
74. Boyd, *Organic Design*, p. 17.
75. Osinga, *Science, Strategy and War*, pp. 36–7 (my emphasis).
76. Hammond, *The Mind of War*, p. 120.
77. See Clausewitz, *On War*; Osinga, *Science, Strategy and War*.
78. See Alan D. Beyerchen, "Clausewitz, Nonlinearity, and the Unpredictability of War," *International Security*, 17, 3 (Winter 1992), pp. 59–90; Alan D. Beyerchen, "Clausewitz, Nonlinearity, and the Importance of Imagery," in David S. Alberts and Thomas J. Czerwinski (eds), *Complexity, Global Politics, and National Security*, Washington, DC: National Defense University, 1997, pp. 153–70.
79. Beyerchen, "Clausewitz, Nonlinearity, and the Importance of Imagery," p. 166 (my emphasis).
80. See Fritjof Capra, *The Tao of Physics: An Exploration of the Parallels between Modern Physics and Eastern Mysticism*, 3rd edn, London: Flamingo, 1982.
81. Osinga, *Science, Strategy and War*, p. 239 (my emphasis).
82. Ibid., p. 124.

83. Robert Jervis, *System Effect: Complexity in Political and Social Life*, Princeton, NJ: Princeton University Press, 1987, pp. 260–1.

84. Osinga, *Science, Strategy and War*, p. 117.

85. Mark Safranski et al., *The John Boyd Roundtable: Debating Science, Strategy, and War*, Ann Arbor, MI: Nimble, 2008, p. 6.

6. ON CHINESE STRATEGIC CULTURE

1. Ken Booth, "The Concept of Strategic Culture Affirmed," in C.G. Jacobsen (ed.), *Strategic Power: USA/USSR*, New York: St Martin's Press, 1990, pp. 121–8.

2. Lawrence Sonhaus, *Strategic Culture and Ways of War*, New York: Routledge, 2006, p. 99.

3. Alastair Iain Johnston, *Cultural Realism: Strategic Culture and Grand Strategy in Chinese History*, Princeton, NJ: Princeton University Press, 1995, p. 173.

4. Andrew Scobell, "Strategic Culture and China: IR Theory versus the Fortune Cookie?" *Strategic Insights*, IV, 10 (Oct. 2005) (electronic version).

5. See Jack Snyder, *The Soviet Strategic Culture: Implications for Limited Nuclear Operations*, RAND R-2154-AF, Santa Monica, CA: The Rand Corporation, 1977.

6. Andrew Scobell, *China's Use of Military Force: Beyond the Great Wall and the Long March*, New York: Cambridge University Press, 2003, pp. 9–10.

7. Alastair Iain Johnston, "Cultural Realism and Strategy in Maoist China," in Peter Katzenstein (ed.), *The Culture of National Security: Norms and Identity in World Politics*, New York: Columbia University Press, 1996, p. 219.

8. Johnston, *Cultural Realism*, p. 71.

9. Ibid., p. 68.

10. Ibid., 62.

11. Ibid., p. 69 (emphasis original).

12. Scobell, *China's Use of Military Force*, p. 21.

13. Johnston, *Cultural Realism*, pp. 45, 168.

14. Lao Zi, *Dao De Jing*, trans. Ames and Hall, p. 124.

15. Johnston, *Cultural Realism*, p. 70.

16. Ibid., p. 170.

17. Ibid., p. 72.

18. Ibid., p. 102.

19. Sun Tzu, *Sun-tzu*, trans. Sawyer, p. 184.

20. Ibid., p. 183.

21. Johnston, *Cultural Realism*, p. 102.

22. Sun Tzu, *Sun-tzu*, trans. Sawyer, p. 193 (my emphasis).

23. Jullien, *A Treatise on Efficacy*, p. 180.

24. Johnston, *Cultural Realism*, p. 164.

25. Ibid., p. 255; Johnston, "Cultural Realism and Strategy in Maoist China," p. 217.
26. Johnston, *Cultural Realism*, p. 149.
27. Ibid., pp. 70, 165.
28. Johnston, "Cultural Realism and Strategy in Maoist China," p. 249 (emphasis original).
29. Ibid., p. 250 (emphasis original).
30. Ibid.
31. Ibid., p. 238.
32. Johnston, *Cultural Realism*, p. 155.
33. Ibid., p. 145 (emphasis original).
34. It is evident that the Marxist aspects in Mao's way of war bear great resemblance to the Taoist dialectics, methodology, and worldview and can be explained in Taoist terms. It is highly probable that Mao was simply reapplying Chinese strategic thought in the name of Marxism. According to John Boyd, Mao synthesized Sun Tzu's ideas, classic guerilla strategy and tactics, and Napoleonic-style mobile operations under an umbrella of Soviet revolutionary ideas to create a powerful way for waging modern (guerilla) war.
35. More on the "strategicness" of Chinese thought will be discussed in the conclusion.
36. Lao Zi, *Dao De Jing*, trans. Ames and Hall, p. 172.
37. Jullien, *A Treatise on Efficacy*, p. 116.
38. Sun Tzu, *The Art of War*, trans. Cleary, pp. 12–13.
39. Ibid., p. 29.
40. Johnston, *Cultural Realism*, p. 108 (my emphasis).
41. Nisbett, *The Geography of Thought*, p. 176.
42. Johnston, *Cultural Realism*, p. 260.
43. Scobell, "Strategic Culture and China" (electronic version).
44. Boyd, *Patterns of Conflict*, p. 66.
45. Jullien, *A Treatise on Efficacy*, p. 84.
46. Johnston, *Cultural Realism*, p. 25.
47. Scobell, "Strategic Culture and China" (electronic version).
48. Mao, "On Protracted War," p. 164.
49. Henry Kissinger, *On China*, New York: Penguin, 2011, p. 2.

CONCLUSION

1. Wylie, *Military Strategy*, p. 71; Coram, *Boyd*, p. 331.
2. Jullien, *A Treatise on Efficacy*, pp. 9–14.
3. Ibid., pp. 9–10.
4. Ibid., p. 24 (emphasis original).
5. Ibid., p. 189.

6. Boyd, *Patterns of Conflict*, p. 66.
7. Wylie, *Military Strategy*, p. 38.
8. Jullien, *A Treatise on Efficacy*, p. 162.
9. Sun Tzu, *Sun-tzu*, trans. Sawyer, p. 173.
10. Antulio J. Echevarria II, *Fourth-Generation War and Other Myths*, Monograph, Carlisle Barracks, PA: Strategic Studies Institute, U.S. Army War College, Nov. 2005, p. 12.
11. Yan Xue Tong et al., *Wang Ba Tian Xa Si Xiang Ji Qi Di* 王霸天下思想及啟迪 [Thoughts of World Leadership and Implications], Beijing: World Affairs Press, 2009, pp. 36–7.
12. Hong Bing, *Zhong Guo Zhan Lue Yuan Li Jie Xi* 中國戰略原理解析 [An Analysis of Chinese Strategic Principles], Beijing: Military Science Publishing House, 2002, pp. 10–13.
13. Hammond, *The Mind of War*, p. 184.
14. Coram, *Boyd*, p. 321.
15. See Qiao and Wang, *Unrestricted Warfare*.

BIBLIOGRAPHY

Chinese Sources

Chen Ku-ying & Bai Xi, *Lao Zi Ping Zhuan* 老子評傳 [A Critical Biography of Lao Tzu] (Nanjing: Nanjing UP, 2001).

Feng Zhen Hao, *Qi Lu Wen Hua Yan Jiu* 齊魯文化研究 [A Study on the Cultures of Qi and Lu] (Jinan: Qi Lu Shu She, 2010).

Gong Yuzhen, Zhong Guo Zhan Lue Wen Hua Jie Xi 中國戰略文化解析 [Analysis of China's Strategic Culture] (Beijing: Military Science Press, 2002).

Gu De Rong & Zhu Shun Long, *Chun Qiu Shi* 春秋史 [A History of the Spring and Autumn Period] (Shanghai: Shanghai People's Publishing House, 2008).

Ho Ping-ti, *Three Studies on* 有關《孫子》《老子》的三篇考證 (Taipei: Institute of Modern History, Academia Sinica, 2002).

Hong Bing, *Zhong Guo Zhan Lue Yuan Li Jie Xi* 中國戰略原理解析 [Analysis of Chinese Strategic Principles] (Beijing: Military Science Publishing House, 2002).

Li Gui-sheng, *Zhu Zi Wen Hua Yu Xian Qin Bing Jia* 諸子文化與先秦兵家 [Cultures of Pre-Qin Masters and Pre-Qin School of the Military] (Changsha: Yue Lu Shu She, 2009).

Li Ling, *Bing Yi Zha Li: Wo Dou Sun Zi* 兵以詐立：我讀《孫子》[Strategy Is Based on Deception: How I Read Sun Tzu] (Beijing: Zhonghua Book Company, 2006).

Li Ling, *Sun Zi Shi San Pian Zong He Yan Jiu* 《孫子》十三篇綜合研究 [A Comprehensive Study of Sun Tzu's Thirteen Chapters] (Beijing: Zhonghua Book Company, 2006).

Li Zehou, *Zhong Guo Gu Dai Si Xiang Shi Lun* 中國古代思想史論 [On the History of Chinese Ancient Thought] (Taipei: San Min Book Co., 2000).

Liu Ke & Li Ke He (eds.), *Guan Zi Yi Zhu* 管子譯注 [An Annotation of Guan Zi] (Harbin: Heilongjiang People's Publishing House, 2003).

Mi Zhen-yu (ed.), *Zhong Guo Jun Shi Xue Shu Shi, Vol. 1* 中國軍事學術史(上卷) [A History of Chinese Military Scholarship, Vol. 1] (Beijing: People's Liberation Army Publishing House, 2008).

BIBLIOGRAPHY

Niu Xian-zhong, *Sun Zi San Lun: Cong Gu Bing Fa Dao Xin Zhan Lue* 孫子三論：從古兵法到新戰略 [Three Discourses on Sun Tzu: From Ancient Art of War to New Strategy] (Taipei: Rye Field Publishing Co., 1997).

Qiao Liang and Wang Xiangsui, *Unrestricted Warfare* (Beijing: PLA Literature and Arts Publishing House, 1999).

Qiu Wen-shan, *Qi Wen Hua Yu Zhong Hua Wen Ming* 齊文化與中華文明 [The Culture of Qi and Chinese Civilization] (Jinan: Qi Lu Shu She, 2006).

Sun Tzu, Yang Bing-an (ed.), *Shi Yi Jia Zhu Sun Zi Xiao Li* 十一家注孫子校理 [The Collation of the Eleven Schools of The Art of War Annotations] (Beijing: Zhonghua Book Company, 1999)

Tian Xu-dong, *Gu Dai Bing Xue Wen Hua Tan Lun* 古代兵學文化探論 [An Exploration of Culture of Ancient Military Studies] (Beijing: China Social Sciences Press, 2010).

Wei Ru-lin, *Sun Zi Jin Zhu Jin Yi* 孫子今註今譯 [The Modern Commentaries on and Annotations of Sun Tzu] (Taipei: The Commercial Press, 2001).

Yan Xue Tong et. al., *Wang Ba Tian Xa Si Xiang Ji Qi Di* 王霸天下思想及啟迪 [Thoughts of World Leadership and Implications] (Beijing: World Affairs Press, 2009).

Yu Ru Bo, *Sun Zi Bing Fa Yan Jiu Shi* 孫子兵法研究史 [A History of the Study of Sun Tzu: The Art of War] (Beijing: Military Science Publishing House, 2001).

Zhang Zhen-ze, *Sun Bin Bing Fa Xiao Li* 孫臏兵法校理 [The Collation of Sun Bin: The Art of Warfare] (Beijing: Zhonghua Book Company, 2010).

English Sources

Alberts, David S. and Thomas J. Czerwinski (eds.), *Complexity, Global Politics, and National Security*, Washington, DC: National Defense University, 1997.

Bassford, Christopher, "Teaching the Clausewitzian Trinity," Jan. 2003 <http://www.clausewitz.com/CWZHOME/Trinity/TrinityTeachingNote.htm>

Beaufre, André, *An Introduction to Strategy*, London: Faber, 1965.

Beyerchen, Alan D., "Clausewitz, Nonlinearity, and the Importance of Imagery," in David S. Alberts and Thomas J. Czerwinski (eds), *Complexity, Global Politics, and National Security*, Washington, DC: National Defense University, 1997, pp. 153–70.

—— "Clausewitz, Nonlinearity, and the Unpredictability of War," *International Security*, 17, 3 (Winter 1992), pp. 59–90.

Black, Jeremy, *Rethinking Military History*, London: Routledge, 2004.

Booth, Ken, "The Concept of Strategic Culture Affirmed," in C.G. Jacobsen (ed.), *Strategic Power: USA/USSR*, New York: St Martin's Press, 1990, pp. 121–8.

Bousquet, Antoine, *The Scientific Way of Warfare: Order and Chaos on the Battlefields of Modernity*, New York: Columbia University Press, 2009.

BIBLIOGRAPHY

Boyd, John, *The Essence of Winning and Losing*, unpublished manuscript, 1995.
—— *Organic Design for Command and Control*, unpublished manuscript, 1987.
—— *Patterns of Conflict*, unpublished manuscript, 1986.
—— *The Strategic Game of ? and ?*, unpublished manuscript, 1987.
Capra, Fritjof, *The Tao of Physics: An Exploration of the Parallels between Modern Physics and Eastern Mysticism*, 3rd edn, London: Flamingo, 1982.
Clausewitz, Carl von, *On War*, ed. and trans. Michael Howard and Peter Paret, Princeton, NJ: Princeton University Press, 1989.
Coker, Christopher, *The Future of War: The Re-Enchantment of War in the Twenty-First Century*, Oxford: Blackwell, 2004.
—— *Waging War without Warriors? The Changing Culture of Military Conflict*, London: Lynne Rienner, 2002.
Coram, Robert, *Boyd: The Fighter Pilot who Changed the Art of War*, New York: Little Brown, 2002.
Corn, Tony, "From Mars to Minerva: Clausewitz, Liddell Hart, and the Two Western Ways of War," *Small Wars Journal* (21 May, 2011) <http://smallwarsjournal.com/blog/journal/docs-temp/767-corn.pdf>
Dellios, Rosita, "Chinese Strategic Culture—Part 1: Heritage from the Past," Research Paper No. 1, Center for East–West Cultural and Economic Studies, Bond University, Apr. 1994.
—— "Chinese Strategic Culture—Part 2: Virtue and Power," Research Paper No. 2, Center for East–West Cultural and Economic Studies, Bond University, Nov. 1994.
De Czege, Huba Wass, "Systemic Operational Design: Learning and Adapting in Complex Missions," *Military Review*, 89, 1 (Jan. 2009), pp. 2–12.
Czerwinski, Thomas J., *Coping with the Bounds: Speculations on Nonlinearity in Military Affairs*, Washington, DC: National Defense University, 1998.
Echevarria, Antulio J. II, *Fourth-Generation War and Other Myths*, Monograph, Carlisle Barracks, PA: Strategic Studies Institute, U.S. Army War College, Nov. 2005.
Fuller, J.F.C., *The Conduct of War 1789–1961*, New Brunswick, NJ: Da Capo Press, 1992.
Gat, Azar, *A History of Military Thought: From the Enlightenment to the Cold War*, Oxford: Oxford University Press, 2001.
Gray, Colin S., *Modern Strategy*, Oxford: Oxford University Press, 1999.
—— *The Strategic Bridge: Theory for Practice*, New York: Oxford University Press, 2010.
Griffith, Samuel B., *Sun Tzu: The Art of War*, London: Oxford University Press, 1963.
Hammes, Thomas X., *The Sling and the Stone: On War in the 21st Century*, Minnesota: Zenith, 2004.

BIBLIOGRAPHY

Hammond, Grant T., *The Mind of War: John Boyd and American Security*, Washington, DC: Smithsonian, 2001.

Handel, Michael I., *Masters of War: Classical Strategic Thought*, 3rd edn, London: Frank Cass, 2001.

Ilichinski, Andrew, *Land Warfare and Complexity, Part II: An Assessment of the Applicability of Nonlinear Dynamic and Complex Systems Theory to the Study of Land Warfare (U)*, Alexandria, VA: Center for Naval Analyses, 1996.

Jervis, Robert, *System Effect: Complexity in Political and Social Life*, Princeton, NJ: Princeton University Press, 1987.

Johnson, Kenneth D., *China's Strategic Culture: A Perspective for the United States*, Monograph, Carlisle Barracks, PA: Strategic Studies Institute, U.S. Army War College, June 2009.

Johnston, Alastair Iain, *Cultural Realism: Chinese Grand Strategy in the Chinese History*, Princeton, NJ: Princeton University Press, 1995.

—— "Cultural Realism and Strategy in Maoist China," in Peter Katzenstein (ed.), *The Culture of National Security: Norms and Identity in World Politics*, New York: Columbia University Press, 1996.

—— "Sun Zi Studies in the United States," Paper, 25 July 1999 <www.people.fas. harvard.edu/~johnston/SunZi.pdf>

Jullien, François, *A Treatise on Efficacy: Between Western and Chinese Thinking*, Honolulu, HI: University of Hawai'i Press, 1996.

Kissinger, Henry, *On China*, New York: Penguin, 2011.

Lao Tzu, *Tao Te Ching*, in Thomas Cleary (ed.), *The Taoist Classics, Volume 1: The Collected Translations of Thomas Cleary*, Boston: Shambhala, 1994.

Lao Tzu, *Tao Te Ching*, trans. D.C. Lau, Hong Kong: The Chinese University Press, 2001.

Lao Zi (Lao Tzu), *Dao De Jing: A Philosophical Translation*, trans. Roger T. and David L. Hall, New York: Ballantine Books, 2003.

Liddell Hart, B.H., *The Decisive Wars of History: A Study in History*, London: G. Bell & Sons, 1929.

—— *Strategy*, 2nd revised edn, New York: Meridian, 1991.

Lind, William S., "FMFM 1-A, Fourth Generation War," Paper 2005. <http:// www.d-n-i.net/lind/4gw_manual_draft_3_revised_10_june_05>

Luttwak, Edward N., *Strategy: The Logic of War and Peace*, rev. and enl. edn, Cambridge, MA: Belknap Press, 2001.

Mahnken, Thomas G., *Secrecy and Stratagem: Understanding Chinese Strategic Culture*, Woollahra, N.S.W.: Lowy Institute for International Policy, 2011.

Mann, Stephen R., "Chaos Theory and Strategic Thought," *Parameters*, XXII (Autumn 1992), pp. 54–68.

Mao Tse-tung, "On Protracted War," in *Selected Works of Mao Tse-tung, Vol. II*, Beijing: Foreign Languages Press, 1967.

BIBLIOGRAPHY

Moran, Daniel, "Strategic Theory and the History of War," Paper (2001) <http://www.clausewitz.com/CWZHOME/Bibl/Moran-StrategicTheory.pdf>

Murawiec, Laurent, "Chinese Grand Strategy and the Chinese Way of War," Written Testimony for US–China Economic and Security Review Commission, 15 Sep. 2005 <http://www.uscc.gov/hearings/2005hearings/written_testimonies/05_09_15wrts/murawiec_laurent_wrts.htm>

Nisbett, Richard E., *The Geography of Thought: How Asians and Westerns Think Differently ... and Why*, New York: Free Press, 2003.

Osinga, Frans P.B., *Science, Strategy and War: The Strategic Theory of John Boyd*, New York: Routledge, 2007.

Peters, Ralph, "Why Clausewitz Had It Backward," *Armed Force Journal* (July 2006) <http://www.armedforcesjournal.com/2006/07/1817576/>

Poole, John H., *Phantom Soldier: The Enemy's Answer to U.S. Firepower*, Emerald Isle, NC: Posterity Press, 2001.

Richards, Chet, *Certain to Win*, Philadelphia: Xlibris, 2004.

Ryden, Edmund S.J., *Philosophy of Peace in Han China: A Study of the Huainanzi Ch. 15 On Military Strategy*, Taipei: Taipei Ricci Institute, 1998.

Safranski, Mark et al., *The John Boyd Roundtable: Debating Science, Strategy, and War*, Ann Arbor, MI: Nimble, 2008.

Sawyer, Ralph D. (trans.), *The Seven Military Classics of Ancient China*, Boulder, CO: Westview Press, 1993.

—— (trans.), *The Tao of War: The Martial Tao Te Ching*, Boulder, CO: Westview Press, 2003.

Scobell, Andrew, *China and Strategic Culture*, Monograph, Carlisle Barracks, PA: Strategic Studies Institute, U.S. Army War College, May 2002.

Scobell, Andrew, *China's Use of Military Force: Beyond the Great Wall and the Long March*, New York: Cambridge University Press, 2003.

Scobell, Andrew, "Is There a Chinese Way of War?" *Parameters*, XXXV, 1 (Spring 2005), pp. 118-22.

Scobell, Andrew, "Strategic Culture and China: IR Theory versus the Fortune Cookie?" *Strategic Insights*, IV, 10 (Oct. 2005) (electronic version).

Snyder, Jack, *The Soviet Strategic Culture: Implications for Limited Nuclear Operations*, RAND R-2154-AF, Santa Monica, CA: The Rand Corporation, 1977.

Sonhaus, Lawrence, *Strategic Culture and Ways of War*, New York: Routledge, 2006.

Sun Bin, *Sun Bin: The Art of Warfare*, trans. D.C. Lau and Roger T. Ames, Albany, NY: State University of New York Press, 2003).

Sun Tzu, Samuel B. Griffith, *Sun Tzu: The Art of War*, London: Oxford University Press, 1963.

Sun Tzu, Ralph D. Sawyer (trans.), *Sun-tzu: The Art of War* (Boulder, CO: Westview, 1994).

BIBLIOGRAPHY

Sun Tzu, Roger T. Ames (trans.), *Sun-tzu: The Art of Warfare* (New York: Ballantine, 1994).

Sun Tzu, Thomas Cleary (trans.), *The Art of War* (Boston: Shambhala, 1988).

Swain, Richard M., "B. H. Liddell Hart and the Creation of a Theory of War, 1919–1933," *Armed Forces & Society*, Vol. 17, No. 1, Fall 1990, pp. 35–51.

Thomas, Timothy L., "The Chinese Military's Strategic Mind-set," *Military Review*, Vol. 87, No. 6, November 2007, pp. 47–55.

Villacres, Edward J. and Bassford, Christopher, "Reclaiming the Clausewitzian Trinity," *Parameters* Vol. XXV, Autumn 1995, pp. 9–19. <http://www.clausewitz.com/CWZHOME/Trinity/TRININTR.htm>

Waldron, Arthur, "China's Military Classics: A Review Essay," *Joint Force Quarterly*, No. 4, Spring 1994, pp. 114–117.

Windsor, Philip, *Strategic Thinking: An Introduction and Farewell* (Boulder, CO: Lynne Rienner, 2002).

Wylie, J. C., *Military Strategy: A General Theory of Power Control* (NJ: Rutgers University Press, 1967).

INDEX

INDEX

INDEX

INDEX

INDEX

INDEX